The
Moral
Teaching

of

Paul

Second Edition, Revised

The Moral Teaching of Paul

SELECTED ISSUES

Victor Paul Furnish

Abingdon Press

Nashville

THE MORAL TEACHING OF PAUL: Selected Issues
Second Edition, Revised

Copyright © 1979 by Abingdon
Second Edition © 1985 by Abingdon Press

Second Printing 1986

Library of Congress Cataloging in Publication Data

FURNISH, VICTOR PAUL.
    The moral teaching of Paul.
    Includes bibliographical references and index.
    1. Ethics in the Bible. 2. Bible. N.T. Epistles of
    Paul—Criticism, interpretation, etc. I. Title.
    BS2655.E8F79 1985   227'.06   84-24549

ISBN 0-687-27181-9

Scripture quotations, unless noted otherwise, are from the Revised Standard
Version Common Bible, copyrighted © 1973 by the Division of Christian
Education of the National Council of Churches of Christ in the U.S.A., and
are used by permission.

Scripture quotations noted NEB are from the New English Bible. © the
Delegates of the Oxford University Press and the Syndics of the Cambridge
University Press 1961, 1970. Reprinted by permission.

MANUFACTURED BY THE PARTHENON PRESS AT
NASHVILLE, TENNESSEE, UNITED STATES OF AMERICA

CONTENTS

PREFACE TO THE FIRST EDITION

This book is written for people who believe that Paul's moral teaching ought to be taken seriously but who are not sure what it means to do so. I have outlined my own convictions about this in chapter 1. In the subsequent chapters, I have sought to demonstrate how some problem texts in Paul's letters can still give moral guidance in our time if we do not force our presuppositions and questions upon them too quickly.

I was encouraged to move ahead with the publication of these short studies by the need, expressed to me often by laypeople, clergy, and students, for sound but nontechnical discussions of these problem texts and topics in Paul's letters. It is for such readers that this book is intended. Several of the chapters have been shaped in no small part by opportunities I have had to discuss these issues in the seminary classroom, at pastors' conferences, and in local churches. Many technical matters have been omitted from the presentation; others have been greatly simplified but, I hope, not misrepresented. The books and articles referred to at the end of each chapter will provide additional information and in certain cases different opinions.

The writing of this book was worked into a schedule which my wife and daughters thought was already too crowded, and without their understanding and support it could not have been accomplished. The manuscript was typed by Mrs. Bonnie Jordan with her usual skill and efficiency.

PREFACE TO THE SECOND EDITION

A number of important studies of particular aspects of Paul's moral teaching have appeared since the first edition of this book was published, and I have sought to take account of these as I have prepared this revision. My fundamental conclusions about Paul's views on the issues considered here remain essentially unaltered, but I have changed my mind about some specific matters. Therefore, while there are alterations of various kinds throughout this new edition, no chapter has been completely rewritten. There have been some additions, however, and certain sections have been completely rewritten, especially those which deal with I Corinthians 7:10-11, I Corinthians 6:9, and I Corinthians 11:2-16, in chapters 2, 3, and 4 respectively.

Some notion of my indebtedness to other scholars can be gained from the bibliographical sections at the end of each chapter, each of which has been brought up to date. I wish to record as well my appreciation to those reviewers of the first edition who raised important questions or made constructive suggestions. Not least, it is a pleasure to acknowledge how much I have gained from the many opportunities I have had to discuss the chapters with lay and clergy groups. These experiences have suggested that this little book has indeed been found helpful by many who (as I wrote in the preface to the first edition) "believe that Paul's moral teaching ought to be taken seriously but who are not sure what it means to do so."

I

THE SACRED COW
AND THE WHITE ELEPHANT

The apostle Paul has the unenviable distinction of having been and remaining one of history's most controversial and misunderstood figures. He was misunderstood, first of all, by his own fellow Christians. His dramatic and unexpected conversion from being a zealous persecutor of the church to claiming to be a qualified apostle of Christ inevitably made him suspect to his new Christian colleagues, as well as making him *persona non grata* to his former colleagues in Judaism. As his mission to the Gentiles increasingly took on momentum and importance, his relationship to the Jerusalem leaders of the Jewish-Christian church became tense and increasingly difficult. Similarly, to his Gentile converts, he often posed a puzzle. How could he, on the one hand, preach freedom from the law, and on the other hand declare that the man or woman in Christ is placed under a yet more total claim to do God's will than the Jews, committed to the fulfilling of the law? In the decades after his death, even as his letters were becoming a fixture in the Christian canon and as he was being increasingly venerated as a person, he continued to be misinterpreted and misunderstood. One indication of this is the famous comment of the second-century author of II Peter who complains of the Pauline letters that "there are some things in them hard to understand, which the ignorant and unstable twist to their own destruction" (3:16).

In the late nineteenth and early twentieth century, it was especially Paul's theology, even more specifically his preaching of Jesus as the Christ, that came under attack by liberal Protestants. The Apostle was portrayed as having, more or less single-handedly, converted "the religion of Jesus" into "a religion about Jesus." Some claimed Paul had infused the simple faith of the Nazarene and his disciples with alien concepts drawn from the Greek philosophical schools and the Eastern mystery cults. Others believed he had imposed on it the burden of rabbinic concerns and methods. The German scholar William Wrede once dubbed Paul "the second founder of Christianity" and lamented that, while Jesus' teaching had exerted "the better" influence on Christianity, Paul's had exerted "the stronger."

Subsequent investigations into the origins of Christianity have shown how naïve it was to label Paul the founder of Christianity as we know it; Paul was converted by and into a Christian movement that already had a rich theological tradition and that had already been nurtured by various religious and cultural sources. Paul made his own theological contributions, to be sure, but the church before him had received its initial and decisive momentum from the recognition by the earliest community that the Jesus who had been crucified lived among them still, as its risen Lord.

Although one may still hear echoes of the old complaint about the "corrupting" influence of Paul's theology on Christianity, at the present time it is more especially his *ethical teachings* that have been thrown into question. While the older, "liberal" view of Paul emphasized his dogmatic interests and argued that all else was subordinate to them, even Wrede had to acknowledge that Paul's ethical interests were also considerable. The Apostle is by no means shy in laying down practical admonitions and exhortations in his letters. He is often bold and blunt in the directions he gives, in the advice he offers, in the opinions he expresses. And so it was, for example, that he had sent Timothy to Corinth to remind the Christians there of all the Apostle's "ways in Christ, as I teach them everywhere in every church" (I Cor. 4:17). What are we to do with these today? The general appeals present no special problem; we may not agree *what* "love" requires in a given instance, but we can agree readily enough *that* we should "make love [our] aim" (I Cor. 14:1), "bear one another's burdens" (Gal. 6:2), and "hold fast what is good, abstain from every form of evil" (I Thess. 5:21). But we begin to have problems whenever Paul's admonitions become specific and concrete, as they so often do: men should not wear long hair (I Cor. 11:14), and women should (I Cor. 11:15); one should not use the secular courts (I Cor. 6:1ff.); one should accept the social status (for example, slavery) in which one finds oneself (I Cor. 7:17ff.); it is better to remain single than to marry (I Cor. 7:7*a*); and many more. How are we to understand these concrete instructions? In what way, if at all, are they applicable to us in our day?

Subsequent chapters will examine several topics of special current interest on which Paul's letters offer concrete advice and instruction. However, it is important first of all to be aware of a fundamental issue that confronts anyone who seeks guidance from the Bible in matters of conduct. The issue, at base, is one's understanding of the nature and authority of the Bible. It is clear that the church has recognized the Bible as authoritative for its faith and life. Unfortunately, Christian people have not always agreed on *how* the Bible's authority should be understood, particularly in its concrete teachings about morality. This important topic cannot be treated fully here, but some fundamental points must be established right at the start so that the subsequent discussions of specific issues can be of maximum benefit. At the risk of caricature, but for the sake of clarity, one may contrast two very different ways Paul's concrete moral teaching has been approached. There are some who venerate it as a sacred cow, and others who dismiss it as a white elephant. As each of these positions is characterized, and the errors in each identified, it will become clear that the approach in the following chapters can be identified with neither.

Paul's Moral Teaching as a Sacred Cow

Some people believe, or at least read the Bible as though they believed, that scripture is the written deposit of God's truth, mediated through inspired writers in centuries past, but valid in both general and specific ways for all times and places. This may be called the sacred-cow view of the Bible. It leads to the conclusion, when applied to the concrete ethical teachings of Paul, that they are in fact God's commandments and thus eternally and universally binding. They are not to be touched, disturbed, or in any sense explained away. They are to be taken at face value. Proponents of this view of the Bible, and of Paul's letters specifically, often quote II Timothy 3:16: "All scripture is inspired by God and profitable for teaching, for reproof, for correction, and for training in righteousness." This text is offered as "proof" that the teachings of the Bible are of divine origin exclusively, and therefore in no way conditioned by the cultural setting of the biblical writers. It would seem to follow, then, that if we are uncomfortable with, for example, the teaching in Paul's letters about slavery or hairstyles or subjection to earthly rulers, that is *our* problem, not the Bible's. Since Paul's words are really God's Word, Christians have no business trying to accommodate them to modern views. Rather, Christians must accommodate *themselves*, by obeying those teachings as the commandments of God.

The fundamental problem with this way of approaching the Bible, and Paul's ethical teaching within it, is the fact that such an approach seriously misrepresents the understanding and intentions of the biblical writers themselves. It is true that the Old Testament prophets, for example, had uttered their oracles as spokesmen for God. But it is also true that those same Old Testament prophets were addressing God's Word to particular situations, and that they understood its applicability within a specific span of time and a particular geographical area. Neither they, nor those who later compiled their oracles and committed them to writing, presumed that the prophets' words could be isolated from the particularities of the situations in which they were originally spoken.

But then what of the text from II Timothy 3:16, quoted so often in defense of a sacred-cow conception of the Bible? To begin with, one must acknowledge a grammatical ambiguity that, in addition to the translation quoted above, permits the alternative found in the RSV footnote: "Every scripture inspired by God is also profitable for teaching. . . ." On this reading the emphasis is not that *all* scripture *is inspired* by God, but that every scripture that is inspired "*is profitable* for teaching, for reproof, for correction, and for training in righteousness." It is also probable that the "scripture" mentioned here means only the *Jewish* scripture, our Old Testament. But most important of all, one must admit that the critical word "inspired" is left vague and unspecific. Only persons can be "inspired," properly speaking, not an inanimate object like a written document. It is already a metaphorical use of the term to apply it to scripture. In and of itself the adjective "inspired" says only that those who have written these words were in some way moved and guided by God. Those who read the word to mean "historically accurate," "inerrant," or the like, are imposing their own ideas upon the text. Neither the word "inspired," nor the equally general term "profitable" (that is, something "helpful" or "advantageous"), requires one to think of scripture as infallible, entirely unaffected by the cultural settings in which the writers labored, wholly consistent, or unconditionally binding for all times and places.

This is confirmed with special clarity in the instance of the Pauline letters. It is important to recognize that Paul was not conscious of contributing to scripture, of writing words that would be read and studied for generations, even centuries to come. He was not writing for us. He was writing to specific Christian congregations, in specific locations, involved in specific situations, at specific times. Since we are *not* the readers Paul had in mind, we must *interpret* his letters, including his moral instructions. They cannot possibly be automatically, and without remainder, applicable to us in our situations. One may speak of Paul's ministry, and therefore of his instructions, as "inspired," but this does not alter the fact that those instructions were meant for others and that what was pertinent in their times and places may not be in ours.

Willi Marxsen has offered a good illustration to make this point. Suppose that Paul sat down to write to the Galatian Christians and to the Thessalonian Christians at the same time (which, of course, was not actually the case). And suppose further that when he addressed the packets in which the letters had been placed for delivery, he mistakenly wrote "To the Thessalonians" on the letter intended for Galatia, and "To the Galatians" on the letter intended for the Thessalonians. What would have happened when the Thessalonians, between whom and Paul there were strong and mutual bonds of love and affection, opened up the letter addressed to them and found the angry and sarcastic words Paul had intended for the Galatians? And what would have happened among the churches of Galatia when they discovered that they had mistakenly been given Paul's letter to the Thessalonians? Now, certainly, the Thessalonian and Galatian Christians had much more in common with each other than we have with either group; and yet in both the churches of Galatia and in the congregation at Thessalonica a good deal of interpretive work would have had to be done in order to make those misdelivered letters intelligible and meaningful for the people. How much more are we in the position of needing to *interpret* Paul's letters, precisely because they were intended not for us, but for others.

An additional factor is that we are separated from Paul's congregations geographically as well as in time. The sociopolitical-cultural conditions and problems of Paul's congregations are vastly different from the sociopolitical-cultural conditions and problems confronting modern Christians. The responsibilities and opportunities of our time and place are different from the responsibilities and opportunities of Christians in Paul's day. Paul was not writing "timeless truths" intended to be valid and relevant for all future ages. There are timeless truths to be found in his letters, but these are embedded within the particularities designed to be relevant to those whom he was addressing. We must remember that what made Paul's letters intensely relevant for his churches serves to accentuate the differences between his day and ours, the differences between the needs of his original readers and our needs. This point may perhaps be formulated more generally as "the law of varying relevancy," because it also applies to other parts of the Bible, and outside the Bible: The more specifically relevant any given moral instruction is to a particular situation, the less specifically relevant it is to other particular situations.

There is yet another reason why one must avoid making Paul's moral teaching into a sacred cow. Paul himself allows for differing ethical judgments, given the differing circumstances of individuals even within the same congregation and at the same time. He shows a sometimes amazing tolerance of rather differing behavior within the Christian communities. He accepts the fact, even affirms it, that some Christians will eat meat which has been ritually slaughtered in a pagan temple, while others will feel bound to abstain from it. He allows that some Christians will marry, while others will remain single; that some Christians will divorce, while others will maintain their marriages; and so forth. Some of these points will be examined in more detail later on. Here it is enough to emphasize that Paul nowhere lays down a rigid, legalistic code of Christian conduct. Taking his moral teaching as a sacred cow, therefore, simply will not work.

Indeed, if one looks beyond the Pauline letters to the New Testament as a whole, the variety of perspectives on practical issues is even greater. It is evident that the earliest church regarded neither its theological nor its ethical traditions as a sacred cow. Within the New Testament itself we see the church interpreting, reinterpreting, correcting, and modifying its traditions for new times and situations. Long before James Russell Lowell ever phrased it so eloquently, the earliest Christians, including Paul, recognized that "new occasions teach new duties; time makes ancient good uncouth." When one talks about the "traditions" in the early church, one should not picture sets of theological and ethical teachings tied up in neat packages, handed on from generation to generation with the warning, "Do not disturb." The theological and ethical traditions within the earliest church remained ever alive and growing; they were not allowed to stagnate and die. For all of his respect for traditions, including the ethical ones, Paul, for example, never confused those traditions, even those compiled into "scripture," with the gospel, the Word of God itself. He constantly reminded his churches, just as Jesus had constantly reminded his hearers, that God's living Word stands *over* and *in judgment upon* every tradition. God's Word is that by which every tradition is to be measured and judged. Whenever we make any of the traditions of the early church, including Paul's moral instructions, into a sacred cow, we are *embalming* the tradition rather than receiving it as a vital and revitalizing force—free to grow, free to develop and change, free to adapt itself to "new occasions and new duties."

Paul's Moral Teaching as a White Elephant

In view of what has been said here by way of criticism of the sacred-cow interpretation of Paul's ethical teachings, it might appear that the only alternative is to judge them to constitute a bulky white elephant. Webster reminds us that we use this phrase "white elephant" to refer to "anything requiring a great deal of care and expense, but yielding little profit; any burdensome possession." Go to any garage sale, and you will see numerous examples of white elephants! A white elephant is anything that is obsolete—perhaps once useful, but now outmoded, irrelevant, maybe even a little ridiculous.

All these terms—"outmoded, irrelevant, ridiculous"—have been applied to Paul's moral teaching. It too, some say, is an imposing but nonetheless unprofitable and burdensome white elephant. Perhaps it was pertinent to other times and places, but no longer. It is an anachronism, like an antique automobile: interesting only to antiquarians, but a real menace when it is driven out onto a modern expressway.

Undoubtedly the most important complaint lodged against Paul's moral teaching by those who would call it a white elephant is this: Paul expected the imminent end of the world, the speedy return of Christ, the close of the age before his own physical death. Moral instructions conveyed in that setting cannot possibly be relevant in a world that no longer lives with that kind of expectation, and whose very existence shows that Paul was mistaken. This is such an important point that it deserves careful examination and response.

More than fifty years ago the great German New Testament scholar Martin Dibelius argued that the early Christian expectation of the imminence of the end of the world automatically precluded any serious concern for ethical behavior within the world in the short time that remained. Dibelius claimed that such moral instruction as did occur among the first-generation Christians was really only a kind of "left-over" from Christianity's Jewish heritage. Dibelius held that the earliest Christians, including Paul, were also influenced by Greek ethical teachings, and adopted many of these along with the Jewish ideals. Then they "christianized" both kinds of materials only insofar as that was necessary. Therefore, in his view Paul's ethical teachings had "nothing to do with the theoretic foundations of the ethics of the Apostle, and very little with other ideas peculiar to him. Rather, they belonged to tradition." That is, in his concrete instructions Paul was simply drawing on the traditions of the church which had, in turn, been adapted from Hellenistic Judaism. In preaching to converts from a Gentile background, Christian missionaries like Paul found it necessary to convey such basic moral exhortation for purely practical reasons, and not because such exhortation was related in any essential way to the proclamation of the gospel. The ethical sections of Paul's letters, then, Dibelius claimed, are there only because of the "didactic habit" Paul had of giving ethical instructions to new converts. On this view, the Pauline ethical teaching is not only unrelated in any significant way to Pauline theology, it is in fact seen as having existed *in spite of* the early church's expectation of an imminent eschaton. And we are left with a white elephant.

An essentially similar conclusion was reached by Albert Schweitzer, but Schweitzer arrived at the conclusion in a different way. He argued that the real Paul is Paul the "mystic," that Paul's theology is oriented fundamentally to the idea of a "mystical" dying and rising with Christ. Paul's ethical teaching was developed, then, "solely from the character of the new state of existence which results from the dying and rising again with Christ and the bestowal of the Spirit." Schweitzer acknowledged that Paul regarded the end of history and of the world as imminent, and for this reason, he said, the idea of a coming judgment and reward still lingers in Paul's ethical teachings. Yet the essential character of Paul's ethics does not derive from the Apostle's expectation of the coming end of the natural world. Its *essential* character derives, instead, according to Schweitzer, from the experience of being in Christ. Paul's mysticism, according to his view, was more important than his eschatology; Paul's mysticism saved him from denying the world in the way that most of his contemporaries did. The "ideal of Paul's ethic," wrote Schweitzer, was "to live with the eyes fixed upon eternity, while standing firmly upon the solid ground of reality." In effect, Schweitzer was saying that Paul's ethical teaching is actually better than one would suppose it could be, considering his sense of standing near the close of history. The Apostle's eschatological doctrine was, in effect, overcome by his "mysticism" and by his "intuition." While Schweitzer admired Paul's ethical teaching, he nonetheless regarded it as existing *in spite of* the Apostle's eschatology.

A more recent discussion of Pauline ethics, that by Jack T. Sanders, echoes several of these ideas, especially those of Dibelius. Thus, Sanders, too, argues that Paul's belief in the shortness of time left for this world has precluded his developing any significant ethical teachings of his own. Paul correctly understood that love (*agape*) is the power of the "new existence," says Sanders, but when, at the same time, he identified that new existence as fully present only in the future, he was rendering the love commandment essentially irrelevant for the present. So, it is claimed, when the Apostle is forced to deal with concrete moral cases, he must fall back on arbitrary legal pronouncements. In effect, Sanders is saying that the concrete moral instructions of Paul should be regarded as a white elephant, as a costly curio without any real present value.

At first, this may appear to be a more reasonable assessment of Paul's ethical teachings than that which venerates them as if they were a sacred cow. There have been some respected scholars who have reached this conclusion, and it certainly avoids the error of interpreting timely instructions as if they had been offered as timeless truths. But this white-elephant interpretation is also involved in a fundamental error. The evidence simply does not support the view that the expectation of an imminent end of the world and history precludes concern for ethical behavior in the present.

The view of Dibelius and others that first Jesus, and then the earliest Christians following him, more or less perfunctorily espoused Jewish or Hellenistic, or Hellenistic-Jewish, morality and traditions, is too superficial a reading of the texts. Jesus' preaching of the nearness of the reign of God did not preclude or cause the subordination of practical ethical concerns, but accentuated the totality of the claim that the sovereign God makes on his people to love him and one another. Jesus' own ministry of compassion, love, and service within the family of God is integrally related to his eschatological message about the imminence of the kingdom. Its nearness brings a new urgency to the ethical appeal. Similarly, as I have tried to show elsewhere, the so-called ethical sections of the Apostle's letters are not loosely tacked on to the weightier, theological parts, as concessions to the practical needs of the less than ideal Christians in Paul's congregations (Dibelius). Rather, Paul's ethical admonitions are closely and significantly related to his preaching of the gospel, and thus to his fundamental theological convictions. What matters most, he insists, is *faith enacted in love* (see Gal. 5:6), and by this he means (as the context of Galatians 5–6 clearly shows), *in the present life of the believer and of the believing community*. Virtually all of the Apostle's concrete moral instructions are intended to show the forms that faith's enactment in love must take in specific cases.

It is true that Paul does occasionally issue fairly arbitrary pronouncements on matters of behavior, what Sanders, following Ernst Käsemann, calls "tenets of holy law." These usually involve some warning about the visitation of God's judgment upon those who fail to keep them. In such passages (for example, I Cor. 3:17; but they are not as numerous as Sanders would have us believe), Paul does seem to be influenced by the form and content of traditional modes of exhortation. But one ought not to isolate such sentences from the wider context of Paul's ethical teaching. They are only elements embedded within larger units of teaching, and a fair appraisal of the relation between eschatolology and ethics in Paul's thought can only result when the broader contexts are considered.

First Thessalonians, probably the earliest letter of Paul's we possess, offers a good illustration of the way his eschatological expectation actually supports his ethical appeals. In chapters 4 and 5, the eschatological hope is keen and vivid. The Apostle is very much concerned here with the future, the destiny under God, of believers. It is also clear in these chapters that Paul believes the decisive eschatological event has occurred already for them in the death and resurrection of Jesus Christ (see 5:10). Paul is saying that, whether the End is upon them or delayed for a little while, the most important thing for the Thessalonians is to know that they belong to the New Age. In Christ, by their faith in him, they are God's people. In certain paragraphs in these chapters, Paul is drawing very heavily upon traditional eschatological pictures he has inherited from Judaism. But when all is said and done, he describes the Christian's future in virtually the same way he talks about the Christian's present experience of being in Christ: "and so we shall always be with the Lord!" (4:17c), that is, "live with him" (5:10). The future for which one hopes is in its essential meaning nothing other than what is already given, a being "with Christ." Paul does not leave us guessing about the ethical implications of this, either. In I Thessalonians 5:5 he points out that the expectation of the Lord's return marks out Christians as "sons of light and sons of the day; we are not of the night or of darkness." Since we belong to the future, we are not ultimately "of this world." Then immediately, without pause or apology, Paul draws the practical ethical conclusion: "So then let us not sleep, as the others do, but let us keep awake and be sober" (vs. 6).

Another outstanding example of this, and one to which we shall return in a later chapter, is to be found in Romans 12–13. This long section of ethical appeals is prefaced in 12:1-2 and concluded in 13:8-14 with eschatological references. "Do not be conformed to this age [RSV footnote], but be transformed . . . "; "The night is far gone, the day is at hand. Let us cast off the works of darkness and put on the armor of light; let us conduct ourselves becomingly as in the day, not in reveling and drunkenness," and so on. In still another letter, to the Philippians, Paul climaxes his admonitions with the reminder that believers are citizens of a heavenly commonwealth, from which they await their Savior, the Lord Jesus Christ (3:20). Their status does not undercut, but makes more urgent, their present ethical responsibilities. There is not, in fact, a major block of ethical teaching anywhere in the Pauline letters in which the practical appeals are not specifically and emphatically supported with reference to the hope by and in which the believer lives, and by and in which the believer has been granted his or her new identity as one "in Christ."

The Role of the Spirit

The interrelationship of Paul's eschatological expectation and his concrete moral instructions may be further clarified when one notes the way in which he sees the Holy Spirit functioning. When the Apostle speaks of the Spirit of God he is thinking primarily of the presence and power of God active in the life of the believing community and in the lives of those who are a part of it. Spatial metaphors tend to predominate in the way most of us think and speak of God and the Holy Spirit: God is "up there," and God's Spirit "comes down" to dwell among and in us. These spatial metaphors are certainly not alien to the Bible. But it is important to notice that Paul at least as often expresses the reality of God and of the Spirit in *temporal* metaphors, using, for example, the categories of present and future. On the one hand, he may conceive of the present moving ahead toward the future (for example, Rom. 13:11-12); and, on the other hand, he may conceive of God's future moving in on the present. In the latter case he writes of the Holy Spirit as the bearer of God's future, establishing the power of the New Age already in the midst of this present age, within the community of those who, by their faith in Christ, are participants in the new creation. This is the meaning of two special metaphors, both temporal in character, by which Paul describes the Holy Spirit.

One metaphor derives from Israel's practice of offering to God, at the annual Festival of the Harvest (or "of Weeks"), the first and presumably choicest portion of the yield. These *first fruits* were not the whole, but they represented and in an important sense embodied the whole, symbolizing that the entire harvest was God's gift and belonged to him. When, in Romans 8:23, Paul refers to believers as those "who have the first fruits of the Spirit," he is thinking of the Spirit as the power of salvation present already with believers, empowering and renewing and, even in the midst of the present age, establishing them in the hope for the full harvest that is to come (see verses 24-25).

Paul's other temporal metaphor for the Spirit derives from the world of business and commerce, and it appears twice in II Corinthians. In these instances the idea is of a *down payment* or *first installment*. "God," writes Paul, "has given us the Spirit as a guarantee" (5:5). Such "earnest money" is not the whole sum, but it represents the whole, and it establishes the credit of the one from whom it has come. Here again Paul is thinking of the gift of the Holy Spirit as the effective presence of God's power in the present—not the fullness of it, but no less the reality of it in the believer's life: "[God] has put his seal upon us and given his Spirit in our hearts as a guarantee" (1:22). This image, like the other, shows that the concept of the Spirit plays a key role in Paul's thinking about the present and the future. The Spirit is the bearer of the power of the New Age, inaugurated, but not yet fulfilled, in the present life of believers.

Now what has this to do with ethics? How does this conception help us understand the vital relationship that exists between Paul's eschatological expectation and his concrete moral instructions? The answer is clear when one recognizes that for Paul the power of the New Age is *love*—not just love in general, but *God's* love, the love through which God has created all that is, in which God wills that it be sustained, and by which God acts to redeem it. For Paul the decisive *event* of God's love is Christ's death. There he finds established that powerful, redeeming love by which the world is reconciled to God and by which those who are open to receive it participate in the new creation (II Cor. 5:14-20; Rom. 5:6-11). This is the love, *God's* love, to which faith is a response, and by which faith itself is empowered to express itself in the believer's life (Gal. 5:6, assuming a double reference in the verb: faith rendered active by God's love and expressed in the believer's love).

If Christ's death is for Paul the decisive *event* by which God's love is established, then it is equally true that for Paul it is God's Holy Spirit that is the decisive *bearer* of God's love, the means by which God's love is made present in the believer's life. "God's love," he writes in Romans 5:5, "has been poured into our hearts through the Holy Spirit which has been given to us." When this affirmation is added to the other cardinal points of Paul's preaching, one may begin to see how, finally, the Apostle's idea of justification by faith, his eschatological expectation, and his ethical concerns are all interrelated, even though he himself has nowhere worked the interrelationships out systematically. They are there, nevertheless, because he understands that faith is *only* faith as it is enacted in *love,* which is the power of the New Age present and active already in the Holy Spirit. It is therefore by the enlivening power of the Spirit that the believer is sustained and guided in his or her new life. "If we live by the Spirit, let us also walk by the Spirit," he writes to the Galatians (5:25), and in the same passage he has indicated that the principal (and all-inclusive) fruit of the Spirit is love (5:22). The three decisive marks of the life in Christ are faith, hope, and love, and of these it is love alone that never ends. That is so because love is understood as God's power, the power of the New Age, reaching back into our present, claiming us for God and endowing our existence with meaning and direction.

Conclusion

It is unacceptable to treat Paul's moral instructions as if they were a sacred cow, and equally unacceptable to treat them as if they were a white elephant. It is not just that these ideas are too extreme, and that one must look for some middle way that will avoid the errors at both ends. Rather, these ideas are both *wrong*. The one approach, for which the sacred cow has been our symbol, misunderstands the nature of the Bible, the intentions of the biblical writers themselves, and the ways in which the moral instructions of Paul are related to the specific needs of Christians living in the Greco-Roman world. The other approach, symbolized here by a white elephant, fails to perceive the interrelationship that exists between Paul's proclamation of the gospel and his concrete ethical teachings and exhortations. In consequence of these points, before the meaning of Paul's moral teaching for our own day can be determined, its meaning for and in Paul's own day must be assessed. This requires that we pay attention both to the sociopolitical context in which Paul's ministry was conducted and to the broader context of Paul's preaching and ministry of which his moral teaching was an integral part.

One final observation about sacred cows and white elephants may help to clarify what is being argued here: *Whenever one treats Paul's moral teaching as if it were a sacred cow, one runs the risk of turning it into a white elephant.* That is, if we regard the particulars of Paul's moral instructions as automatically applicable and binding in *our* times and circumstances, we are sure to end up with a good many requirements that are either irrelevant or, what is worse, clearly inappropriate. Moreover, we shall be disappointed to find that Paul has nothing to say about problems that are real and urgent ones in the modern world: overpopulation and world hunger, nationalism, environmental pollution, the threat of nuclear holocaust, the unprecedented moral dilemmas posed by developments in the fields of genetic engineering and medical science, to name but a few. These are distinctively issues of the modern, technological age, and they must be faced and thought through even though no biblical writer could have addressed them in any specific way. But if we try seriously to understand and assess what Paul did have to say about the issues of his own day, how his teaching applied in the situations to which it was addressed, and how it functioned within the overall theological perspective of the Apostle, then it can take on new meaning for us in our day.

In the following chapters, attention will be focused on several topics that Paul discussed and that continue to be of concern for modern Christians. Even so, the principles enunciated above still apply. Just because the general *topics* are the same does not mean that the issues are the same. It must be our task to inquire, in each case, into the issues as Paul faced them and into the resources Paul had at hand as he responded to them. We should not expect to find clear and specific answers to our particular ethical questions. Paul's instructions were shaped to meet the situations that confronted him and his congregations in their world, and their relevance for Paul's first readers must be distinguished from their relevance for us. Their importance for us, as we shall see, is less in the particular patterns of conduct they promote than in the underlying concerns and commitments they reveal. They show us faith being enacted in love, and love seeking to effect its transforming power in the midst of this present age.

For Further Reading

Three valuable books on the general topic of biblical ethics are *Bible and Ethics in the Christian Life,* by Bruce C. Birch and Larry L. Rasmussen (Minneapolis: Augsburg Publishing House, 1976); *Biblical Ethics and Social Change,* by Stephen Charles Mott (New York/Oxford: Oxford University Press, 1982); and *The Use of the Bible in Christian Ethics,* by Thomas W. Ogletree (Philadelphia: Fortress Press, 1983). Wolfgang Schrage's article, "Ethics in the New Testament," in *The Interpreter's Dictionary of the Bible,* Vol. 5 (Nashville: Abingdon, 1976), is especially helpful on Paul's teaching. On the topic of New Testament eschatology in general, see the article in the same volume by Elizabeth Schüssler Fiorenza. I have treated certain points in the foregoing chapter more extensively in *Theology and Ethics in Paul* (Nashville: Abingdon, 1968) and in a chapter on Paul in *The Love Command in the New Testament* (Abingdon, 1972). Leander E. Keck's *Paul and His Letters* (Philadelphia: Fortress Press, 1979) and the book he and I have co-authored for the Interpreting Biblical Texts series, *The Pauline Letters* (Nashville: Abingdon Press, 1984), provide brief introductions to the apostle's life, letters, and teaching as a whole.

Books referred to or quoted in this chapter: William Wrede, *Paul,* trans. E. Lummis (London: Philip Green, 1907); Willi Marxsen, *The New Testament as the Church's Book,* trans. J. E. Mignard (Philadelphia: Fortress Press, 1972), an important discussion of the apostolic norm in the earliest church; Martin Dibelius, *From Tradition to Gospel,* trans. B. L. Woolf (London: Nicholson and Watson, 1934), especially pp. 238-39; Albert Schweitzer, *The Mysticism of Paul the Apostle,* trans. W. Montgomery (London: Adam and Charles Black, 2nd ed. 1953), quotations taken from pp. 297, 311, 333; and Jack T. Sanders, *Ethics in the New Testament* (Philadelphia: Fortress Press, 1975), chapter 3.

II

SEX: MARRIAGE AND DIVORCE

Among the most difficult and misunderstood passages in the Pauline letters are those which have to do with women, specifically with their role in marriage and their role in the church. On the one hand, there are those who fasten on these texts to prove how "unchristian" the movement for women's rights is. On the other hand, there are those who believe that in these matters, at least, the Apostle's personal biases were so substantial that his teaching can no longer be taken seriously. For this reason it will be important to examine that teaching with some care. In this chapter, only the question of marriage and divorce will be discussed; the issue of a woman's place in the church has been reserved for chapter 4.

Paul's principal comments on marriage and divorce occur in a passage, I Corinthians 7, where the fundamental issue is not the family, but whether sex ought to have any place in the life of a Christian. In Ephesians and Colossians there are passages that focus directly on the Christian household and the respective roles of husbands, wives, children, and slaves; but there are persuasive reasons for believing that those letters were written after Paul's death by a later interpreter of his teaching. It is precarious to base one's estimate of Paul's own teaching on those passages. (See below, pp. 89-90.) The place to begin is I Corinthians 7, where Paul is responding to some issues that have been raised by the Corinthians themselves.

The Situation in Corinth

The Corinthians have written to Paul asking for instruction on a series of matters which had stirred up controversy in their congregation. The Apostle refers to their letter in I Corinthians 7:1, and most of the remainder of his own letter is in response to it. In chapter 8 we see him dealing with the question of whether Christians should eat meat that has been ritually slaughtered in pagan temples. In chapter 11 the question concerns head coverings in church. In chapters 12–14 it is the question of spiritual gifts, in chapter 15 the future resurrection, and in chapter 16 the collection for the Christians in Jerusalem. But underlying all of these, including the question about sex discussed in chapter 7, is the belief, held apparently by a sizable number of Corinthians, that salvation has already been granted in its fullness. These Corinthians seem to have been ecstatics, convinced that they were gifted with a spirituality that in effect lifted them above the worldly and the physical. They probably regarded their speaking in tongues as one evidence of this, and perhaps they identified it with the language of the angels themselves (see I Cor. 13:1).

In I Corinthians Paul is more than once sharply critical of those who presume to possess a superior religious knowledge. " 'Knowledge' puffs up, but love builds up," he says (8:1). And in one of the most scathing indictments to be found anywhere in his letters, he caricatures these spiritually pretentious Corinthians by presenting them as claiming a status to which neither he nor any apostle could dare aspire: "Already you are filled! Already you have become rich! Without us you have become kings! And would that you did reign, so that we might share the rule with you!" (I Cor. 4:8). These naïvely arrogant Corinthians, claiming for themselves spiritual wisdom, knowledge, and glory, have missed the meaning of the cross. Such is the burden of Paul's message in the first four chapters of I Corinthians.

This special Corinthian brand of Christianity also had concrete moral implications. These were of two very different kinds. On the one hand, a view of salvation which, like the one

Paul criticizes, demeans the worldly and physical, can lead to a reckless libertinism. If the spiritual existence is completely independent of the physical, then why be concerned about morality at all? "All things are lawful" must have been the libertinistic slogan of some of the Corinthian ecstatics. Paul quotes it back to them in I Corinthians 6:12 and 10:23 in order to correct it with the reminders, "but not all things are helpful" and "not all things build up." They were also saying, "Food is meant for the stomach and the stomach for food," by which they meant that being in Christ allows one to give free rein to all physical desires. This slogan, too, Paul quotes in order to refute. He warns: "and God will destroy both one and the other. The body is not meant for immorality, but for the Lord, and the Lord for the body" (6:12-13).

Other Corinthians, however, doubtless equally convinced of their superior religious status, were reading the ethical implications in quite a different way. They did not think that their special experience of salvation permitted them to give free rein to physical, worldly impulses and desires. They held that these must be denied, repressed, held in constant check. In matters of ethics they were not libertines but ascetics, especially in the matter of sex. The ascetics also had their slogans, and from Paul's standpoint the asceticism of this group was just as misguided as the libertinism of the other. It is above all the concern to correct the ascetic error that moves Paul to write to the Corinthians as he does about marriage and divorce.

Marriage

Paul's comments about marriage in I Corinthians 7 have been an embarrassment to many modern readers. One commentator has opined that "the best [Paul] can say for marriage in this entire chapter 7 is that it is no sin." And the same writer thinks the discussion reads like something that comes from a person who "had been through a marriage that almost but never quite succeeded." We shall see that these statements are not really fair to Paul.

To begin with, we must remember that Paul's topic is not marriage as such, but the place of sex in the Christian's life. Many recent interpreters agree that quotation marks should be placed around the second half of verse 1, thus: " 'It is well for a man not to touch a woman.' " No such punctuation marks were available to Paul, so their inclusion or omission has to be an editorial decision of the translator. In I Corinthians 6:12, 13; 10:23, as noted above, the translators of the Revised Standard Version have seen fit to include them, indicating that Paul was quoting the Corinthians. That must also be the case in 7:1b (despite the RSV), otherwise the subsequent statements make no sense. The statement that a man should not "touch" (engage in sexual relations with) a woman is a slogan of the Corinthian ascetics. It was probably quoted to Paul in the letter sent to him from Corinth, along with the request that he give his authoritative opinion about its validity. This he proceeds to do at once (verses 2-7):

> (2) Because of the temptation to immorality each man should have his own wife and each woman her own husband. (3) The husband should give to his wife her conjugal rights, and likewise the wife to her husband. (4) For the wife does not rule over her own body, but the husband does; likewise the husband does not rule over his own body, but the wife does. (5) Do not refuse one another except perhaps by agreement for a season, that you may devote yourselves to prayer; but then come together again, lest Satan tempt you through lack of self-control. (6) I say this by way of concession, not of command. (7) I wish that all were as I myself am. But each has his own special gift from God, one of one kind and one of another.

Paul begins by affirming the traditional Jewish view of marriage: a husband shall have one wife, and a wife, one husband. The word here translated as "immorality" refers in particular to sexual immorality, and in effect the Apostle is emphasizing that apart from the covenanted relationship between a husband and a wife that marriage represents, sexual relationships are immoral. Paul's argument reflects the rabbinic teaching to which he was heir. The rabbis insisted on marriage for two main reasons. First, it was necessary for the purpose of procreation. Significantly, Paul does not use this argument. Because of his sense of living at the close of history, he could not have accorded such an argument any validity. But the rabbis also argued for the importance of marriage because without it one might be tempted by immoral forms of sexual activity. This argument does have meaning for Paul, and is doubtless echoed here in his phrase, "Because of the temptation to immorality."

Although Paul's response to the problem at Corinth has been influenced in part by one familiar rabbinic argument for marriage, that argument itself is not the Apostle's main point. It would be quite wrong to interpret either Paul or his rabbinic contemporaries as saying that marriage exists solely as an outlet for the sexual appetites. Such an interpretation is, in Paul's case, explicitly ruled out by his own sharp criticism of "the heathen" who enter into marriages precisely out of their "lust" (I Thess. 4:3b-5). Rather, the main point Paul wants to make is that sex is not only permissible (moral) within marriage, but is something *due* to each partner and therefore something for which each partner is *obligated* to the other. This is the point registered in verse 3, and it is one directed especially to the Corinthian ascetics, who were denying the propriety of sex for Christians under any conditions. They were apparently arguing that the new life in Christ precludes a sexual union even between a husband and a wife.

In I Corinthians 6:15-16a Paul had reminded the Corinthians about the incompatibility of membership in Christ's body and sexual union with a prostitute. This was probably a standard part of his missionary teaching. Some Corinthians had misunderstood this to mean that *any* kind of sexual union defiles the temple of God, and thus the body of Christ. It is likely that they believed conversion to Christ required married persons either to separate or to maintain "celibate marriages." In the paragraph before us, however, we see Paul going on record as emphatically opposed to this view. The scriptural injunction of Genesis 2:24, which he had quoted in *opposition* to prostitution (I Cor. 6:16), would have led Paul just as readily to the *affirmation* of a sexual relationship between husband and wife: it is God's will that the two shall become "one flesh."

An outstanding feature of Paul's discussion in chapter 7 of I Corinthians is his emphasis on the need for a husband and wife to recognize their complete *mutual* responsibility in matters of sex (verses 3-4). One interpreter has called this an "incredible" and "repulsively external requirement," saying that "the mechanical sexuality envisioned for these marriages, is almost emetic in its conception." This is a gross distortion of Paul's meaning. His point is, first, that sex is a meaningful part of marriage, and meaningful only within marriage. And the second point is that neither partner should peremptorily thrust himself or herself upon the spouse in a way that would exploit the other person sexually. The statement about not ruling over one's own body (verse 4) is applied to *both* partners precisely in order to establish the point that *sex must be a shared relationship between two persons of equal standing.* What Paul is saying about mutuality in matters of sex (because sex is the issue being discussed here), he would say also about other aspects of the marriage relationship. This is shown by the important aside of I Corinthians 11:11, where, in a more general statement about the interdependence of male and female, he insists that "in the Lord woman is not independent of man nor man of woman."

In I Corinthians 7:5 Paul recognizes that sexual abstinence may have a place within marriage, but only under three conditions: that it be temporary, that it be by mutual agreement, and that it be for prayer. Otherwise, as in the more extreme case of celibate marriages, one may be tempted to seek the fulfillment of one's sexual desires elsewhere, and that would be immoral. It is probable that this allowance for temporary sexual abstinence within marriage is the "concession" (RSV) of which the Apostle speaks in verse 6, even though many have taken that as a reference to marriage itself. In either case, the word "concession" has come to have connotations in English that are not present in the Greek word Paul himself uses. We speak of a candidate "conceding" the election to an opponent and our picture is of something reluctantly, maybe even bitterly acknowledged. But Paul's word connotes a different attitude, rather like "fellow-feeling" or "forbearance." It refers to an allowance made empathetically, out of concern, with constructive goodwill. So even if he does mean to say that marriage itself is allowed as a "concession," his point would be that it is allowed out of consideration for the well-being of those to whom it is permitted, and not just to be rid of their importuning. It is much more likely, however, that the concession concerns temporary abstinence from sexual intercourse; otherwise Paul would be playing into the hands of the ascetic Christians whose views he is seeking to correct in these paragraphs.

Then what of verse 7, in which Paul expresses his wish that all were single as he himself is? (It is useless to speculate on whether he ever had been married; we have no evidence on the subject.) Doesn't verse 7 prove that Paul regards marriage as an inferior way of life for Christians? That the single state is his own preference is clear. It is equally clear, however, that he regards his celibacy as a "gift" and that this gift is not shared by all. Later in the letter he will tell the Corinthians that there are many diverse kinds of gifts, and that the possession of one or another is no reason for one member of Christ's body to claim pride of place over another—all the gifts are from the one Spirit (chapter 12). Whether or not Paul means to imply that the *married* Christian may also regard his or her status as a gift, he at least does not flaunt his celibacy as proof of some superior religious or moral attainment. That, again, would have played into the hands of the ascetics whose opposition to all sexual relationships he is anxious to correct.

It is often observed that Paul's teaching in this chapter of I Corinthians is conditioned in large part by his belief that "the form of this world is passing away" (verse 31*b*). It is true that this sense of standing on the border between the old age and the new inhibits, if it does not actually preclude, a concern for the nature and quality of marriage as an ongoing social institution. What the times demand above all else, Paul believes, is single-minded devotion to "the affairs of the Lord," to the preaching of the gospel of Christ and the building up of his body into an authentic community of faith. Paul knows that marriage imposes special cares and responsibilities upon the partners—"worldly troubles," he calls them in verse 28. He wishes that Christians could be spared these in order to give their "undivided devotion to the Lord" (verse 35). A significant assumption underlies Paul's comments here. Committing oneself to a marriage means committing oneself in a special way to the existence of another by involving oneself with the spouse in a relationship of care and concern. It is significant that Paul does not *criticize* married persons for having anxieties and worldly cares. He accepts the fact that these are part of marriage. He is just thankful that he himself is not burdened with them. One might reasonably infer from this that had Paul been writing about the responsibilities of marriage, he would have emphasized the caring that must be exhibited by both partners. Indeed, in verses 32-34 what is said of the man is also said of the woman; because marriage is a partnership, obligations run both ways. Mutuality and interdependence are again presumed.

Paul's sense of living at the close of the old age and at the dawning of the New Age also helps to explain the otherwise curious remark in verse 29 that "those who have wives [should] live as though they had none." By this he cannot possibly mean that Christians should eliminate sex from their marriages. That is the view in Corinth which he has been opposing. Nor can he mean that Christians should abandon the responsibilities normally associated with the married state. As we have seen, he presumes these must continue, and for that very reason he rejoices in his own gift of celibacy. The remark in question appears in a whole series of injunctions delivered in view of the "shortness" of the time (verses 29-31). Not only should those with wives "live as though they had none," but also "those who mourn as though they were not mourning, and those who rejoice as though they were not rejoicing, and those who buy as though they had no goods, and those who deal with the world as though they had no dealings with it." In none of these cases does Paul mean that the Christian should opt out of his or her worldly responsibilities. Earlier in this same letter, for example, he had chided the Corinthians for having mistakenly thought it was even *possible* "to go out of the world" (5:9-10). Therefore, Paul's meaning must be that no ultimate value is to be placed on worldly institutions or relationships. No mundane responsibility, however noble or important in this present age, should be allowed to make an *absolute* claim upon the Christian. The Apostle is not denying the *importance* of the responsibilities worldly existence entails, but he is denying their *ultimacy*. Here, formulated with rhetorical skill, Paul is saying in effect that the Christian does not finally belong to this world, but exists within it, always under a higher claim.

Before moving on to what Paul writes to the Corinthians about divorce, we need to be aware of two special questions about marriage on which he comments. One of these questions pertains to Christians who once had spouses, but who have them no longer. Widows are mentioned specifically (verses 8-9 and 39-40). The other special question is about Christians who are pledged to each other, but whose marriages have not been consummated (verses 36-38). In each case, and consistent with his counsel to those who have never been married, Paul says it is preferable not to marry (or to consummate the marriage). Once more, however, he allows that marriage is better for those whose sexual feelings are strong (verses 9a and 36).

The oft-quoted comment in verse 9b, "For it is better to marry than to be aflame with passion," has to be read in the context of Paul's whole discussion. One must remember, first, that he is not discussing marriage in general, or seeking to provide a Christian rationale for it. Rather, he is having to deal with people who claim that Christians should abstain from sexual relations no matter what. In correction of their view, he wants to say that there is nothing edifying about being celibate if one is all the while "aflame with passion." One must also remember that Paul regards celibacy as a *gift*. Considering the urgency of the present times, he regards it as the eminently more practical gift, but not as an inherently "superior" one. To espouse celibacy is no gain if it means to be tortured by strong, unfulfilled sexual desires. For such persons the married status is not just a poor "second best," but *the best;* for them it is the proper way in Christ.

Finally, then, Paul affirms that it is good to be married (verse 38*a*). The added comment that it is "better" not to be is prompted by his conviction that history is drawing to a close, that the responsibilities that are necessarily involved in marriage belong, like other worldly claims, to the realm of what have been called "preliminary concerns" (Paul Tillich) and that it is preferable for the Christian's fullest energies to be devoted "to the Lord." This is no disparagement of marriage. It is Paul's effort to cope with the realities of the present time as he understands them.

Divorce

The matter of separation or divorce from one's partner also claims Paul's attention in I Corinthians 7, presumably because it was another of the points in dispute among the Corinthian Christians. It is taken up in two different connections.

The topic arises first of all in verses 10-11: "To the married I give charge, not I but the Lord, that the wife should not be separated from her husband (but if she is, let her remain single or else be reconciled to her husband)—and that the husband should not divorce his wife." It is significant that Paul says his authority for this teaching is "the Lord." This is one of the very few instances in his letters where the Apostle appeals directly to Jesus' teaching. (The other instances are in I Cor. 9:14 and 11:23ff.; possibly also I Thess. 4:14-15.) We know that these teachings had been kept alive in the traditions of the church through their oral repetition and interpretation, as well as through their practical application.

Finally, but not until after Paul's death, they were committed to writing. Jesus' teaching on divorce to which Paul is referring here has been preserved, although in different forms, in all three Synoptic Gospels, indeed twice in Matthew (Matt. 5:31-32; 19:9; Mark 10:11-12; Luke 16:18). Most commentators have argued that the Gospel of Mark (followed closely in the Gospel of Luke) has provided us the earlier form of Jesus' teaching, and that in the Gospel of Matthew one sees how the church softened that in the concrete application. On the face of it, this would appear to be the case, because the prohibition of divorce is apparently absolute and unconditional in Mark, while in both Matthean passages divorce "on the ground of unchastity" is allowed. It has also been held, however, that the exception-clause was an original part of the teaching. On this view, in Matthew 5 and Mark 10 the saying of Matthew 19:9 has been "abstracted" into a community regulation, and while in Mark permission for divorce "on the ground of unchastity" is not specifically indicated, it is nonetheless presumed. But the more immediate question for us is what Paul understands the requirements to be in this matter.

It was the Greco-Roman world of the first century that Paul knew, and in which Christianity emerged. In that milieu, marriages were just as easily dissolved as they were made in the first place. In society as a whole, no religious sanctions or ideals influenced very significantly either the making or breaking of marriages. Under Roman law, specifically, either husband or wife could initiate the divorce. Within Judaism, however, the situation was different. There the marriage bond was regarded as profoundly important. The union of male and female was regarded as an essential ordinance of God, an integral part of God's creation. There was allowance for divorce, but—at least within the Judaism known by Jesus and Paul—only at the husband's initiative, not the wife's. Ordinarily, only one reason for divorce was acknowledged, namely (as in Matthew) infidelity. And in practice, divorce seems to have been infrequent among the Jews.

There are several striking things about Paul's comments in verses 10-11, in addition to his appealing to the authority of "the Lord." First, the wife is addressed before the husband is; second, the Apostle uses a passive-voice verb when he instructs that she "should not be separated from her husband" (here I have altered the RSV translation, which renders the verb as if it were in the active voice); third, a parenthetical remark reckons with the possibility that a separation may take place, despite Paul's counsel against it; and fourth, while he appears to prohibit any remarriage for the woman (except to her former husband), no such prohibition is addressed to the man. How are these features of verses 10-11 to be explained?

To begin with, one need not be distracted by the fact that Paul uses two different verbs in these verses, "to separate" (verse 10) and "to divorce" (verse 11). There is ample evidence from other ancient sources to show that "separation" was sometimes used as another technical term for "divorce," and that is unquestionably the case here. A more difficult question is why, in verse 10, the passive voice of the verb is used. One plausible explanation is that Paul knows about a specific case in the Corinthian congregation where a husband has threatened to divorce his wife because she does not share his ascetic view that their marriage ought no longer to involve a sexual relationship. Thus, the controversy with Corinthian ascetics which forms the background for verses 1-9 continues to be the background for verses 10-11. In the preceding verses Paul had urged that conversion to Christianity does not require, or really even allow, a husband and a wife to abstain from sexual union. Now he is saying, in addition, that conversion to Christianity does not require divorce, either— although at least one particular Corinthian husband thinks so. In verse 10, the wife is being counseled to resist her husband's attempt to effect a divorce, at least until it is clear whether he is going to persist in his ascetic views despite Paul's arguments against them in this letter. This counsel to her, and the corresponding counsel addressed to the husband in verse 11, are supported by a reference to the Lord's prohibition of divorce, which the apostle obviously takes very seriously. Marriage is a good thing, and it should be maintained.

What, then, of the parenthetical remark in verse 11, which presumes that divorce may occur within the Christian community? One possibility is that the parenthesis was added at a later time to the text of I Corinthians, either accidentally or deliberately. This could easily happen as the ancient scribes copied and recopied manuscripts that, not infrequently, contained marginal notations placed there by earlier readers. There is no evidence that such has occurred in this instance, however.

Assuming that the parenthetical remark originated with Paul, the specific case of that Corinthian ascetic who wants to divorce his wife must still be in view. What if the divorce takes place before this letter reaches Corinth, or despite Paul's advice to the contrary? These are the contingencies that are taken into account when the Apostle adds that, if a divorce does occur, the woman should not remarry—unless it is possible for her to remarry her former husband. Perhaps the most important thing to notice here is that neither party to the divorce is condemned, nor is the congregation instructed to exclude them from its fellowship or to discipline them in any way. Paul's charge to the woman not to remarry is consistent with his principle that it is better to be single, and therefore free to give one's undivided devotion to the Lord. Although there is no specific provision in verse 11 for the possibility that the woman may not have the "gift" to remain single, Paul may intend that what he has just written about "the unmarried and the widows" who have strong sexual desires (verses 8-9) should apply here as well. If, as seems likely, the Apostle is addressing a case where the man has divorced his wife because of his ascetic views, that is enough to explain why the prohibition of remarriage is addressed only to the woman; her ex-husband certainly would not want to remarry so long as he continued to believe that marital union was incompatible with commitment to Christ.

Paul has some further comments about divorce in verses 12-16. Here, however, the specific issue is different. The concern is about what course of action a Christian should follow when she or he converts to Christianity and the other partner in the marriage does not. (Whether a Christian should enter into a marriage with a non-Christian is not raised or answered. Paul has already dealt with the more fundamental question of whether the Christian should marry at all.) This matter is probably still related to the more general subject of sex in the Christian life. The earliest Christians had inherited from Judaism the belief that the sexual union between a man and a woman is a union of *persons*, of *whole beings*, not just a superficial physiological connection. Therefore, it is not entirely surprising to find the Corinthian ecstatics particularly distressed about the sexual union of a man or woman "in Christ" with an unbelieving spouse, even though it appears that they were divided on how this situation should be handled.

In verses 12-14 Paul addresses those in the congregation who believe that it is wrong for a believer to continue in a marriage with an unbeliever. One may suppose that they thought it would be a violation of Christ's body, into which they had been incorporated by faith, to maintain such a marital union. The Apostle thinks not, however, for his instruction is that whether it be the husband or the wife who has been converted to Christianity, the marriage should continue so long as the unconverted spouse is willing (verses 12-13). One should not miss the fact that here as elsewhere Paul presumes that the marriage, if it is continued, should be based on mutual agreement—only if the unbelieving wife "consents" to live with her Christian husband and the unbelieving husband "consents" to live with the Christian wife. It is also worth noting that Paul does not presume that the wife will automatically pledge herself to her husband's religion. The Greek moralist Plutarch, born about A.D. 46, reflects the usual view of Paul's contemporaries when he advises newlyweds that

it is becoming for a wife to worship and to know only the gods that her husband believes in, and to shut the front door tight upon all queer rituals and outlandish superstitions. For with no god do stealthy and secret rites performed by a woman find any favor. ("Advice to Bride and Groom," 140.19)

For Paul, however, faith must have the character of a genuine decision, a free commitment of will, or else it is not really faith. Therefore, he does not seem to presume that a husband's conversion to Christianity will automatically mean the wife's espousal of the new faith, any more than he presumes that a husband's refusal to convert will preclude his wife's conversion.

The Apostle's supporting argument for the instruction of verses 12-13 comes in verse 14. Here he reasons that these mixed marriages must be "holy" marriages, since the church does not in fact consider children born of one to be "non-Christian" in the same way the unbelieving partner is. Paul's argument can be laid out best in the form of a syllogism:

Major premise: Holy children are produced by holy marriages.
Minor premise: Mixed marriages produce holy children.
Conclusion: Mixed marriages are holy marriages.

Admittedly, the Apostle himself has not formulated his argument this clearly, but this is the implicit logical structure of it. The minor premise is quite apparent in the remark of verse 14*b*, addressed to believers married to unbelievers, that "your children . . . are holy." The major premise, left unexpressed, would have been axiomatic, given Paul's belief that sexual union is an essential part of marriage. And the conclusion is legitimately inferred from verse 14*a*, where Paul says that the new life (holiness) brought to the marriage by the Christian partner may effect new life in the unconverted spouse. In effect, this conclusion becomes the minor premise of a second syllogism. Thus:

Major premise: Holy marriages should be maintained. (See verses 10,11.)
Minor premise: Mixed marriages are holy marriages.
Conclusion: Mixed marriages should be maintained.

The question about "mixed marriages" between believers and unbelievers is still in view in verses 15-16, but now the Apostle comments on what the believing partner should do when the unbelieving spouse wants a divorce. In that case, Paul says, the Christian "is not bound" to the Lord's word prohibiting divorce (verse 15*a*). This instruction is based on the Apostle's conviction that, because "God has called us to peace" (verse 15*b*), a marriage can only be "holy" if it is marked by genuine harmony and concord. Perhaps the Apostle has in mind cases where an unbelieving spouse would make the partner's renunciation of his or her faith a condition for continuing the marriage. Or he may be thinking of the difficulties created where marriage partners are committed to different priorities, goals, and values. Whichever the case, he would appear to be unwilling to sanction the idea that marriage is an end in and of itself that must be maintained at any cost. Here Paul shows a sensitivity to the importance of the *quality* of a marriage relationship for which he is seldom given credit. When, practically, the relationship between a husband and wife is no longer characterized by mutual respect, love, and faithfulness, then separation is permissible.

From Paul's comment in verse 16 we may surmise why some Corinthian Christians resisted the efforts of a non-Christian spouse to dissolve the marriage—because they have hoped that the unbelieving spouse could eventually be converted to the gospel. Paul does not rule out this possibility, but verse 16, taken in its context, suggests that he finds that prospect an insufficient reason for continuing such a marriage; the missionary opportunity it may conceivably provide is less important than whether the partners can live together in peace and concord.

Conclusion

May the instructions about marriage and divorce in I Corinthians 7 still have meaning for modern Christians? The realities of Christian existence as Paul understood them in the first century were, in some major respects, different from the realities we face in the twentieth. Unlike Paul, we must reckon with a social and political order of indefinite duration. We are aware, sometimes painfully so, that "the form of this world" is constantly—and rapidly—changing, but we cannot share his view that its "passing" is imminent. Although the characteristics of "Corinthian" Christianity—its ecstatic experiences, its arrogant spirituality, its wavering between libertinism and asceticism—have appeared in one way or another throughout the history of the church, the forms they take in modern Christianity are significantly different from the conditions Paul saw in Roman Corinth. Nevertheless, if we keep these differences in mind, and do not expect all of our twentieth-century problems and questions to be solved for us, Paul's instructions here can still provide guidance in our day.

One more basic caution. We must remember that I Corinthians 7 is addressed to a specific dispute about sex in Corinth. It is not an essay on "the Christian family." If it seems, as laypersons have on occasion complained to me, that "Paul is preoccupied with the sexual part of marriage," that is because sex in marriage is the issue that the Corinthians had appealed to him. We shall be disappointed if we expect to find more than hints of the Apostle's views on other aspects of marriage and family life. He says nothing, for example, about the responsibilities of parenthood, or how these might figure into the question of maintaining or breaking up a marriage. So let us take what we find here, and not chastise Paul for what we do not find. What one does find here is, in fact, rather impressive.

1. *A consistent emphasis on the mutuality of the marriage relationship.* Paul regards the husband and wife as equal partners. They are to share decisions and responsibilities. They are to respect and care for each other. They are to remain faithful to each other. The Apostle emphasizes the importance of mutuality in connection with two areas where conflicts between persons are most apt to arise, religion and sex. We have already seen how, unlike his contemporary, the Greek moralist Plutarch, Paul presumes that a wife's religious

commitments must be genuinely her own, not dictated by her husband's. And we have also noted Paul's emphasis on mutual sexual satisfaction. In this area, too, the contrasting attitude voiced by Plutarch helps us appreciate the distinctiveness of Paul's Christian teaching. The "true mistress of the household," writes Plutarch, is "not to avoid or to feel annoyed at [sexual advances] on the part of her husband if he begins them, [but] on the other hand [she is not] to take the initiative herself; for the [latter] course is meretricious and froward, the [former] disdainful and unamiable" ("Advice to Bride and Groom," 140.18). Paul's teaching on this matter also contrasts with the Jewish view of sex in marriage. The Apostle follows good rabbinic precedent when he teaches the maintenance of regular sexual relations within marriage. But in rabbinic teaching the responsibilities for this are placed on the husband exclusively. A rabbinic saying found in the Talmud (Pes. 72*b*) is typical: "A man is required to make his wife happy." According to the rabbinic view, a marriage must be clearly and entirely under the husband's direction.

At this point something should be said about the passages in Ephesians and Colossians that have been quoted so often in support of the idea that the wife's role in marriage is to serve her husband and to be subordinate to him in every way (Eph. 5:21-33; Col. 3:18-19). Don't these contradict the emphasis on mutuality that is so prominent in I Corinthians 7? As noted earlier, there are good reasons to think Paul did not write Ephesians or Colossians. Specifically, the passages in question are oriented to marriage and the family as ongoing social institutions. We have seen that Paul's own teaching was not. Even so, as careful studies of the admonitions in Ephesians and Colossians have shown, the importance of mutual respect and care between the parties of a marriage is still emphasized, and in this and other ways these passages differ fundamentally from the ideas about marriage and family that were widespread outside the Christian community. (See further below, pp. 89-90.)

2. *A concern for the character of the relationship between husband and wife*. Even though, because of the special issues

in Corinth, this concern is not spelled out, it is pervasive. Paul had reminded the Thessalonians that a man should "take a wife for himself in holiness and honor, not in the passion of lust like heathen who do not know God" (I Thess. 4:4-5). In common with the Judaism out of which he came, the Apostle regards marriage as a part of the goodness of God's creation. Thus, in the apocryphal book of Tobit from the second century B.C., the creation story of Genesis 2 is invoked as offering the prototype of a true marriage. On the night of his wedding to Sarah, Tobias, Tobit's son, prays:

> Thou madest Adam, and Eve his wife to be his helper and support; and those two were the parents of the human race. This was thy word: "It is not good for the man to be alone; let us make him a helper like him." I now take this my beloved to wife, not out of lust but in true marriage. Grant that she and I may find mercy and grow old together. (8:6-7 NEB)

There is no reason to think that now, as Paul writes to the Corinthians, he is any less aware than usual of the importance of the quality of married life. He knows full well that exploitation (for example, sexual) of another person can occur as well within a marriage as apart from marriage. When he says that persons with strong sexual feelings should marry, he is certainly not reducing marriage to the status of a safety valve for pent-up lusts. That is what he sees it to be among the "heathen who do not know God." For those in Christ, the marriage relationship must be characterized by "holiness" and "honor." For Paul, this means that it must be characterized by mutual trust and caring, and by the absolute faithfulness of one to the other. He allows no exception to the principle that a man should have but one wife and that a woman should have but one husband. He emphasizes that the authentic expression and fulfillment of one's specifically sexual drives and desires can take place only within this kind of covenant relationship. While he offers no counsel on how such a relationship may be nurtured (that is not one of the items on his agenda here), he is clearly concerned that

47

harmony and concord should prevail there, according to the peace of God to which all believers are called.

3. *A recognition that individual cases may be different, and that different circumstances may require different actions.* As we have just noted, Paul allows for no exceptions to the principle that sexual relationships are appropriate only within marriage, or to the further principle that absolute mutuality and fidelity should obtain within a marriage. (We know too little about betrothal and marriage customs in the Pauline congregations even to conjecture what the Apostle's attitude may have been toward "pre-marital sex," or even to know whether he would have understood the issue as it is faced by modern Christians.) We have also seen that he allows for no variation from the principle that there should be no permanent abstention from sex within marriage. As he sees it, sexual union is both a legitimate and an important part of the relationship, part of the bonding together of two persons committed to one another.

Apart from these three fundamental points, however, it is remarkable how many varied patterns of action Paul allows for in this chapter. Some should remain single, others should marry. Some should maintain their marriages, others should probably separate. Some formerly married persons should remain unmarried; others may remarry. Some betrothals should proceed to marriage, some should not. And at one point Paul interrupts his instructions to say he is intending not to lay down *restraints*, but "to promote good order and to secure [the Christian's] undivided devotion to the Lord" (verse 35). Flexibility, then, is a prominent characteristic of the teaching here. The Apostle is keenly aware of the way circumstances may vary from case to case, and he takes account of this so far as it is possible for him to do so.

4. *A conviction that believers have been graced by God with different gifts and thus called to different tasks.* This plays a major role in I Corinthians 12 where Paul emphasizes that these varied gifts come from "the same Spirit," but it is also involved here in chapter 7 when, referring to the gift which

makes it possible for him to remain single, he recognizes that most others do not have this gift. He neither flaunts his own gift as the only legitimate one, nor demeans those who do not share it. Rather, he urges them to be mindful of what is right for them, given their own individual situations, even though he could wish that all might share his gift to be single.

Two final observations about Paul's preference for the single state are in order. First, one may legitimately wonder whether Paul does not go too far when he supposes that marriage inevitably distracts and detracts from one's undivided devotion to the Lord's work. He of course recognizes that for those with strong sexual feelings marriage will be less distracting than celibacy. But why does he not recognize that in some instances marriage may actually enhance one's service of the gospel? One thinks of Paul's own dear friends and associates, Priscilla (Paul uses the familiar form, "Prisca") and her husband Aquila; and one wishes that Paul had thought of them, too, as an instance of persons whose service of the gospel seems not to have been diminished by their marriage (see, e.g., Rom. 16:3-4; I Cor. 16:19).

Second, the Apostle's commendation of the single state is not at all what one would expect from someone with his Jewish background. Among the Jews, marriage and procreation (which was understood to be the primary objective of marriage) were regarded as obligatory, and it was considered morally and socially irresponsible to remain single. For Paul, however, it is not the possibility of procreation that legitimates a marriage, but the need of two people for each other and their ability and willingness to commit themselves to each other in a caring relationship. However, where these conditions do not obtain it is both legitimate and good for a person to remain single. When Paul even goes so far as to commend the single state as preferable to marriage, that is not because he shares the ascetic views of those in Corinth he has criticized. It is because he believes that singleness may be regarded as a genuine gift of God, and one which provides a special opportunity for serving the Lord.

For Further Reading

There is no shortage of books and articles on the topics discussed in this chapter. Unfortunately, many of them are highly biased and based on an uncritical analysis of the biblical materials. Responsible, basic information can be found in the various articles on "Marriage," "Divorce," "Kinship and Family," "Sex," and "Sexual Behavior" in *The Interpreter's Dictionary of the Bible,* 5 volumes (Nashville: Abingdon, 1962 and 1976), especially in the Supplementary Volume. Further basic bibliographical information is appended to each article.

The book by Evelyn and Frank Stagg, *Woman in the World of Jesus* (Philadelphia: Westminster Press, 1978) is helpful in several ways. The chapter on "The Domestic Code and Woman," which treats relevant materials in I Peter and the Pastoral Epistles as well as Ephesians and Colossians, is especially good, and a valuable supplement to the more restricted discussion above. I am in less accord with the interpretation of I Corinthians 7 in the chapter on Paul, chiefly because I think the peculiar situation Paul faced in Corinth has not been taken seriously enough. Nevertheless, this discussion, too, supplements mine in certain ways, and it is in agreement with mine in some basic ways. Separate chapters on women in Judaism and in Greek and Roman society provide good general background, and there is a bibliography.

The quotation on pages 31-32 above is taken from Kenneth J. Foreman's exposition of I Corinthians in *The Layman's Bible Commentary,* Vol. 21 (Richmond: John Knox Press, 1961), p. 85, and the quotation on page 34 is from David L. Dungan, *The Sayings of Jesus in the Churches of Paul* (Philadelphia: Fortress Press, 1971), p. 85. A detailed discussion of I Corinthians 7:10-11 in relation to the passages in the Synoptic Gospels constitutes about one-half of Dungan's book. It is here that one may find the argument that the exception-clause belongs to the earliest, not the latest, version of Jesus' saying.

The quotations from Plutarch's "Advice to Bride and Groom" are from Frank C. Babbitt's translation in The Loeb Classical Library, *Moralia,* Vol. II (Cambridge, Mass.: Harvard University Press, 1928). Plutarch's whole essay is worth reading for the light it sheds on non-Christian ideas about marriage in the first century A.D. A useful discussion of marriage practices in Judaism at that time may be found in Leonard Swidler's *Women in Judaism: The Status of Women in Formative Judaism* (Metuchen, N.J.: The Scarecrow Press, 1976), chapter 6; see also Rachel Biale, *Women and Jewish Law: An Exploration of Women's Issues in Halakhic Sources* (New York: Schocken Books, 1984), esp. chapters 2, 3, and 5.

Among the more detailed commentaries on I Corinthians, those by H. Conzelmann, trans. J. W. Leitch for the Hermeneia series (Philadelphia: Fortress Press, 1975), and C. K. Barrett in the Harper's New Testament Commentaries series (New York: Harper, 1968), are the most adequate. Two excellent, briefer commentaries are those by Jerome Murphy-O'Connor, Vol. 10 in the New Testament Message series (Wilmington, Del.: Michael Glazier, 1979), and John Ruef in the Westminster Pelican Commentaries series (Philadelphia: Westminster Press, 1977). My views on Ephesians and Colossians are set forth in *The Interpreter's One-Volume Commentary on the Bible* (Nashville: Abingdon, 1971).

III

HOMOSEXUALITY

When a group of representative laypersons and clergy in a major Protestant denomination were asked to indicate the sources that had contributed to their "present attitudes and opinions concerning homosexuality," *scripture* was named significantly more often than any other source as having contributed the most. The same poll disclosed that a high percentage of those questioned agreed that "homosexual activity is a sin." Their views, it would appear, are accurately mirrored in a letter written to the editor of a large metropolitan newspaper about the "sin" of homosexuality:

> I can much more easily respect and understand an atheist or agnostic accepting homosexuality than an individual who alleges to take the Bible seriously. Scripture is unequivocal on the subject, and to interpret it in any other way is to play fast and loose with God's word. (Dallas *Times Herald,* March 31, 1978)

As it happens, the scriptural texts that are most directly relevant to this question are found in Paul's letters. Because they have been so often invoked and so variously interpreted in the debates about the church and homosexuality, they deserve our careful consideration.

Several questions must be addressed in this chapter. First, what did Paul actually say about homosexuality? Second, what meaning does Paul's teaching on the subject have in our day? In order to answer these, two further questions will have to be considered. What were the realities of homosexual practice in Paul's day; that is, what empirical data were available to him? And, finally, what are the realities of homosexual practice in our day; what empirical data are available to us? Before turning to these questions, however, some preliminary remarks must be made about the status of the biblical evidence in general.

Finding the Biblical Texts

I once had an urgent telephone call from the host of a local television program. He was scheduled to interview a "gay rights" leader in a few days, and he wanted to confront him with the biblical injunctions against homosexuality. He could not find the passages, he confessed, and would I please help him?

That interviewer had already discovered something important although he scarcely realized it: *Homosexuality is not a prominent biblical concern.* The earliest ethical codes of the Hebrews make no mention of homosexual behavior. There is nothing about it in the Ten Commandments. The four Gospels record no saying of Jesus on the subject. The texts that are discussed in this connection are few and far between, and not even all of these are really pertinent. As we begin an investigation of the biblical teaching about homosexuality, then, we must keep our sense of proportion. We are not dealing with a fundamental biblical theme. We are not dealing with a major biblical concern. We have to *hunt* for relevant passages.

It must also be stressed that a Bible concordance is of only limited help in locating these passages. There were no words in Hebrew or in ancient Greek equivalent in meaning to our English words "homosexual" and "homosexuality." Indeed, the term "homosexuality" was not coined until the latter half of the nineteenth century (by a Hungarian writer commenting on the Prussian legal code), and that and related words came into usage in English only toward the end of the nineteenth century. Thus, one will search the King James Version of 1611 in vain for any mention of homosexuality. In fact, the first use of the term "homosexuals" in an English Bible did not come until 1946, with the publication of the Revised Standard Version of the New Testament. In that translation it represents two Greek words included in a list of "vices" in I Corinthians 6:9; however, in the second edition of the RSV New Testament (1971), and thus in the RSV Common Bible (1973), it is dropped in favor of the phrase "sexual perverts" (see below). Some other modern versions continue to employ it in this passage, either as the noun "homosexuals" (for example, *The Living Bible* and the New American Standard Version), or as an adjective ("homosexual perversion" in the New English Bible and "homosexual perverts" in Today's English Version).

Other recent translations, for example the Jerusalem Bible and the New American Bible, use the noun "sodomite" to refer to a male who engages in homosexual activity. This word has a much longer history of use in the English language than "homosexual" and, along with "sodomy," has become a technical term for a type (or types) of sexual activity prohibited by law. The King James Version uses "sodomite(s)" in Deuteronomy 23:17; I Kings 14:24; 15:12; 22:46; II Kings 23:7. Here, again, however, one must beware of placing too much confidence in an English concordance.

The English words "sodomy" and "sodomite" are formed from the name of the ancient city of Sodom. According to Genesis 19, two angels disguised as men came to Sodom and were offered hospitality in Lot's house. After dinner, and before Lot's guests had retired for the night, all the men of Sodom surrounded the house and shouted, "Where are the men who came to you tonight? Bring them out to us, that we may know them" (19:5). The Hebrew word "to know" can be used with reference to sexual relations, and it certainly is used so here, despite occasional claims to the contrary. Lot offers his virgin daughters instead (19:8). The men of Sodom decline the daughters, however, and press forward to do violence to Lot as well as to his guests. Their attack is repulsed only when the visitors cause them to be blinded (19:11). Thereupon Lot is advised to leave Sodom because, his visitors tell him, "The Lord is about to destroy the city" (19:14). Thus it was that brimstone and fire rained down from heaven on Sodom and neighboring Gomorrah (19:24-25), so that the next morning only the smoking ruins could be seen (19:27-28).

Many recent writers, sponsors of what may be called a revisionist interpretation of the story of Sodom, have argued that homosexuality is not involved at all here. They insist that the men of Sodom were guilty only of inhospitality to the visiting strangers. In their view, the verb "to know" does not have a sexual meaning in this case, but only its usual meaning of getting acquainted, finding out who the strangers are and what they are about. This interpretation is not persuasive, however. For one thing, the context makes the sexual meaning of "to know" likely; certainly that is how Lot understands the demand when, in response, he offers his own daughters to the men who make it. Moreover, in Judges 19 there is a similar story of an Ephraimite who stops over in Gibeah for a night's lodging. He, too, is besieged by the men of the city, who cry out to his host that they want to "know" the stranger (Judges 19:22). Again the host offers to substitute his own virgin daughter, or else the visitor's concubine. The offer was declined, but when the concubine was put out to them anyway, "they knew her, and abused her all night until the morning" (Judges 19:25). Clearly, the objective of the men of Gibeah was sexual. Had the Ephraimite himself been attacked it would have been an act of homosexual rape. As it turned out, they abused his concubine instead. It is likely that this story in Judges has been influenced by the Genesis story of the men of Sodom. In each case the men of the city intended a homosexual assault on the visiting stranger. In this respect the revisionist interpretation must be corrected. The story is about sexual lust and violence—in the instance of Sodom, the unfulfilled lust of men directed against men.

We must recognize, however, that later biblical writers were not themselves preoccupied with this homosexual dimension of the old story. The reference to the "abominations" of Sodom in Ezekiel 16:47 probably has the (homo)sexual lust in view, but those abominations are described principally as having to do with "pride, surfeit of food, and prosperous ease," and with a refusal to "aid the poor and the needy" (Ezek. 16:48-50). In some other Jewish writings the crime is understood to have been not the desire of men to have sexual relations with men, but the desire of human beings to have sexual relations with angels, for that is who Lot's visitors really were. (See *The Testament of Naphtali* 3:4-5.) Echoes of this point of view are heard in Jude 6 and 7 and II Peter 2:4-8 in the New Testament. But elsewhere in the New Testament, as very often in the Old, it is the totality of the *destruction* of Sodom and not the particular nature of its crime for which the city is remembered. Thus, Sodom is a symbol for the reality of God's judgment, not a symbol for homosexuality—or even for sexual lust more generally. See, for example, Matthew 10:15 and the parallel in Luke 10:12, and Matthew 11:23-24. The one mention of Sodom in Paul's letters falls into this same category. It is, in fact, not even Paul's own reference, but is quoted by him from Isaiah 1:9. The scriptural text is used by Paul in order to assure his readers of the plight that befalls those against whom God has cause to direct his wrath (Rom. 9:29).

Two Jewish writers contemporary with Paul do refer to the homosexual aspect of the crime at Sodom. One of these is the Alexandrian philosopher Philo, who, in a vivid passage in his essay *On Abraham,* details the various excesses of the Sodomites including the practice of intercourse between males (XXVI.133-136). The other is the historian Josephus, a sometime confidant of Roman emperors. In his *Jewish Antiquities* (I.200-201) he comments that "the Sodomites, on seeing these young men of remarkably fair appearance whom Lot had taken under his roof, were bent only on violence and outrage to their youthful beauty." Significantly, however, homosexual practice is only one of a number of charges Philo lists against them (his remarks will be discussed further below), and the main criticism Josephus has for the Sodomites is their pride, insolence, and refusal to respect the rights and needs of strangers in their midst (see especially *Jewish Antiquities* I.194-195, where, contrary to what some have claimed, Josephus does *not* use the term "sodomy" to mean homosexual intercourse; the term is not used at all.) It is really first of all in the Christian literature of the second century A.D. that Sodom becomes an unambiguous symbol of homosexuality, specifically of the sexual exploitation of a youth or young man by an older male. Subsequently, the terms "sodomy" and "sodomite" came to be used as they are today in English.

It must be emphasized that the development of the sodomitic symbolism sketched above is not in evidence in the Bible itself. Although one may find the word "sodomite" used in some English versions, even recent ones like the second edition of the RSV New Testament (I Tim. 1:10), the Jerusalem Bible, and the New American Bible, no Hebrew or Greek word formed on the name "Sodom" ever appears in the biblical manuscripts on which these versions are based.

In every instance in the King James Version where the term "sodomite" is used, the reference is to male prostitutes associated with places of worship. The practices of the ancient Canaanite and Babylonian fertility cults persisted in Palestine after the Hebrew settlement there, and their rites included the use of both male and female prostitutes. The potential, and in some cases actual, influence of these ancient practices was a persistent concern of the leaders of Israel. It is important to notice that our Old Testament texts attack the male prostitutes not because they engage in sexual relationships with other males; they, like the female prostitutes, are attacked because they serve alien gods. "Sodomite," therefore, is an improper translation; the one adopted in the RSV and other modern versions is much superior, "male cult prostitute." These passages are not about homosexuality, but about foreign idolatries. Thus, for example, King Asa is praised because "he put away the male cult prostitutes out of the land, and removed all the idols that his fathers had made" (I Kings 15:12).

Where, then, can we find the biblical texts worth considering in relation to the question about homosexuality?

The only Old Testament references that still require discussion are to be found in the so-called Holiness Code of Leviticus, chapters 17–26. Here we encounter the earliest specific legislation in Israel against homosexual practices (Lev. 18:22 and 20:13). These laws are part of Paul's heritage from Judaism, and they will be discussed in that connection below.

In the New Testament, apart from occasional references to Sodom (which do not mention the nature of the Sodomites' crime), we have three passages only. Two of these are Pauline—Romans 1:26-27 and I Corinthians 6:9. The third text is I Timothy 1:10. Not only is this the least helpful of the three New Testament passages, but it also stands in a writing that most scholars are unwilling to attribute to Paul himself. The first two passages are those which will have to claim our closest attention.

Homosexuality in Paul's World

Before we can evaluate Paul's remarks about homosexual practice or determine his intentions in the two relevant passages, we must understand something about the place of homosexuality in Greco-Roman society. We must also make ourselves aware of the attitudes toward it expressed in the moral teachings of Paul's contemporaries, Greco-Roman, rabbinic, and Hellenistic Jewish. Only when we have some acquaintance with the phenomenon of homosexuality as Paul's world observed and analyzed it will we be able to deal sensitively with the original meaning of the Pauline texts and with their significance for modern Christians.

Beginning in the sixth century B.C., homosexual love had a relatively prominent place in Greek social life. As several historians have noted, this coincided with the development of a commercial economy based on the institution of slavery and the use of money in business transactions. It coincided also with the increasingly subordinate role assigned to women in Greek society. Women had come to be valued only for their part in helping to ensure the continuation of the race. In this male-dominated society, even when the young female form became the model for beauty, the youthful male was regarded as embodying the ideal. Thus, the more a youth resembled a female, the more he was admired by older males, and the more apt he was to become the object of their erotic attentions. The word for this is *pederasty*, the love of an older man for a boy or male youth, and it was extolled by Plato and many other philosphers as the purest form of love. On the island of Crete it was thought shameful for a boy not to have a lover, a custom that may have derived from ancient puberty rites. In Boeotia, it was reported, men and boys paired off into actual marriages.

Among the Greeks, it appears, pederasty played an important role in a youth's education. Moreover, when Plato described pederasty as among the noblest of all human relationships, his thought was not of a physical relationship but of a "higher" form of love uniting two persons—what we have come to call a Platonic relationship. More than likely these relationships were often physical as well, but it was not the physical as such that called forth the praise of the philosophers. Much the same may be said about the early-sixth-century poetess, Sappho. She presided over an intimate community of young women on the island of Lesbos and was famous, even in antiquity, for her love poems, many of them lyric odes to the beauties of her young proteges. The description of female homosexuality as "lesbianism" derives from this community of women and young girls, even though Sappho herself was married and had a daughter.

During the Roman period, including the first century A.D., in which Paul lived, pederasty as we have just described it was still practiced, and its merits were still sometimes argued in the philosophical literature. Increasingly, however, two other forms of pederasty claimed the attention of moral philosophers, evoking from most of them strong words of condemnation.

One of these involved the sexual exploitation of a youthful male slave by his master, and the other involved the voluntary sale of sexual favors by a "call-boy" to older male patrons. These, and particularly the latter, as Robin Scroggs has shown, would have been the types of "homosexuality" most evident in the great urban centers of the Roman world, and therefore the forms with which the apostle Paul would have been most familiar. Several examples from literature essentially contemporary with Paul's life and ministry are worth citing. Taken together, these help to give us a picture of what Paul must have had in mind when he spoke of homosexual practices. They also indicate what some other thoughtful—and in each case non-Christian—writers were saying about such practices.

The distinguished philosopher, moralist, and statesman Seneca was named a Roman praetor in A.D. 49 and simultaneously appointed tutor to the young Nero. Nero's mother was at that time married to the Emperor Claudius, and upon Claudius' death five years later, Nero became his successor. Seneca thereupon became the new emperor's political adviser, and remained so until A.D. 62 when, disillusioned with Nero's policies, he retired from public life. Seneca's *Moral Epistles* were written during this period of retirement, and they reflect his concern about the lack of moral reason and responsibility in his society. Seneca deplores the way dissolute men of luxury exploit their slaves, and he offers one example that, for our present topic, is of special interest. At a banquet, Seneca complains, the slave who serves the wine

> must dress like a woman and wrestle with his advancing years; he cannot get away from his boyhood; . . . he is kept beardless by having his hair smoothed away or plucked out by the roots, and he must remain awake throughout the night, dividing his time between his master's drunkenness and his lust. (*Moral Epistles* XLVII, "On Master and Slave," 7)

Seneca has here given us a picture of homosexual practice that springs from lust, is associated with idle luxury and moral debauchery, and that takes the form of a grotesque exploitation of another person, a male slave kept artificially youthful in appearance and forced into transvestitism. We are here far removed from the Greek ideal of pure love as it was hymned by Plato.

Plutarch, the Greek biographer, essayist, and moralist, was born about A.D. 46 and died about A.D. 120. His works also give us helpful information about the social environment in which Paul's ministry was conducted. Plutarch was well acquainted with Athens; he had traveled in Egypt, lectured in Rome, and for several decades served as a priest in the important city of Delphi. In his *Dialogue on Love* he has several young men debate whether handsome young Bacchon should marry the rich widow of Thespiae, a certain Ismenodora. Anthemion and Pisias, rivals for Bacchon's affections, have been asked to decide. Anthemion, joined by his friend Daphnaeus, is for the marriage, but Pisias, joined by his friend Protogenes, is against it.

Pisias argues, against the marriage, that decent women are incapable of either receiving or giving sexual pleasure (752B, C). Daphnaeus, on the other side, insists that "if union contrary to nature with males does not destroy or curtail a lover's tenderness, it stands to reason that the love between men and women, being normal and natural, will be conducive to friendship developing in due course from favour" (751C). The same speaker goes on to argue that "to consort with males . . . is a completely ill-favoured favour, indecent, an unlovely affront to Aphrodite [the Greek goddess of love and fertility]" (751D,E). In an aside, Daphnaeus distinguishes between homosexual intercourse "without consent, in which case it involves violence and brigandage," and that which is "with consent," in which case "there is still weakness and effeminacy on the part of those who, contrary to nature, allow themselves in Plato's words 'to be covered and mounted like cattle.' "

In Plutarch's dialogue there is a concern for the sexual exploitation that homosexuality involves, even where there is consent. There is also the typically Stoic aversion to whatever is "contrary to nature." This second point plays an especially important role in the strong condemnation of homosexual practice found in the works of another first-century writer, Dio Chrysostom. He was born about A.D. 40 and died sometime after A.D. 112. Banished from Rome early in the reign of Domitian (A.D. 81–96), Dio wandered for many years through Greece, the Balkans, and Asia Minor, preaching the standard ideas and values of the Stoics and Cynics. Two particular features of homosexual practice as he knew it stand out in his writings.

First, like Seneca, Dio saw homosexuality as essentially exploitative. In one place (*Discourse* LXXVII/LXXVIII.36) he refers to dissolute males "who, though there are women in abundance, through wantonness and lawlessness wish to have females produced for them from males, and so they take boys and emasculate them. And thus a far worse and more unfortunate breed is created, weaker than the female and more effeminate." In another place (*Discourse* XXI.6-10) Dio provides a concrete, and famous, instance of just such a thing. In A.D. 67, after the death of his second wife, Poppaea Sabina, Nero had his male lover, Sporus, mutilated. Sporus was then renamed "Sabina," and publicly married to the Emperor.

Second, Dio understood homosexuality to be an expression of absolutely insatiable lust. In his so-called Euboean discourse (*Discourse* VII) he identifies brothel-keeping as one occupation that is legitimate for neither the rich nor the poor. Brothel-keepers, he complains, "bring individuals together in union without love and intercourse without affection, and all for the sake of filthy lucre" (133). Like Daphnaeus in Plutarch's dialogue, Dio asserts that prostitution blasphemes the goddess Aphrodite, "whose name stands for the normal intercourse and union of the male and female" (135). Moreover, he argues, in cities where the young women are thus corrupted, the corruption of young men is likely to follow. He reasons that men will grow weary of satisfying their lust for women, especially when, for a fee, they have ready access to the town prostitutes. Then, he warns,

> the man whose appetite is insatiate in such things, when he
> finds there is no scarcity, no resistance, in this field, will have
> contempt for the easy conquest and scorn for a woman's love,
> as a thing too readily given . . . and will turn his assault against
> the male quarters, eager to befoul the youth who will very soon
> be magistrates and judges and generals, believing that in them
> he will find a pleasure difficult and hard to procure. (151-152)

Such men, concludes Dio, are like people addicted to wine who, when they have finally lost their taste for it, must "create an artificial thirst by the stimulus of sweatings, salted foods, and condiments." In his view, then, lust and the violation of the natural order go closely together as the cause and the result of homosexual behavior.

Before concluding these observations about homosexual practice and attitudes toward it in the Greco-Roman world, some comments must be made about Jewish teaching on the subject. The earliest specific law against homosexuality in Israel occurs in Leviticus. In 20:13 it had been decreed: "If a man lies with a male as with a woman, both of them have committed an abomination; they shall be put to death, their blood is upon them." The same law is present in Leviticus 18:22, but without reference to the death penalty. The Holiness Code in which this law stands (Leviticus, chapters 17–26) had its origin in the sixth century B.C., either during or just after the Babylonian Exile of the Hebrew people. The purpose of this legislation, made plain early on in the Code, was to establish the distinctiveness of the Jewish cultus over against all foreign cults:

> You shall not do as they do in the land of Egypt, where you
> dwelt, and you shall not do as they do in the land of Canaan, to
> which I am bringing you. You shall not walk in their statutes.
> You shall do my ordinances and keep my statutes and walk in
> them. I am the Lord your God. (18:3-4)

The original purpose of this Holiness Code should be remembered when considering the specific prohibitions contained within it. These are numerous and detailed, and include strictures against various kinds of incestuous relationships (chapter 18), against idolatry (19:4), against cross-breeding cattle, sowing two kinds of seed in one field, or wearing two kinds of fabrics (19:19), as well as against theft, lying, and many kinds of social injustice. In all of these ways the people of Israel were required to maintain their identity and integrity as the people of the one true God. The prohibition of males lying with males, like many of the other laws in this code, sought to identify practices that had been, and ought always to remain, essentially foreign to Israel's life.

Among the Jews, in contrast to the Greco-Roman world as a whole, homosexual behavior was not common. The later rabbis regularly invoked the Levitical prohibitions of it and applied them to intercourse between females as well as to intercourse between males. The rabbis regarded homosexual behavior as a typical Gentile vice, and from a passage in Josephus one can get some idea of how widespread this suspicion was among the Jews. When Antony asked Herod to send his young brother-in-law, Aristobulus, to Rome, Herod decided that it "would not be safe" because Antony was surely set on using the handsome youth "for erotic purposes" (*Jewish Antiquities*, XV.28-29). Josephus himself, in an eloquent defense of Jewish morality and culture, *Against Apion*, echoes the Levitical laws when he writes proudly about the Jews' abhorrence of intercourse between males and of their specifying the death penalty for those who engage in it (II.199).

A passage in which Philo describes the vicious behavior of the Sodomites has already been mentioned. The Alexandrian philosopher's embellishments of the biblical account provide further evidence of the revulsion felt toward homosexual behavior even by Jews who had in many ways fallen under the influence of Hellenistic culture. The men of Sodom, writes Philo, had been debauched by their wealth. Corrupted by their own opulence and satiety,

> they threw off from their necks the law of nature and applied themselves to deep drinking of strong liquor and dainty

feeding and forbidden forms of intercourse. Not only in their mad lust for women did they violate the marriages of their neighbors, but also men mounted males without respect for the sex nature which the active partner shares with the passive. . . . Then, as little by little they accustomed those who were by nature men to submit to play the part of women, they saddled them with the formidable curse of a female disease. (*On Abraham* 135-136)

Here the traditional Jewish abhorrence of homosexuality has found expression in terms current among Gentile moralists like Seneca and Dio Chrysostom. Such behavior is said to contravene "the law of nature" and to spring from unbridled lust.

These representative descriptions of and comments about homosexual behavior in the first century A.D., all from thoughtful, contemporary observers and critics of the social scene, suggest three important points that must be borne in mind as the Pauline texts are studied.

First, not only the terms, but also the concepts "homosexual" and "homosexuality" were unknown in Paul's day. These terms, like the terms "heterosexual," "heterosexuality," "bisexual," and "bisexuality," presume an understanding of human sexuality that was possible only with the advent of modern psychological and sociological analysis. The ancient writers quoted above were operating without the vaguest conception of what we have learned to call "sexual orientation." Dio Chrysostom, for instance, presumed that the same lusts that drove men to engage female prostitutes could drive them eventually to seduce other men. Similarly, Philo wrote of the Sodomites' sexual intercourse with men as if it were one form of their "mad lust for women." Moreover, both writers presumed, with their contemporaries, that one could by force of will *control* these appetites and conform oneself to the sexual behavior dictated by reason or "the law of nature."

Second, then, the critics of homosexual behavior invariably associated it with insatiable lust and avarice. Seneca portrayed it as a rich man's sport, Dio Chrysostom as the ultimate sexual debauchery, and Philo, with reference to Sodom, as one of the vile consequences of wanton luxury and self-centeredness. By Paul's day the old Platonic ideal of the pure, disinterested love between a man and a boy was coming to ruin on the hard realities of Roman decadence. One of the speakers in Plutarch's dialogue could acknowledge the possibility of genuine homosexual love, but even he saw a need to repeat Plato's warning about homosexual seduction; and his real point was that a man's love for a woman is potentially finer than one's love for another man.

Finally, the writers of this period who were concerned about homosexual behavior seemed convinced that it necessarily involved one person's exploitation of another. Stoicism, especially, maintained that one's life must be conducted in accord with the immutable law of nature and in ways appropriate to the created order. The influence of this popular philosophical movement was widespread, and is detectable not only in several of the writers quoted above but also, as we shall see, in the teaching of Paul. The physiological complementarity of male and female and the obvious necessity of heterosexual intercourse for the purposes of procreation would have seemed to many adequate proof that intercourse between persons of the same sex was "unnatural," a violation of "the law of nature." Thus, Plutarch's Daphnaeus admitted, even when both parties consent to homosexual intercourse, that the passive one is bound to be violated. He becomes what he is not—"weak" and "effeminate," and his weakness and effeminacy are more demeaning than that of a woman because they do not belong to the role nature has assigned him. On this view, if there is exploitation of one person by another even where there is consent, how much more where there is none? One thinks of the Sodomites' attempted rape of Lot's visitors, of the actions of a debauched master toward his slaves, or of lustful men toward helpless youth. (The point had not been lost on Philo, who, in the passage quoted above, mentions "the sex nature which the active partner shares with the passive.") To discerning ethical teachers in the Greco-Roman world it seemed just as obvious that homosexual practices were necessarily exploitative as that they were inevitably born of insatiable lust.

The Pauline Texts

The preceding section sought to indicate the ways in which certain writers contemporary with Paul perceived and criticized homosexual behavior. When we turn now to Paul's remarks about such conduct, it becomes apparent that he perceived it in essentially the same way. The picture we have obtained, notably from Seneca and Dio Chrysostom, of homosexual practices in Greco-Roman society, must closely approximate the picture Paul would have had in his mind as he, too, condemned such behavior. But Paul's ethical teachings, one must remember, are integrally related to his fundamental theological convictions, the most definitive of which were not shared by the writers we have considered so far. Therefore, in our analysis of the two relevant Pauline texts we shall need to be aware not only of the social context they presume, but also of the literary-theological contexts within which they stand. The reference in I Corinthians 6:9 is the briefer, more problematic, and overall less informative of the two. It will be well to start with this one, if for no other reason than that it has chronological precedence over the longer and more substantial remarks on the subject in Romans 1:26-27.

1. I Corinthians 6:9

In several recent English versions a reference to homosexuals appears in this verse. Thus, the first edition of the RSV lists "homosexuals" among those excluded from God's kingdom, and so does *The Living Bible*. The New English Bible uses "homosexual perverts," and the New American Bible has "sodomites." The second edition of the RSV New Testament (incorporated into the RSV Common Bible) broadens the concept with a reference to "sexual perverts," with which one may compare the rendering of the New International Bible, "the sexually immoral."

This picture becomes still more confused when one realizes that all the translations cited are using *one* word or phrase to render *two* distinct nouns in Paul's original Greek. Some other translations do try to reflect Paul's use of two different words, but here again the translations are quite varied. The King James Version had rendered them as "effeminate" and "abusers of themselves with mankind" respectively. The American Standard Version changed "mankind" to "men," and recently the New American Standard Version, while retaining the word "effeminate," has translated the second word as "homosexuals." James Moffatt's translation had used the words "catamites" and "sodomites," and these have been more recently revived in the Jerusalem Bible. Goodspeed, on the other hand, had interpreted them as references to those who are "sensual" and "given to unnatural vice," and in the version of J. B. Phillips one reads of the "effeminate" and the "pervert."

The two Greek words in question are *malakoi* and *arsenokoitai*. The root meaning of the first term is "soft" or "weak," and by extension, "effeminate," as in some translations of I Corinthians 6:9. It is significant that this is the very term the critics of "call-boys" often used to describe those who offered their bodies for pay to older males. That Paul is using it this way here seems likely, because it stands in a list where several other terms referring to sexual immorality also appear, for example "fornicators" (RSV renders this term too broadly, as "the immoral") and "adulterers."

The second disputed term is compounded of the word for "male" or "masculine" and a word that refers to "ones who go to bed." Its literal meaning, therefore, is something like, "those who go to bed with males." Although I Corinthians 6:9 is the first documented use of the word, because it is associated here with the term *malakoi* it probably refers to males who engage in sexual activity with other males. Indeed, Robin Scroggs argues plausibly that the word is simply a literal rendering in Greek of the Hebrew phrase *mishkav zakur,* "lying with a male," which was the usual early rabbinic way of referring to male homosexual intercourse. Since *malakoi* would refer to the "effeminate" or passive partner in such a relationship (thus, "catamite" in Moffatt's version and the Jerusalem Bible), *arsenokoitai* doubtless refers to the male who assumes the more active role (translated "sodomite" by Moffatt and the Jerusalem Bible).

Since no English version is fully satisfactory, I offer here my own translation.

> Don't you know that unrighteous persons will not get into God's kingdom? Don't deceive yourselves: neither the sexually immoral, nor idolators, nor adulterers, nor effeminate males, nor men who have sex with them, nor thieves, nor money-grabbers, nor drunkards, nor slanderers, nor swindlers will get into God's kingdom. Some of you were like that; however, you have been cleansed, set apart for God's service, affirmed as righteous, in the name of the Lord Jesus Christ and in the Spirit of our God. (I Cor. 6:9-11)

Granting that this is what Paul *says* to the Corinthians, what does he *mean*, what is his *point*? To understand this we must take a broader look at the passage, considering its literary-theological context.

In chapters 5 and 6 of I Corinthians, Paul is discussing various problems of sexual immorality. Beginning in chapter 7, as we have seen (above, chapter 2), he will deal with some questions (including some about sex) that had been put to him in a letter from Corinth. Here, however, he is responding, first of all, to some troubling news received by means of an oral report, perhaps from the bearer of the letter. He has learned that a member of the Corinthian congregation has taken up living with his stepmother, presumably now widowed (5:1). Paul directs that the man should be put out of their church because of his aberrant behavior (5:2-5). One gathers that the Corinthian Christians had not, themselves, been very worried about the matter. Paul is astonished at their smug complacency ("And you are arrogant!" 5:2) and he criticizes their spiritual pride (5:6-8).

This specific case of sexual immorality in Corinth—we should note that it involved "heterosexual," not "homosexual" behavior—prompts Paul, in 5:9-13, to clarify something he had said in an earlier letter (now lost). He had warned the Corinthians not to associate with persons guilty of sexual (and other) immoralities (5:9). Evidently the Corinthians had taken this to mean (or at least Paul thought they had taken it to mean) that they were to dissociate themselves from society at large. Not at all, says Paul! That is quite impossible (5:10). What he actually meant was that they should break off fellowship with other *Christians* who, like this fellow who is living with his stepmother, are guilty of serious immorality (5:11-13).

Paul's instruction to the Corinthians about disciplining errant members of their congregation moves him, in 6:1-11, to comment on the impropriety of Christians' taking their disputes to secular judicatories for settlement. Of course, it is a shame that any such disputes even arise within the church (6:7-8), but if they do, they should also be heard and settled there, not before "unbelievers" (6:6). Implicit in the argument of these verses is the Apostle's conviction that Christians do not belong, ultimately, to this world. Although they are for the present in this world (see 5:10), they are not "of" it. The world is not to judge them; indeed, because they are God's people the world is in a sense judged by them (6:2). Those who belong to the world are called "unbelievers" (6:6) and, later, "unrighteous persons" (6:9); Christians, on the other hand, are called "saints," people set apart for the service of God (6:1, 2). The question, "Don't you know that unrighteous persons will not get into God's kingdom?" (6:9a), simply emphasizes the distinction that had been implicit in the preceding discussion. On the one hand are the "saints" who belong to God's kingdom even while they are in this world; on the other hand are the "unbelievers" or "unrighteous" people who are not only in this world but belong to it, insofar as they submit to its claims and not to God's.

In 6:9b-10, to make his point yet more concrete, Paul offers a list of unrighteous types, examples of those who belong to this world rather than to God's kingdom. He uses similar lists in I Corinthians 5:10,11, Galatians 5:19-21, and Romans 1:29-31. Catalogs of vices are present elsewhere in the New Testament as well, and as in the Pauline letters are probably to be attributed to the writer's drawing on traditional ethical lists rather than to the writer himself. The author of the so-called Pastoral Epistles, who wrote some years after Paul's death but under his name, incorporates such lists in several passages. The one in I Timothy 1:9-10 includes the second of the two disputed words in I Corinthians 6:9, and in I Timothy the RSV has translated it "sodomites." In this list, as in Paul's own, it is one of a miscellaneous handful of vices chosen to identify actions displeasing to God.

No two New Testament vice lists are identical. Moreover, none is offered as a definitive formulation of all, or even of the chief evils Christians should avoid. When Paul closes the list in Galatians with the phrase "and the like" (5:21), it is clear that he intends such lists to be only exemplary. They only illustrate the kind and range of vices that he deems incompatible with the ways in Christ he teaches in all his churches. These catalogs have been assembled more or less at random. For the most part they contain the kinds of vices that Jews identified with pagan behavior, and similar catalogs are present in the moral literature of Hellenistic Judaism. Paul is probably thinking of the Gentile background of some (perhaps the majority) of the Christians in Corinth when he reminds them, "Some of you were like that" (6:11a). However, their baptism into Christ has now marked them as persons gifted with God's righteousness and God's Spirit, and set apart for his service.

Now, having examined the words Paul uses in I Corinthians 6:9, and having acquainted ourselves with the literary-theological context of the verse, we are ready to ask what it discloses about the Apostle's view of homosexuality. Even as we turn to this task, however, we must acknowledge that "homosexuality" is not the topic in this passage, and that the two words which, taken together, constitute a reference to it, are part of a traditional list of miscellaneous vices commonly attributed by Jews to Gentiles. Paul uses the list as a reminder to his readers that, as Christians, they should have put their old ways behind them. There is no indication that he is aware of or has been asked about any particular problem of homosexual practice in Corinth. In fact, the sexual immorality with which he is specifically concerned in this context is heterosexual in nature (I Cor. 5:1-5; 6:12-20).

Despite all of this, it is legitimate to ask what Paul would have in mind as he recites a list of vices which includes references to "effeminate males" and "men who have sex with them." Given what we have learned about the forms of homosexual activity with which Paul's world was most familiar, it would appear that these references are, respectively, to youthful call-boys and to their customers. According to various ancient writers who condemn this practice, the one partner has violated the male role that by nature is his; and, by taking advantage of this, the other partner has also violated his proper role. Such conduct Paul regards as one of the forms of unrighteousness by which "unbelievers" are distinguished from "saints." Neither here nor elsewhere are such examples of wickedness identified as "sins." In fact, whenever the plural form, "sins," does appear in Paul's letters, it is either a quotation from scripture (once) or in a more or less set formula Paul has taken over from church traditions (four times). The Apostle himself thinks of sin (singular) both as a power that drives a wedge between God and his people and as the condition of alienation from God that results. The various kinds of vice and wickedness listed here and elsewhere are understood by Paul to be symptomatic of sin, not as its roots and essence. This important point becomes especially clear when we analyze the second passage and its context.

2. Romans 1:26-27

This is the most extensive biblical reference to homosexual practice, even though it is still brief, and even though homosexual practice as such is not the topic under discussion. The passage is also notewothy because here, for the first and only time in the whole Bible, one encounters the condemnation of female homosexuality as well as of male. Again with special reference to the immorality of pagan Gentiles, Paul writes: "Their women exchanged natural relations for unnatural, and the men likewise gave up natural relations with women and were consumed with passion for one another, men committing shameless acts with men and receiving in their own persons the due penalty for their error."

One is struck immediately by the similarities between this condemnation of homosexual behavior and that of Paul's non-Christian contemporaries. Like them Paul supposes that homosexual behavior is something *freely chosen* by an individual; in Greek as in English the verbs "exchanged" and "gave up" imply a conscious decision to act in one way rather than another. Like them Paul associates this choice with *insatiable lust;* the men, he says, were "consumed with passion" for other men. And like them, Paul regards such activity as *a violation of the created order;* "natural" heterosexual relations were abandoned in favor of those which were "against nature" (RSV: "unnatural"). These similarities make it reasonable to suppose that the picture of homosexual practice Paul had in his mind corresponded closely to the depiction of it we have seen in the works of Seneca, Dio Chrysostom, and Philo.

The text in Romans, no less than the one in I Corinthians, needs to be appraised in the light of its literary and theological context in the letter of which it is a part. Romans, however, is not addressed to a congregation with which Paul is very well acquainted. He had not founded the church there, as he had the one in Corinth, and he had not even visited there. So far as we know, the Roman Christians had never written him, and it is debated whether any of the ethical teachings of Romans have specific "Roman problems" in mind.

The verses with which we are concerned here stand in a long discussion that begins at Romans 1:18 and continues through Romans 3:20. The best summary of this section of the letter is supplied by Paul himself as he moves into a new phase of his argument (3:22*b*-23): "For there is no distinction; since all have sinned and fall short of the glory of God. . . ."

When he says "all," the Apostle means that Jews no less than Gentiles stand in need of God's gracious gift of justification. How justification comes—"by faith"—and what justification means are important themes from Romans 3:21 through chapter 8. In these chapters we are at the very heart of Paul's gospel. To this the preceding section, 1:18–3:20, provides an important introduction.

Put briefly, Romans 1:18–3:20 stresses the need of all people for the saving grace of God. In 1:18-32 the Apostle is denouncing the wickedness of the Gentiles in terms and with arguments that were the stock-in-trade of much Hellenistic-Jewish teaching. Paul is heir to this, and commentators have long recognized the correspondence between his condemnation of the Gentiles here in Romans and that which appears in the apocryphal Wisdom of Solomon, written in Greek in the preceding century, probably by an Alexandrian Jew. In Wisdom 13:1-9, for example, the author argued that "all men who were ignorant of God were foolish by nature," unable to know God "from the good things that are seen," that is, from his creation (13:1). "For from the greatness and beauty of created things comes a corresponding perception of their Creator" (13:5). This writer is briefly tempted to admire the Gentiles, searching for God (13:6-7), but he finally has to conclude that "not even they are to be excused; for if they had the power to know so much that they could investigate the world, how did they fail to find sooner the Lord of these things?" (13:8-9). It was of course profoundly ironic that the Gentiles had failed to acknowledge the Lord and Creator of the very world that they seemed to understand so well in so many ways. But it was more than ironic; here it is regarded as the essence of their depravity. They mistook the stars of heaven for gods (13:2) and prayed to wooden figures they themselves had carved and painted (13:13-19). This is the ultimate folly, to be caught up with one's own devices and thereby alienated from one's own Creator.

The same interplay of ideas is present in Romans 1:18-32. Here again it is asserted that the world itself is testimony to the existence and sovereignty of God: "Ever since the creation of the world his invisible nature, namely, his eternal power and deity, has been clearly perceived in the things that have been made" (1:20*a*). Here again the Gentiles are given some credit: they do have a certain knowledge of God, Paul admits (1:21). Here again the conclusion follows that the Gentiles are all the more "without excuse" (1:20*b*) for their failure to recognize their sovereign Lord: "they did not honor him as God or give thanks to him" (1:21). And here again Gentile religions are denounced as foolish idolatries: "they became futile in their thinking and their senseless minds were darkened. Claiming to be wise, they became fools, and exchanged the glory of the immortal God for images resembling mortal man or birds or animals or reptiles" (1:21, 22-23). Paul understands the old lesson very well: the grossest depravity of which human beings are capable is "[to exchange] the truth about God for a lie and [to worship and serve] the creature rather than the Creator" (1:25). The word "sin" does not happen to occur in Romans 1:18-32, but the taproot of sin is being described nonetheless. It is the refusal to acknowledge the true source and meaning of one's existence, and therefore the failure to acknowledge the grace and the claim under which one's whole life stands.

The closing paragraphs of Romans 1 have not yet been analyzed, and because Paul's remarks about homosexual conduct occur in them, this phase of the argument needs to be given our particularly close attention. It is opened in verse 24 with the statement that God "gave up" the Gentiles "to impurity." This is restated in verse 26*a* as his having given them up "to dishonorable passions." Then in verse 28 it is restated again, now in such a way as to connect this last phase of the argument with the earlier phases: "And since [the Gentiles] did not see fit to acknowledge God, God gave them up to a base mind and to improper conduct."

Here Paul is still under the influence of the traditions of Hellenistic Judaism, and the Wisdom of Solomon once more helps us grasp his meaning. In Wisdom 11:16 it is claimed that the Gentiles learned "that one is punished by the very things by which he sins." Since they had engaged in the idolatrous worship of "irrational serpents and worthless animals" (11:15; compare Rom. 1:23), their punishment came in the form of savage beasts like ravenous bears and lions (11:17-20). The point is not, however, that their wickedness automatically generated its own punishment. The punishment was *sent* upon them by God (11:16), even though in a form appropriate to the root idolatry. Similarly in Wisdom 12:17—the Gentiles first recognized the true God when they saw his hand in the punishment visited upon them by the very creatures that they had mistakenly worshiped. Paul, too, understands God to be the agent of punishment. He is the one who "gives up" the Gentiles to the appropriate consequences of their idolatries. It is thus "the wrath *of God*" that is *revealed "from heaven* against all ungodliness and wickedness of men" (Rom. 1:18).

In these closing paragraphs Paul is also being influenced by the traditional connection made in Hellenistic Judaism between idolatry and sexual immorality. The Wisdom of Solomon affords us an example.

> For the idea of making idols was
> the beginning of fornication
> and the invention of them was the
> corruption of life. (14:12)

Specific forms of immorality to which the Gentiles have submitted are cataloged in Wisdom 14:25-26: "All is in chaos—bloody murder, theft and fraud, corruption, treachery, riot, perjury, honest men driven to distraction; ingratitude, moral corruption, sexual perversion, breakdown of marriage, adultery, debauchery" (NEB). At the close of this listing it is reiterated that "the worship of idols, whose names it is wrong even to mention, is the beginning, cause, and end of every evil" (14:27 NEB). It is not surprising, then, to find Paul including sexual immoralities among those vices to which the pagans have been led by their own idolatry: lustful impurity and the degradation of their bodies (1:24), and "dishonorable passions" as evidenced by homosexual intercourse (1:26-27).

In this connection he too can speak of the Gentiles having received "the due penalty for their error" (1:27).

The pattern of thought in Romans 1:18-32 should now be clear. It is a denunciation of the Gentiles formulated in accord with traditional Jewish reasoning. Although God's sovereign power was evident to the Gentiles in the created order, they chose to worship gods of their own making. They are therefore without excuse for their refusal to acknowledge their true Creator and Lord. This is their sin, their attempt to exist apart from God. In consequence, God has now been "revealed" to them through his wrath (see Rom. 1:18), and the vices typical of Gentile society are the specific evidences of this. They are the penalties appropriate to the idolatries that have been committed.

Homosexual intercourse is mentioned as one of these typically Gentile practices (1:26*b*-27). It is regarded not as one of the "sins" of the Gentiles, but as one of the *consequences* of their root sin of refusing to let the one true God be *their* God. There is nothing in Paul's description of homosexual conduct, if we abstract it from the context in Romans 1:18-32, which could not have been written by Paul's non-Christian contemporaries, like Plutarch and Dio Chrysostom. And even granting the context, a Hellenistic Jew like Philo could just as well have written it. The particular function Romans 1:18-32 has in the whole of Romans 1–8, is another matter, however. Paul's condemnation of the Gentiles is only preludial to Romans 2:1–3:20, where he argues that also the Jews are sinners before God. Because they presume that they are justified by doing what the law requires (see, for example, 3:20), they too are guilty of trying to live on the basis of their own devices. So Paul can conclude (and he quotes scripture to prove it) that all peoples, "both Jews and Greeks, are under the power of sin" (3:9, followed by citations from the Psalms in verses 10-18). This is why God had acted in Christ to reconcile his people to himself, and this is the very gospel for which Paul had been made an apostle. The redemptive grace of God in Christ is the one great theme of all of Paul's letters and the fundamental theological basis of all of his ethical teaching.

Conclusion

In common with many "secular" moralists of his time and in accord with the teachings of the rabbis and of Hellenistic Judaism, Paul condemns homosexual practices. However, he is not preoccupied with this matter (we have at most only two relevant texts in his letters), and there is no evidence that he ever had to deal with a specific case of homosexual conduct. His references to it are brief and formulated under the influence of traditional ideas about its causes and characteristics. In Romans, the most important text, his remarks do not even occur within a specific section of ethical teaching. They are a relatively incidental part of his argument that all people are sinners who stand in need of salvation. In the light of all of this, what shall we do with these texts today?

1. *Since Paul offered no direct teaching to his own churches on the subject of homosexual conduct, his letters certainly cannot yield any specific answers to the questions being faced in the modern church.* Shall practicing homosexuals be admitted to church membership? Shall they be accorded responsibilities within a congregation? Shall they be commissioned to the church's ministry? The Apostle never asks or answers these questions. He assumes that homosexual conduct is symptomatic of an individual's fundamental refusal to acknowledge God, so it is doubtful that such questions could ever have occurred to him. On these points there are no proof texts available one way or the other. It is mistaken to invoke Paul's name in support of any specific position on these matters.

2. *Paul, in common with the traditions by which he was influenced and in accord with the wisdom of his day, saw the wickedness of homosexual practice to inhere in its lust and its perversion of the natural order.* In this connection, however, we must remember that it was the more degraded and exploitative forms of pederasty that the Apostle and his contemporaries had in view when they condemned homosexual practice. Paul, like many of his contemporaries, doubtless regarded such behavior as a matter of deliberate choice born

of an insatiable sexual appetite. The moral legacy Paul had received from Hellenistic Judaism certainly left no doubt in his mind that pederasty was a specifically Gentile vice and one of the numerous signs of pagan idolatry. In Romans 1 we have seen homosexual intercourse named as one of the dreadful consequences of the Gentiles' refusal to receive the world as it was created and their own lives within it as gifts from God.

But what Paul accepted as a matter of course about homosexual behavior, we can no longer take for granted. The modern behavioral sciences are still baffled by many aspects of this phenomenon; yet there is broad agreement on a number of points. To begin with, one must now acknowledge that homosexuality is an exceedingly complex phenomenon. The description and analysis of it offered by ancient writers are as outdated as their descriptions of the bodily organs. The present scientific consensus is that homosexuality has multiple causes. Important psychological and social factors, and perhaps even some biological conditions, play a role in the formation of a person's "gender identity." Moreover, the forms and evidences of homosexuality are now understood to be many and varied. Modern students of the subject are reluctant to speak of homosexuality and heterosexuality as mutually exclusive categories. They much prefer to speak of homosexual and heterosexual aspects in the sexual orientation of a given individual. They refer to "latent" and "active" homosexuality, and allow that the latter can manifest itself in different ways, some of them more and some of them less socially acceptable. It is also clear that homosexual behavior does not necessarily involve the sexual exploitation of another person, and that it does not necessarily take the bizarre forms that were so evident in Paul's time.

If Paul had said somewhere that all mushrooms are "naturally poisonous," therefore those who eat mushrooms or cause others to eat them will not get into God's kingdom, we should think it important to reconsider his verdict in the light of our present-day knowledge. When in I Corinthians 11:14-15 he actually does say that it is unnatural for men to wear long hair and for women to wear their hair short, we find the judgment eccentric (the only "natural" thing is to let one's hair grow as long as it will!). Of course, human sexuality is an infinitely more complex phenomenon, indeed, far more complex than Paul and his contemporaries could have realized. Precisely for this reason, the Apostle's judgments in the matter require careful interpretation and evaluation if they are to be meaningful in the light of our present knowledge.

It would be unfair to charge Paul with naïveté or ignorance in the matter of homosexuality. Such evidence as we have suggests he was as informed as anyone could have been in his day. Indeed, *we* should be the naïve ones were we to ignore the data available to us in our own day, supposing that Paul's teaching alone is sufficient to answer our questions about right and wrong in this difficult matter.

3. *Paul's fundamental concerns about homosexual practice (as he understood it) are as valid in the twentieth century as they were in the first.* When Paul referred to homosexual behavior he was illustrating the wretchedness of the human condition where there has been no acknowledgment that life is God's gift and that one's existence stands always under God's claim. To Paul it represented a rebellion against the Creator and his creation, a surrender to one's own lusts, the debasement of one's own true identity and the exploitation of another's. It is no longer possible to share Paul's belief that homosexual conduct always and necessarily involves all these things. But it can be said with certainty that whenever a homosexual *or* heterosexual relationship does involve one or more of these, it stands under the judgment of scripture.

4. *Paul's remarks about homosexual behavior must not be isolated from the wider theological context in which they stand.* One must remember the function of Romans 1:18-32 in the letter as a whole. Paul repeats the standard Jewish accusations against the Gentiles in order to be able to say, respecting the Jews, "they are no better," and to emphasize that all stand in need of God's grace (2:1–3:20).

One must also remember that homosexual practice is mentioned in this context as just one of numerous vices that are symptomatic of sin. For Paul neither homosexual practice nor heterosexual promiscuity nor any other specific vice is identified as such with "sin." In his view the fundamental sin from which all particular evils derive is idolatry, worshiping what is created rather than the Creator, be that a wooden idol, an ideology, a religious system, or some particular moral code.

And finally, one must remember that 1:18–3:20 is itself prefatory to the good news about the reality of God's grace, which is expounded in the rest of Romans. Romans 5:6-11 is one classic summary of Paul's gospel: While we were still "weak," still "sinners," and still "enemies" of God, he reconciled us to himself through the love revealed and made real for us in Christ's death.

For Further Reading

D. S. Bailey's discussion of the biblical materials in his book *Homosexuality and the Western Christian Tradition* (London: Longmans, Green, 1955) has influenced much of the subsequent literature, though biblical scholars and others have challenged many of his conclusions. A more recent and more comprehensive examination of the biblical texts is Tom Horner's *Jonathan Loved David: Homosexuality in Bible Times* (Philadelphia: Westminster Press, 1978). Horner corrects Bailey in a number of important ways. It is unfortunate, however, that Horner feels constrained to argue for at least the possibility of homosexual relationships between Jonathan and David and Ruth and Naomi, respectively, and to hint at the homosexual characteristics of Jesus and Paul. Our sources simply do not provide the data to support such ideas. Horner's treatment of the Old Testament passages is, on the whole, better than his treatment of the Pauline texts.

Especially to be commended is the book by Robin Scroggs, *The New Testament and Homosexuality: Contextual Background for Contemporary Debate* (Philadelphia: Fortress Press, 1983), whose careful study of the literature contemporary with Paul documents points that I have been able to make only briefly in the present chapter. In particular, his discussion of I Corinthians 6:9 has contributed substantially to my understanding of that text, and has enabled me to sharpen my own comments on it. His more general reflections on the role of the Bible in current discussions about homosexuality are also commendable. Numerous other treatments of the pertinent texts can be found by consulting Tom Horner's *Homosexuality and the Judeo-Christian Tradition: An Annotated Bibliography,* ATLA Bibliography Series, No. 5 (Metuchen, N.J.: The Scarecrow Press, 1981).

In citing and quoting from non-Christian contemporaries of Paul, I have relied on The Loeb Classical Library as follows: Josephus, *Jewish Antiquities,* Book I, trans. H. St. J. Thackeray (1930), Book XV, trans. Ralph Marcus and Allen Wikgren (1963), and *Against Apion,* trans. H. St. J. Thackeray (1926); Philo, *On Abraham,* trans. F. H. Colson (1935); Seneca, *Moral Epistles,* XLVII, trans. R. M. Gummere (1917); Plutarch, *Dialogue on Love,* trans W. C. Helmbold in Vol. IX of the *Moralia* (1961); Dio Chrysostom, *Discourse* VII, trans. J. W. Cohoon (1932) and *Discourse* LXXVII/LXXVIII, trans. H. Lamar Crosby (1951).

The most important commentaries on Romans are those by Ernst Käsemann (Grand Rapids: Eerdmans, 1979) and C. E. B. Cranfield, *The Epistle to the Romans,* 2 vols. in the International Critical Commentary series (Edinburgh: T. & T. Clark, 1975 and 1979). Commentaries on I Corinthians are noted at the end of chapter 2.

IV

WOMEN IN THE CHURCH

Our examination of Paul's references to marriage (chapter 2) disclosed that he regards the man and woman as fully equal partners and mutually responsible for the quality of the relationship. It is difficult to find real parallels to this emphasis in the ethical writings of Paul's contemporaries, either Jewish or non-Jewish. Now in this present chapter we must ask whether the Apostle holds any corresponding view about the equality of men and women within the life and ministry of the church.

In many Protestant denominations and in Roman Catholicism, the role of women within the church continues to be debated. The appropriateness of ordaining women has been bitterly contested, and the decision to do so in one major denomination led some local congregations to sever their ties with the national body. Even in denominations where the ordination of women has not been seriously questioned on doctrinal grounds, women clergy have often found the opportunities for ministry more limited for them than for their male counterparts. On this subject, as on the others we are surveying, Pauline texts have frequently been invoked by one side or the other, but probably more often by those who argue that women should *not* be accorded equal status in the church's ministry. The following two examples will illustrate the point.

An urban church in the Southwest, which belongs to a denomination in which the local congregations decide who shall be ordained, was proposing to ordain a woman into the ministry. Just before the final vote, one of its members arose to argue that this was not a proper role for a woman to have. He based his case primarily on the teaching of Paul. Appealing, for example, to the eleventh chapter of I Corinthians, he declared that there "Paul had set up roles for the kingdom of God," because Paul described God as the head of Christ, Christ as the head of man, and a man as the head of a woman. "These roles," he went on,

> were not culturally conditioned, but were begun with Adam and Eve. The roles for men and women are not the same and it is no disgrace or shame to either sex that their roles are different. The church structure is set up by God in line with the family structure. As Christ is head over the church and as the husband is head over the family, so men are to be the authorities in the body of believers.

He cited several other texts as well, including I Corinthians 14:34 ("the women should keep silence in the churches") and I Timothy 2:12 ("I permit no woman to teach or to have authority over men").

A more extreme example is that of a Protestant minister in the lower Midwest who conducted a question-and-answer column in a local newspaper. In response to a reader's question, he argued on the basis of I Timothy 2:11-12 that women are to have no major leadership roles in the church as a whole, thus no part in preaching, teaching, (solo) music, or prayer when men are present! When women assume such roles, he concluded, "they violate the positive command of God through Paul."

Both of these examples reflect the sacred-cow view of Paul's ethical teaching which was criticized in chapter 1. And they both illustrate how Paul's teaching on practical matters can be grossly distorted if one does not take account of *all* the evidence available and interpret it within the total context of Paul's world, of his gospel, and of his ministry.

The Problem of Sources

Before we can proceed very far with the topic before us, we must make some decisions about sources. There has been occasion earlier to note that Ephesians, Colossians, and the Pastoral Epistles (I, II Timothy, and Titus) should probably be regarded as non-Pauline letters. These are, in a sense, the earliest "commentaries" on Paul, insofar as they represent the attempts of later writers to interpret and apply the Pauline teaching to needs and situations the Apostle himself had not confronted and could not have foreseen. Opinions vary on how well these interpreters did their job and on how much they may have altered, rightly or wrongly, Paul's most fundamental convictions. We shall need to make at least a provisional decision about them, however, because they contain passages that often play a major role in discussions about Paul's view of women.

In this book these letters are not regarded as Paul's own. The arguments against Pauline authorship are given in the commentaries on Colossians and Ephesians listed at the end of chapter 2 and in the commentaries on the Pastoral Epistles listed at the end of this one. Even those who are not persuaded by these arguments should be aware of the problematic nature of their results when they include the disputed letters as evidence for Paul's views on any subject. The letters that most Pauline scholars agree are certainly the Apostle's own (Romans, I and II Corinthians, Galatians, Philippians, I Thessalonians, Philemon) provide the most secure information about Paul's mission and message. These must always be given the major weight in any exposition of his concrete ethical teaching. However, because I Timothy, Ephesians, and Colossians are so often cited for Paul's view of women in the church, we must pay some attention to the relevant passages in them as well. To these we shall add I Corinthians 14:33*b*-36, which stands in an authentic letter but may itself be non-Pauline.

1. I Timothy

The important passage for our topic is 2:8-15. In the preceding verses (2:1-7) instructions had been given about public prayer, what it should include and why it is important. Then in verse 8 the author enjoins the *men* to pray with uplifted hands (as was traditional in the Jewish synagogues) and "without anger or quarreling." As for the *women,* they should

> adorn themselves modestly and sensibly in seemly apparel, not with braided hair or gold or pearls or costly attire but by good deeds, as befits women who profess religion. Let a woman learn in silence with all submissiveness. I permit no woman to teach or to have authority over men; she is to keep silent. For Adam was formed first, then Eve; and Adam was not deceived, but the woman was deceived and became a transgressor. Yet woman will be saved through bearing children, if she continues in faith and love and holiness, with modesty. (I Tim. 2:9-15)

There is nothing specifically Christian about these comments on women. They could have been written by a Hellenistic Jew or—save for the references to Adam and Eve and to the virtues of faith, love, and holiness—by any "secular" moralist of Paul's day. It was a commonplace among the ethical teachers of the Greco-Roman world that women should groom themselves modestly and refrain from public displays of any kind. To do otherwise would either mark them as women of easy virtue or else lead them to become such. A few examples will suffice to make the point.

Neopythagoreanism was a movement with philosophical and ethical interests which dated from the first century B.C. and reflected the influence of various older teachings and traditions. One ethical treatise that originated in this movement maintained that

> women who eat and drink all sorts of extravagant dishes and dress themselves sumptuously, wearing things that women are given to wearing, are decked out for seduction into all manner of vice, not only the bed but also the commission of other wrongful deeds. . . . The beauty that comes from wisdom and not from these things brings pleasure to women who are well born.

Plutarch's "Advice to Bride and Groom" has already been quoted in chapter 2. In the same essay he argued that a woman's speech can be as seductive as her physical appearance:

> Not only the arm of the virtuous woman, but her speech as well, ought to be not for the public, and she ought to be modest and guarded about saying anything in the hearing of outsiders, since it is an exposure of herself; for in her talk can be seen her feelings, character and disposition. (142B)

A bit later he advises, "A woman ought to do her talking either to her husband or through her husband" (142D, 32). An ancient Latin dictum that asked specifically, "What have women to do with a public assembly?" went on to supply the answer: "If old-fashioned custom is preserved, nothing."

Similar teachings are present in the rabbinic traditions of Judaism, specifically with reference to the participation of women in public prayers. For such prayer a quorum was necessary, and for this *minyan,* as the quorum was called, ten adult males had to be present. A woman's presence was allowed; but since she was under no obligation to participate, her presence did not count. And she was *not* permitted to lead in the prayers. Rather, the rabbis taught that her place was to develop an inner spirituality, and they insisted that her primary role was a domestic one. In the setting of the home she had the chief responsibility for the children's instruction, but when she was in the synagogue among the men she was to keep quiet.

That during Roman and Byzantine times, certain women had certain kinds of leadership roles in some synagogues, is suggested by inscriptions which have been studied by Bernadette Brooten. These roles seem to have been primarily administrative, however. The evidence is too fragmentary and ambiguous to allow the conclusion that Jewish women regularly had responsibilities equal to those of the men for teaching or for synagogue worship. Indeed, numerous Jewish sources emphasize how gullible and therefore undependable women are. For example, in the second century B.C. *Letter of Aristeas,* a man is quoted to the effect that he is able to get along with his wife because he recognizes "that womankind are by nature headstrong and energetic in the pursuit of their own desires, and subject to sudden changes of opinion through fallacious reasoning, and their nature is essentially weak" (250). A similar point is made by the first century A.D. Jewish philosopher Philo, when he comments on Adam and Eve:

> And woman is more accustomed to be deceived than man. For his judgment, like his body, is masculine and is capable of dissolving or destroying the designs of deception; but the judgment of woman is more feminine, and because of softness she easily gives way and is taken in by plausible falsehoods which resemble the truth. (*Questions and Answers on Genesis* I, 33)

It should be apparent that the comments about women in I Timothy 2:8-15 reflect the values and customs of both Hellenistic and Jewish culture. It is also clear that the ideas in these verses are very far from Paul's own, as disclosed in the unquestionably genuine letters. For example, contrary to I Timothy 2:14, Paul implies that Adam *was* deceived (Romans 7:11), and it is Adam (not Eve) whom Paul identifies as the first transgressor (Rom. 5:12-21; I Cor. 15:21-22); and contrary to I Timothy 2:15, Paul regularly insists that salvation comes as a gift, not as the result of one's good deeds (Rom. 3:21-28; 5:6-8, etc.). Still other differences from Paul will become apparent below.

The instructions about women in I Timothy 2:8-15 should not, then, be attributed to Paul. One still has to deal with them, of course, but with reference to the historical context and religious concerns of a man who was writing in Paul's name perhaps as many as sixty-five years after the Apostle's death. It is probable that he was intent on refuting an aberrant form of Christianity that regarded complete abstention from sex as a prerequisite for salvation. Considered in this light, the author's comment that women are saved by bearing children and continuing faithful in their domestic role would be an attack on a rigidly ascetic form of Christianity which regarded sex, marriage, and family as evils.

2. Ephesians and Colossians

Although nothing is said in Ephesians and Colossians about the role of women in the church, these letters are often cited in confirmation of the view that women are to be subordinate to men in all ways and in every sphere of activity, including the church. The texts quoted are Ephesians 5:22-24 ("Wives, be subject to your husbands, as to the Lord," verse 24) and Colossians 3:18 ("Wives, be subject to your husbands, as is fitting in the Lord"). When Josephus sums up the Jewish view of marriage, the tradition lying behind these admonitions becomes clear: "The woman, says the Law, is in all things inferior to the man. Let her accordingly be submissive, not for her humiliation, but that she may be directed; for the authority has been given by God to the man" (*Against Apion,* 201).

The texts cited from Ephesians and Colossians stand within passages that scholars describe as "tables of household duties," or family codes. These speak not only about the responsibilities of wives to husbands, but also about the responsibilities of husbands to wives (Eph. 5:25-33; Col. 3:19), of children to parents (Eph. 6:1-3; Col. 3:20) and parents to children (Eph. 6:4; Col. 3:21), and of slaves to masters (Eph. 6:5-8; Col. 3:22-25) and masters to slaves (Eph. 6:9; Col. 4:1). The principle of mutual responsibility that Paul had stressed must operate between husbands and wives (I Corinthians 7) has been extended in Ephesians and Colossians to apply to other kinds of relationships as well. In both of these later writings this mutuality is grounded in the common status of all family members as persons in Christ, responsible finally to God alone. For example, the whole list of family duties in Ephesians is prefaced with the injunction, "Be subject to one another out of reverence for Christ" (5:21). It is the *codification* and *expansion* of Paul's own teaching which characterizes these various post-Pauline codes (in addition to those in Ephesians and Colossians, see especially I Pet. 2:11–3:12). The codification systematizes and generalizes Paul's teaching, and the expansion enables it to cover more cases.

In the ethical codes of such writings as Ephesians, Colossians, and I Peter, and in the rules and regulations of the Pastoral Epistles, we see a concern for social institutions and structures, political, ecclesiastical, and domestic, that surpasses anything in Paul's own letters. These later writers did not share Paul's sense of the imminent close of history. They were reckoning with an indefinite delay in Christ's return and were concerned to help the church and individual Christians settle down in society. It was perhaps natural, given the political, social, and ecclesiastical pressures that confronted them, that their initial impulses were conservative. They were third-generation Christians. The pioneers in the faith were gone, and theirs was a time that required "regrouping" around the traditions they had received. It required them to think hard about the meaning of those traditions for their life in a world that did not appear to be "passing away" very quickly. They were having to grapple, as Paul himself had not, with the problem of a "social ethic." Perhaps they may be pardoned if they did not always clearly perceive the distinction between accommodation to the realities of the world and capitulation to its values and claims. We can gratefully receive these later writings as an important part of our Christian heritage. Let us not, however, confuse their teachings with those of the Apostle, whose moral instruction they themselves sought to interpret.

3. I Corinthians 14:33*b*-36

In chapters 11 through 14 of this letter, Paul is instructing the Corinthians to maintain order in their worship. Beginning in chapter 12, the matter of spiritual gifts is of special concern because of a dispute in the Corinthian congregation about speaking in tongues. This is still the subject in chapter 14. Paul's overall conclusion is that speaking in tongues is permissible but less edifying to the church than prophesying, which is the gift of intelligible speech (see, for instance, 14:39). And if there is to be speaking in tongues, he warns, it must proceed in orderly fashion and always with an interpreter (14:27-28). This, like all else in the Christian community, "should be done decently and in order" (14:40).

Near the end of this discussion stand the words about women in church, which the RSV, like many other versions, prints as a separate paragraph:

> (33*b*) As in all the churches of the saints, (34) the women should keep silence in the churches. For they are not permitted to speak, but should be subordinate, as even the law says. (35) If there is anything they desire to know, let them ask their husbands at home. For it is shameful for a woman to speak in church. (36) What! Did the word of God originate with you, or are you the only ones it has reached?

There are two striking things about this paragraph. First, it disrupts the flow of Paul's argument. Immediately before it and after it he is discussing the relative merits of prophecy and tongue-speaking. Several ancient manuscripts of I Corinthians remove verses 34-35 to the end of the chapter, showing that some early scribes were also puzzled about their appropriateness just here. Second, this admonition that women should not talk in church and should rely on their husbands to explain things at home sounds very much like the teaching of I Timothy 2:11-12 and the tradition of which it is a part. It is not what one would expect to come from someone who, like Paul earlier in this same letter, was concerned to emphasize the equality of husbands and wives in marriage.

Indeed, many commentators believe that the verses before us (or at least verses 34-35) were not written by Paul. On this view, they may have originated as the marginal notation of some later scribe who, recalling the instruction of I Timothy 2:11-12 and finding nothing comparable in I Corinthians, added a similar provision near the end of Paul's discussion of

Christian worship. In time, yet another scribe, using this manuscript as his master copy, could have mistaken the marginal notation for something that had been left out of his exemplar. By dutifully inserting it in the body of the text in his own copy, it thus became a part of I Corinthians! This is one of the ways an "interpolation" of later material could have occurred.

Several additional points lend support to the hypothesis that these verses constitute a non-Pauline interpolation. The expression "are not permitted" seems to look backward to a regulation previously formulated (for instance, in I Tim. 2:12); it is not Paul's way of phrasing his ethical teaching. The expression "be subordinate" echoes the stereotyped formula we have seen in the family codes of Ephesians and Colossians. Finally, but certainly not least, these verses stand in tension with, if they do not actually contradict, I Corinthians 11:2-16. There, as we shall see, Paul presumes not only that women may speak during public worship, but that they participate on an equal footing with men in both the prayers and the prophesying.

Galatians 3:27-28

Where shall we turn for firm evidence of Paul's teaching about women in the church? The passage with which to begin is unquestionably one in his letter to the Galatians, the two famous sentences in 3:27-28: "For as many of you as were baptized into Christ have put on Christ. There is neither Jew nor Greek, there is neither slave nor free, there is neither male nor female; for you are all one in Christ Jesus."

Paul is probably quoting or alluding to a traditional affirmation in the church's baptismal liturgy. The same formula is echoed in Romans 10:12, I Corinthians 12:13, and Colossians 3:11. In Galatians it is used as part of his argument that Christ frees one from the law and enables one, by faith, to become a child of God. The statement that immediately precedes the baptismal formula suggests what may have called it to his mind in this context: "For in Christ Jesus you are all sons of God through faith" (Gal. 3:26). *In* Christ Jesus—that is, in the community of faith—*all* believers are "sons of God." (What may sound like sexist language to modern ears would not have sounded so to Paul; with reference to God's people, Paul uses "son/sons" and "child/ children" quite interchangeably, as in this very passage in 4:1-7.) Baptism into Christ means that all worldly distinctions become irrelevant. What is important before God is not whether one is Jew or Greek, slave or free, male or female. What is important above all is that one is "in Christ" and has "put Christ on."

The Apostle does not presume that these distinctions are erased. As a Christian, one necessarily retains one's ethnicity (Jew, Greek) and sexuality (male, female). As for legal status, Paul recognized that one's condition as "slave" or "free" was not necessarily permanent in Roman society. In I Corinthians 7:21 he counseled slaves to gain their freedom if possible, and he himself wrote to Philemon in an effort to get Onesimus his freedom. But "in Christ" it does not matter that one is a slave, because "in Christ" one's social class is of no more consequence than one's race or sex.

It is not a coincidence that the same baptismal affirmation is reflected in I Corinthians 12:13 when Paul begins to develop his image of the church as the "body of Christ" (12:12-27). This imagery provides us a closer look at what he understands the traditional formula to mean. It means that those who are baptized into Christ, though they have different gifts, are bound together in their dependence on the same God (12:4-11). It means that though they serve in diverse ways they all "have the same care for one another" (12:25). It means, because the body cannot function without all its parts, that what the world values as "honorable" or what it rejects as "inferior," "weak," or "unpresentable" does not matter; all the members of Christ's body are equally valued as "indispensable" to its life (12:14-26).

But is it not significant, someone may ask, that Paul omits the reference to male and female equality in Christ when he uses the baptismal formula in I Corinthians 12:13? Doesn't this show that he is not really committed to it? The omission is significant, but not because of any doubts in Paul's mind about the full partnership of men and women in the body of Christ. The omission probably results from the state of affairs in the Corinthian congregation. In chapter 2 we saw that some Corinthian Christians believed their commitment to Christ required them to abstain from marriage and sex altogether. Such a view might have been prompted in the first place by the principle that "there is neither male nor female." Even if it had not, for Paul to repeat it now might only support one of the errors he wants to correct. Paul himself certainly did not interpret that principle to require the denial of one's sexuality. Therefore, its omission from the letter to Corinth perhaps shows how *seriously* the Apostle takes it, and how intent he is on preventing its misuse.

In his discussion of the diversity of gifts and functions in I Corinthians 12, there is not the slightest suggestion that one's racial or ethnic origin, one's position in the class structure, or one's being a man or a woman is in any way involved. There, by his allusion to the baptismal formula of Galatians 3:27-28, he is affirming without compromise the principle that all are one in Christ. But does he honor this principle in his own concrete ethical teaching? Our answer to this question must come from yet another passage in I Corinthians.

I Corinthians 11:2-16

Paul's instructions to the Corinthians on "good order in public worship" really begin in I Corinthians 11:2 and extend clear through chapter 14 of the letter. His advisories about their common meal (the Lord's Supper) in 11:17 ff. and about spiritual gifts in chapters 12–14 are well known. We tend to be much less familiar with the opening paragraphs, 11:2-16. This is not surprising, because the concern here seems remote, even somewhat ridiculous, to the modern reader. Contrary to the impression given by the RSV and other familiar translations of these verses, the topic is not women's "veiling" or otherwise "covering" their heads in church. The word "veil" does not occur, and many interpreters now agree that the topic is, rather, women's *hair*styles in public worship. This is suggested by the remarks in verses 14-15, and also by evidence that the word which the RSV translates as "unveiled" in verse 5 and as "uncovered" in verse 13 sometimes refers to "loose" or "unbound" hair. Therefore, the instruction here is probably that a woman should not let her hair fall loosely from her head when she prays or prophesies in church. It should be done up properly, just as any decent woman in Paul's day would have it whenever she went outside her residence.

The argument in verses 3-16 is not easy to follow, and a number of specific points are unclear. Some interpreters, moreover, believe that what is said here about the relation of man and woman is much more akin to the views about women we have seen in the non-Pauline Pastoral Epistles than those that are present in Paul's own letters. Various scholars, in fact, have proposed that I Corinthians 11:3[or 2]-16 should be regarded, like I Corinthians 14:33*b*-36, as a later, non-Pauline interpolation; or, that, in verses 3-7*b*, the Apostle is simply describing what he understands to be the practice in Corinth, but which he proceeds to criticize in verses 7*c*-16. Some plausible arguments have been advanced for these theories, and they cannot be ruled out altogether. However, unlike the case of I Corinthians 14:33*b*-36, there is no evidence of any textual disturbance in chapter 11; and it takes considerable imagination to read verses 3-7*b* as merely descriptive of Corinthian customs. Let us begin, therefore, with the assumption that the passage is attributable to the Apostle. How should it be understood?

The discussion opens with a commendation of the Corinthians for maintaining "the traditions" Paul has delivered to them. The plural form, "traditions," shows he is not thinking of the fundamental apostolic tradition, which he will later summarize in 15:3-5: "that Christ died for our sins . . . , that he was buried, that he was raised on the third day . . . and that he appeared to Cephas, then to the twelve." Rather, in 11:2-16 he is thinking of the ordinary and familiar ways of doing things in church. As he closes this first subtopic he refers specifically to what the established custom (RSV: "practice") is in "the churches of God" (verse 16), including (he hopes) the church in Corinth.

Paul's initial commendation of the Corinthians for maintaining the worship customs is immediately qualified, however. In one particular there is reason for concern. At least some of the women of their congregation have been going to church with their hair left hanging loose. This is indicated first of all in verse 5, only after Paul has started to develop his argument in favor of the usual practice: "Any woman who prays or prophesies with her hair not bound up on her head dishonors her head—it is the same as if her head were shaven." The following verses confirm that this is the point at issue. Paul's arguments in favor of a woman's wearing her hair in the generally accepted mode when she is in public are varied and complex. In at least one instance, the argument that women should be veiled "because of the angels" (verse 10), scholars have made several different proposals about Paul's meaning, none of them fully convincing. Readers may consult the commentaries for discussion of this and many other points in the passage which cannot be treated here.

Our special concern is whether these instructions about women in the church correspond to Paul's espousal of the principle that "there is neither male nor female" in Christ. Although there are many details in I Corinthians 11:2-16 hard to explain, several things relevant to our study can be established with some degree of confidence. The conclusion to which they lead may be summarized as follows: No general theory of woman's inferiority is presumed or promoted in this passage, nor is it the Apostle's intention here to argue that women must always be subordinate to men in the church or in their marriages. In fact, Paul's commitment to the baptismal affirmation that "there is neither male nor female" is visible in this very context, in what he says as well as in what he seems to presuppose. Support for this conclusion may be presented under four points.

(1) The issue addressed in I Corinthians 11:2-16 has arisen, like much else in this letter, because of the peculiar kind of religious frenzy which characterizes some—perhaps even many—in the Corinthian congregation.

(2) Paul's theme here is not the subordination of one sex to the other.

The argument of verses 3 through 9 needs to be observed with some care (I quote the RSV with various alterations):

> (3) But I want you to understand that the head of every man is Christ, the head of a woman is the man, and the head of Christ is God. (4) Any man who prays or prophesies having long hair coming down dishonors his head, (5) and any woman who prays or prophesies with her hair not bound up on her head dishonors her head—it is the same as if her head were shaven. (6) For if a woman will not arrange her hair properly, then she should cut it off; but if it is disgraceful for a woman to be shorn or shaven, let her arrange her hair properly. (7) For a man ought not to arrange long hair on top of his head, since he is the image and glory of God; but woman is the glory of man. (8) (For man was not made from woman, but woman from man. (9) Neither was man created for woman, but woman for man.)

One's initial impression is apt to be that Paul is arranging "God-Christ-man-woman" in a hierarchical order moving from superior to inferior, each member subordinate to and controlled by the preceding. This impression is probably fostered most of all by the man-woman part of the set and the fact that the subordination motif is so familiar to us from the family codes of Hellenistic Judaism and the later New Testament epistles. We are thus inclined to understand the headship metaphor as emphasizing the authority that the superior member exercises over the inferior. However, there are reasons to think that the authority-subordination theme is not in Paul's mind.

(a) Earlier in this same letter the formula "you are Christ's; and Christ is God's" (3:23) had been used to complete and in a sense support the claim, "all things are yours" (3:21-22). Paul was affirming that the one who belongs to Christ and through him to God is no longer in bondage to anyone ("whether Paul or Apollos or Cephas") or to anything ("or the world or life or death or the present or the future"). In 11:3 the "you" of the earlier formula has been differentiated into male and female for the purposes of the argument about women's hairstyles. The original affirmation about the sovereignty of God, which relativizes all other claims, is still implicit however. Indeed, it becomes explicit in 11:12*b*, "And all things are from God."

(b) The Greek word "head" may be used metaphorically, as in English, to mean "one who is in charge." But it may also be used as a metaphor to designate "source" or "point of origin" (as in the English term "headwaters"). This second meaning, as Robin Scroggs has suggested, seems to be the one present in I Corinthians 11. Paul's comment in verses 8-9 that woman was created from and for man, not the reverse, shows that he is thinking of Genesis 2:18-23. There it is said that God took a rib from man's side and fashioned a woman from it to be like him. The Genesis story itself does not speak of woman's inferiority or subjection to man. It emphasizes, on the contrary, her being "like him." It says that she was created from his own flesh and bone in order to be his companion, because he was lonely. It does not say or suggest that she was created because man needed someone over whom to exercise control. Nor does Paul, here in I Corinthians, speak of man's control over woman or of woman's subordination to man. His concern is only to distinguish man from woman in the created order, and thus to provide some basis for the customs he wants the Corinthians to follow in their worship. Even though his schematization suggests a certain dependence of woman on man, it is clear that he understands this relationship to be for her ennobling, not demeaning. We must not forget that the point of this whole discussion is not to suppress the Christian women of Corinth, but to make their participation in the congregation's worship more meaningful and effective.

(c) In verse 7 Paul substitutes the words "image" and "glory" for "head." In this context he has no interest in belaboring the role of Christ, so now the set is abbreviated to "God-man-woman." This allows the Apostle to give closer attention to the issue he is addressing as well as to the scriptural passages upon which his argument is based. His reference to man as "the image and glory of God" derives specifically from Genesis 1:27, which states that "God created man in his own image, in the image of God he created him; male and female he created them." It is important to notice that the term "man" is generic here. Thus, the text affirms that male and female originated in the same creative act of God and that both were created in God's image. This is the text that lies behind Paul's comment in verse 7*ab*. In verses 7*c*-9, however, the Apostle has in mind the account of creation in Genesis 2, according to which man (the male) was created first and then woman (the female) was formed later from his side. Although Paul's combining of these two separate creation stories is not in accord with modern principles of biblical interpretation, it is typical of Jewish biblical interpretation in his day, and we simply have to grant him that if we want to follow his argument. Here his point continues to be that man and woman occupy different places in the created order. By "different," however, we are not to understand "inferior." It is significant that the Apostle does not say that woman is man's "image," but only that she is his "glory" (verse 7*c*). He seems not to question the view of Genesis 1:27 that woman, like man, was created in the image of God. It is also significant that he proceeds to speak of a woman exercising "authority over her head" (verse 10, where the main RSV translation uses the word "veil"). Given the context, this could be the authority she exercises—when her hair is appropriately dressed—through her contributions (praying and prophesying) to the congregation's worship.

(3) In the midst of this very discussion, Paul in effect reaffirms the principle that "there is neither male nor female."

Reference has already been made to the complexity of Paul's argumentation in I Corinthians 11:2-16. In the present discussion we have sought only to keep his major intentions and points in focus, not to follow his reasoning in detail. We have seen that his concern here is very specific—to bring order and discipline to public worship in Corinth, where religious frenzy threatens to make it appear like madness. Paul believes that one thing contributing to the present chaos (he will address others in subsequent chapters) is the custom that the congregation's prophetesses leave their hair unbound, like prophetesses and priestesses in the Hellenistic cults. We have seen, further, that Paul's opposition to this practice is supported not only by appeals to apostolic authority, to ecclesiastical custom, and to what is "natural," but also by an appeal to woman's place in the created order.

While this part of the argument has often been used as a proof-text by those who want biblical support for their idea that women are inferior to and should be subordinate to men, that is not the Apostle's point at all. If one still harbors any doubts about this, the important affirmation of verse 11 should dispel those. Recent studies of the terminology here suggest that the RSV translation should be altered to read: "In any case, in the Lord woman is not different from man nor man from woman." It is not difficult to recognize in these words Paul's rephrasing of the traditional baptismal affirmation that there is neither male nor female in Christ. Two supporting points are registered in verse 12. First, alluding once more to the creation story in Genesis 2, Paul notes that even though woman had in the beginning been made from man, ever since then man had been born from woman (verse 12a). It would appear that the Apostle doesn't want his earlier argument about woman's place in the created order to be used to deny her equality with man. For the same reason, he offers a further supporting point: "And all things are from God" (verse 12b). The oneness and equality of all people, whatever their ethnic origin, social status, or sex, is assured, finally, by their common dependence upon the one God from whom they all have their life.

(4) Paul's entire discussion in this passage presumes that women as well as men participate in the leadership of public worship.

No arguments are advanced in support of the legitimacy of women's playing leading roles in public worship because they are not needed. Paul takes this for granted and must know that the Corinthians do too. This important presupposition of the passage is apparent in verses 4-5 where Paul phrases his remarks about a man and a woman in exactly parallel ways: "any man who prays or prophesies . . . , any woman who prays or prophesies. . . ." The issue is not whether a woman *may* utter prayers and prophecies in public worship, but only whether her hair should be bound up or loose when she *does*.

There is nothing in the teaching of I Corinthians 11:2-16 that is incompatible with Paul's espousal elsewhere of the principle that "there is neither male nor female." Only if one approaches this passage as if it were a family code comparable to those in Ephesians and Colossians and applies Paul's arguments to subjects for which they were not devised will he be found deserting that principle. In fact, however, the presupposition of the whole discussion is that women can and do share fully in the leadership of worship. When we add our findings about this passage to our findings about Paul's remarks concerning the role of women in marriage relationships, it is clear that there is nothing in his teaching that compromises the affirmation of Galatians 3:27-28.

But does Paul adhere to his own teaching? What about his own practice? This will be the acid test of the depth of his conviction.

Women in Paul's Ministry

We know next to nothing about the women in Paul's family. There is only the notice in Acts 23:16 that "the son of Paul's sister" alerted the Apostle to the plot of some Jews to assassinate him. Of his own mother we know nothing. If he was ever married it was before his conversion, because he implies in I Corinthians 9:5 that he had not been "accompanied by a wife" during his apostolic ministry. The domestic side of Paul's life, therefore, gives us no inkling of Paul's relationships with or attitudes toward women.

On the other hand, we are fortunate in being able to piece together a good deal of information about Paul's dealings with women in the church. For this we shall rely chiefly on passages in his letters where specific women are mentioned. What emerges is the picture of an apostle who in practice as well as in principle supports the view that in Christ Jesus "there is neither male nor female."

1. Chloe

Paul's opening appeal in I Corinthians is that the dissensions and disagreements that have fractured the Corinthian congregation be overcome (1:10). In the next sentence he indicates the source of his information about the present difficulties: "For it has been reported to me by Chloe's people that there is quarreling among you" (1:11). The reference is literally to "those who belong to Chloe," and these could have been family members, friends, or slaves. The name itself tells us that Chloe was a woman. Obviously, she is someone known to the Corinthians as well as to Paul. Perhaps Chloe herself was a member of the Corinthian church, one of those widows Paul advises to remain as they are (I Cor. 7:8, 39b-40a). Or perhaps, since Paul is writing this letter from Ephesus, Chloe lived there and her "people" had been in Corinth on business. It is inherently more probable that Chloe was a Christian than that she was not, and it would appear that her standing with the Corinthian church and with Paul was such that both they and he knew a report from her "people" deserved to be taken seriously.

2. Euodia and Syntyche

The church at Philippi had been founded by Paul, and his subsequent relationship to the Philippian congregation remained warm and cordial. According to Acts 16:11-15, Paul had preached first to some women of the city; and one of them, Lydia, was baptized by him. Her home, we are told, became a hospice for Paul and his companions. The same narrative goes on to say that after he and Silas were miraculously released from jail, Paul made it a point to visit Lydia before leaving the city (Acts 16:40). Yet Paul himself never mentions this person, and, as so often in the case of the stories in Acts, we are left wondering about the reliability of the information.

Two other women of Philippi are mentioned by Paul himself, however. In a letter to the Philippians he writes:

> I entreat Euodia and I entreat Syntyche to agree in the Lord. And I ask you also, true yokefellow, help these women, for they have labored side by side with me in the gospel together with Clement and the rest of my fellow workers, whose names are in the book of life. (4:2-3)

There are several things here one could wish to know more about. What was the matter about which these two women, Euodia and Syntyche, disagreed? It is idle to speculate. Who is the "true yokefellow" whom Paul urges to step in and help settle the dispute? We do not know. Nor do we have any idea who Clement is, save for what is indicated right here. The name appears nowhere else in Paul's letters or in Acts. Despite such unanswered questions as these, the verses do tell us some important things about women in Paul's ministry.

First, the disagreement between Euodia and Syntyche was of enough consequence to prompt Paul to give it specific attention, to name the disputants and to address them each individually, and to call upon a third party to help effect a reconciliation. This ought not to be shrugged off as "just a case of two bickering women" and used as the basis for another "Ladies' Aid" joke. Paul believes it to be a serious matter for the whole congregation. This by itself suggests that the women involved may have held positions of special responsibility in their church.

Their importance in Philippi is confirmed when Paul says that the two of them have "labored side by side . . . in the gospel" both with himself and "with Clement and the rest of my fellow workers." Whenever Paul speaks of laboring "in the gospel" he is speaking of his own apostolic ministry (Rom. 1:9; II Cor. 10:14) or of the ministry of his closest associates (of Timothy in I Thess. 3:2 and of an unnamed brother— Apollos?—in II Cor. 8:18). It is no insignificant thing for Euodia and Syntyche to be included in this company. Moreover, Paul makes it a point to indicate that their labor for the gospel has been no less important than that of "Clement and the rest." Although we cannot know anything specific about these persons, the reference to their names being "in the book of life" suggests they may have been early leaders of the Philippian church now deceased but still remembered for their illustrious service "in the gospel."

As little as we know about Euodia and Syntyche, then, it is still enough to permit us the conclusion that they were important leaders of the Philippian congregation. It is enough to show us that Paul himself respected them as such, just as he regarded them along with men like Timothy and Clement as fully engaged in the ministry of the gospel.

3. Prisca (Priscilla)

Our evidence suggests that the woman closest to Paul was the one we know from the Book of Acts as Priscilla, and whom Paul himself always refers to as Prisca, using the familiar form of her name. She was married to Aquila who, according to Acts 18:2, was "a native of Pontus," a Roman province in northern Asia Minor on the Black Sea. There is no reason to doubt the further report in Acts that this couple had for a while resided in the capital of the Empire, but then removed to Corinth when the Emperior Claudius "commanded all the Jews to leave Rome" (18:2). The exact year of this order is disputed, but it was sometime in the 40s, and it was during a period when, according to other ancient sources, the Jewish community in Rome was "in tumult" because of the presence among them of some believers in Christ. By no means "*all* the Jews" were expelled by Claudius, but the agitators certainly were. Maybe some other Jews or Jewish Christians fled the city at the same time.

Whether Prisca and Aquila were already Christians when they arrived in Corinth, or whether they were converted there, perhaps by Paul himself, we do not know. That they did meet Paul in Corinth is likely (Acts 18:1-2), and they may have been associated with him in the same trade, as Acts also reports (18:3). Prisca and Aquila accompanied Paul when he went on to Ephesus, but they did not accompany him when he took ship from there for Caesarea (Acts 18:18-19). Their residence in Ephesus is confirmed in the earliest mention of them to be found in Paul's own letters. This comes in I Corinthians, written from Ephesus to the church in the city from which Prisca and Aquila had removed to Ephesus. Near the close of that letter Paul writes: "Aquila and Prisca, together with the church in their house, send you hearty greetings in the Lord" (16:19). The reference to "*their* house" sounds natural enough to us, but it would have sounded far less so in Paul's day. Both law and custom assigned to the male special rights and duties as the head of the household, and one might have expected Paul to refer to "the church in *Aquila's* house." That he uses instead the plural possessive, "their," may suggest something about Paul's view of the marriage itself as well as about his understanding of Prisca's importance as a leader in the church.

Paul's other reference to these two friends is more informative. It occurs in Romans 16:3-5 where, this time, Paul is sending his greetings to them and "the church in their house." "Greet Prisca and Aquila, my fellow workers in Christ Jesus, who risked their necks for my life, to whom not only I but also all the churches of the Gentiles give thanks; greet also the church in their house." There are several reasons why it is unlikely that chapter 16 in our "book" of Romans was originally part of the letter to Rome. One of them is that it would require us to believe this couple has now returned to the city they had left earlier, yet we have no evidence from Acts or Paul's other letters that they ever did. But where they are as they receive these greetings is not important, anyway.

Wherever it is, they are still leaders in a local congregation. Now we learn in addition, however, that they had "risked their necks" for the Apostle's life. For that, both Paul and the churches he has founded are profoundly grateful.

In what way had they "risked their necks" for Paul? We cannot even be certain whether the expression is meant literally or metaphorically, although something similar is said about Epaphroditus of Philippi, and that seems to be meant literally (Phil. 2:30). The most important thing is that husband and wife are both mentioned, and that both are included without any hesitation or any hint of a distinction as Paul's "fellow workers in Christ Jesus." Moreover, in mentioning these friends, Paul again departs from normal usage in his day by naming the wife before the husband. Prisca's name also stands first in two of the three places in Acts where both are mentioned. It would appear reasonable to suppose that Prisca was recognized not only by Paul but also by the later church as being the more important of the two.

One of the instances in Acts where Aquila's name is preceded by his wife's is especially interesting. It is reported that after Paul's departure from Ephesus the renowned and eloquent Apollos arrived in the city and began to preach (Acts 18:24-25). Prisca and Aquila heard him in the synagogue but must not have been entirely satisfied with the gospel he proclaimed. This, at least, is what the writer of Acts wants us to believe, because he says that "they took him and expounded to him the way of God more accurately" (18:26). "They" refers to Prisca and Aquila, and thus we are confronted with the remarkable picture of a woman (named first) and her husband engaged in the theological instruction of one of the most famous preachers of their day. The scene is in direct contradiction to the rule of I Timothy 2:12, which "permit[s] no woman to teach or to have authority over men"! It is difficult to know what factual basis there may be for this story. The writer of Acts, after the fashion of many ancient writers, tends to mold history and traditions in keeping with his own ideas and objectives. The Gospel of Luke is also from his hand, and there he shows a special interest in portraying the importance of the women around Jesus. Nevertheless, enough is known about Prisca from Paul's own comments about her to make this story in Acts believable. Its net effect therefore, is to strengthen the impression that women held positions of importance and authority in the Pauline churches.

4. Phoebe

Another name on the roster of women in Paul's ministry is that of Phoebe. She is mentioned in Romans 16:1-2. "I commend to you our sister Phoebe, a deaconess of the church at Cenchreae, that you may receive her in the Lord as befits the saints, and help her in whatever she may require from you, for she has been a helper of many and of myself as well." Whether this chapter was part of Paul's original letter to Rome, or whether it was a separate note sent originally to some other church, perhaps Ephesus, as many believe, does not affect our discussion. In either case it (or some part of it) is Paul's letter of recommendation for Phoebe, introducing her and asking that she be received hospitably.

Cenchreae was one of the port cities of Corinth, and this mention of it shows there was a Christian congregation there as well as in Corinth proper. Phoebe, we are informed, was an official of the congregation there. The RSV calls her "a deaconess," but to be quite fair to Paul's Greek we should call her a "deacon." The use of the masculine form here precludes the possibility that Phoebe belonged to some special order of "deaconesses," perhaps inferior in status and authority to other church officials. Not even the form of her title distinguishes her from male leaders! In Paul's letters "deacon" is often used nontechnically as a reference to "one who serves." Thus, the RSV uses the words "servant(s)" or "minister(s)" to translate it when it refers to Paul and other apostles in I Corinthians 3:5; II Corinthians 3:6; 6:4 (compare II Cor. 11:15, 23). In I Thessalonians 3:2 it describes Timothy's service of God. It is also used with reference to Christ's ministry, once explicitly (Rom. 16:8) and once by implication (Gal. 2:17, where the RSV translates it as "agent").

In Philippians 1:1 Paul addresses "all the saints in Christ Jesus who are at Philippi, with the bishops and deacons." These persons seem to exercise special offices within the congregation, and the reference to Phoebe as a "deacon of the church at Cenchreae" suggests the same for her. The word itself, however, gives us no clue as to the specific kind of responsibility she may have had as a deacon. More instructive is the concrete description of her as "a helper of many and of myself as well." The crucial term here is the one rendered "helper" by the RSV and "good friend" by the NEB and Today's English Version. None of these translations, however, does justice to the Greek word Paul has used. Etymologically it means "one who stands before," and in ancient Greek texts it is often applied to a presiding officer. It could also mean a "patron" or "benefactor," and there is evidence of its use to describe an officer in a religious association. In an inscription pertaining to one specific Hellenistic cult, the word stands first in a list of various cultic officers, the others being chief priest, scribe, custodians, and trustees. Paul's use of a feminine form of this noun has no known precedent.

However we choose to translate the term in question, Phoebe turns out to have been someone of considerable importance both in her own church and in Paul's ministry. In Romans 16:2 he says that she has served "many," including himself. She is commended to an unusually long list of persons (16:3-16), as would be appropriate for one setting out for strange and distant places. These Christian friends of Paul are being asked to welcome and support her on her mission—the nature of which, unfortunately, Paul does not indicate.

5. Junia

The most striking Pauline reference to a female leader in the church has, unfortunately, been written out of most modern versions of the Bible and explained away by most modern commentators. The reference comes, again, in the long list of persons to whom Paul sends greetings in chapter 16 of Romans. Verse 7 is usually translated just about as it is in the RSV: "Greet Andronicus and Junias, my kinsmen and my fellow prisoners; they are men of note among the apostles, and they were in Christ before me." Increasingly, however, interpreters are recognizing that this is a serious mistranslation of the verse. The second name mentioned can be translated as "Junia," the Greek equivalent of a common Roman name for females; or as "Junias" (not "Junius"), conceivably a shortened form of the male name Junianus. Since the name "Junias" is otherwise unattested, however, the correct translation must certainly be "Junia." This means that the RSV must also be corrected when it intrudes the word "men" into a subsequent phrase. We should therefore translate the verse as follows:

> Greet Andronicus and Junia, my kinfolk and my fellow prisoners; they are outstanding among the apostles, and they were in Christ before me.

Neither of these persons is named elsewhere in the New Testament, so we know only what the present brief lines disclose about them. When Paul refers to them as "kinfolk" he probably means they are "kinfolk by race" (a phrase he employs in Rom. 9:3), not that they are relatives. That he calls them also "fellow prisoners" could mean that he and they had at some point been imprisoned together, or it could mean that they, like himself, had on occasion been imprisoned on account of their faith. In either case, their devotion to the gospel is stressed. Most significantly, however, he numbers both of them—Junia as well as Andronicus—among the apostles, that group of itinerant missionaries who, like Paul himself, were recognized to have been especially commissioned to preach the gospel of Christ. They are described, moreover, as "outstanding" apostles (not "regarded as outstanding by the apostles," as commentators have sometimes understood the phrase). Finally, Paul notes that their conversion to the gospel had preceded his own, which probably also means that they were senior to him with respect to their apostolic labors.

We could wish to know more about these two people, and especially about what made them "outstanding among the apostles." It is likely that they were husband and wife, and if so they can be identified with those "other apostles" who, according to Paul in I Corinthians 9:5, exercise their right to be married.

6. Some Other Women

Among those to whom Phoebe is commended in Romans 16 are several other women concerning whom Paul has high praise: Mary ("who has worked hard among you," 16:6); Tryphaena and Tryphosa, perhaps twin sisters ("workers in the Lord," 16:12); the "beloved Persis" (who has also "worked hard in the Lord," 16:12); the unnamed mother of Rufus ("his mother and mine," 16:13); Julia; and the sister of Nereus (16:15). When, finally, we note that Apphia is one of those Paul is addressing in Philemon (verse 2), our catalog of women mentioned by Paul is complete. Apphia may have been Philemon's wife, but that is not certain. It is certain that she was a prominent member in the congregation to which Paul is sending that letter.

Conclusion

We have seen that it is crucial, particularly on the subject of women in the church, to distinguish between the letters of indisputably Pauline origin and those of the Apostle's later interpreters, penned in his name. One cannot ignore the views and practices of those who came after Paul. Ephesians, Colossians, and the Pastoral Epistles are also part of the church's canon of scripture. But only when we have made all of the proper distinctions between Paul's letters and the later ones will we be able to interpret each one in terms of its own social, historical, and religious context. Apart from some brief suggestions about the needs of the churches for which the later ethical codes were formulated, our attention here has been focused on Paul's own view of women in the church. The results are clear.

1. *Paul was committed to the fundamental principle that there is neither male nor female in Christ Jesus.* This principle was based on his conviction, firmly held, that the believers' common dependence upon God's grace and their joint incorporation into Christ brought them into a new relationship to one another. Their new identity, and ultimately their only significant one, was now "in Christ." The racial, national, legal, and sexual identities were not destroyed, but they were transcended and their meaning was relativized. They continued to exist in the world as Jew or Greek, slave or free, male or female—and, one might add, as single or married, artisan or farmer, and so on. But even their continued existence in these roles was understood by Paul to be radically qualified and transformed by their new being "in Christ."

2. *There is nothing in Paul's concrete teaching on matters pertaining to women that is incompatible with the principle he had affirmed.* The main passage that has to be tested in this connection is I Corinthians 11:2-16, since it is often used in support of the view that women are to remain subordinate in all ways to men. We have seen, however, that one must consider the situation Paul was addressing in that passage and avoid applying his arguments to matters for which they were not formulated. When his own intentions there are honored and when his own words about the equality of man and woman are heeded, one sees that his concrete teaching not only accommodates but actually exhibits the principle that "there is neither male nor female" in Christ.

3. *There is ample evidence that the principle was affirmed by Paul not only in words but also in practice.* There are women among his closest associates in the ministry and women among the most prominent leaders in his churches. Their gifts, functions, and accomplishments are in no way distinguishable because they are female. Such distinctions do exist within the body of Christ, but there is no hint that one's sex is tied up with them in any way. Paraphrasing Paul, one

might ask: Must all apostles be males and Jewish? Must all prophets be Gentiles? Must all teachers be women? Must all helpers be slaves? Paul's response would be unequivocal: Of course not! The evidence from his letters is so overwhelming that one knows as soon as these questions have been formulated that they are ridiculous. On the topic of women in the church, certainly, Paul seems fully committed to the baptismal affirmation that "there is neither male nor female." Not only was his teaching compatible with this, but his own practice was a demonstration of it.

For Further Reading

There are three excellent articles on "Woman" in *The Interpreter's Dictionary of the Bible,* Vol. 5, one dealing with the Ancient Near East (Rivkah Harris), another with the Old Testament (Phyllis Trible), and a third with the New Testament (Robin Scroggs). Each includes a bibliography.

In the first edition of this book I had to note that relatively few biblical scholars had devoted much attention to Paul's teaching and practice with respect to women in the church. Happily, in the intervening years this has changed, so that the list of books and articles in which this topic is addressed by competent interpreters is now extensive. One of the most important of these, partly because it takes account of the contributions of many other scholars, is Elisabeth Schüssler Fiorenza's *In Memory of Her: A Feminist Theological Reconstruction of Christian Origins* (New York: Crossroad, 1984 [copyright 1983]). In particular, her discussions of Galatians 3:28 and of I Corinthians 11:2-16 (chapter 6) have prompted me to rethink and reformulate my own earlier judgments about these passages. Jerome Murphy-O'Connor also deals helpfully with I Corinthians 11:2-16 in a book that is directed to a more general audience, *Becoming Human Together: The Pastoral Anthropology of St. Paul,* 2d rev. ed., Good News Studies, 2 (Wilmington, Del.: Michael Glazier, 1982), pp. 193-97.

Two articles on special topics are also worth noting here. In "The 'Theology of Woman's Place' and the 'Paulinist' Tradition" (*Semeia* 28 [1983]: 102-12), William O. Walker, Jr., argues that I Corinthians 11:3-16, as well as I Corinthians 14:34-35 should be identified as a later addition to Paul's letter. These passages, he suggests, represent the same later "Paulinist" teaching one finds in Colossians, Ephesians, and the Pastoral Epistles. Even though I have not yet been persuaded that I Corinthians 11:3-16 belongs to that later tradition, the idea has gained some support and certainly needs to be taken seriously. On the whole matter of Romans 16:7 and the female apostle Junia, one should consult Bernadette Brooten's article, " 'Junia . . . Outstanding among the Apostles' (Rom. 16:7)," in L. and A. Swidler, eds., *Women Priests: A Catholic Commentay on the Vatican Declaration* (New York: Paulist Press, 1977), pp. 141-44, with which one may compare the remarks on the passage in C. E. B. Cranfield's commentary on Romans, Vol. 2 (listed at the end of chapter 3).

For general background information (apart from Judaism) the book of Sarah B. Pomeroy, *Goddesses, Whores, Wives, and Slaves: Women in Classical Antiquity* (New York: Schocken Books, 1975) is excellent; Flora Levin's translation of the Neopythagorean treatise from which I have quoted may be found there, pp. 134-36. A useful collection of primary sources, translated and briefly introduced, is *Women in Greece and Rome,* by Mary R. Lefkowitz and Maureen B. Fant (Toronto and Sarasota: Samuel-Stevens, 1977). On women in Judaism see, in addition to Leonard Swidler's book mentioned at the end of chapter 2, *Women Leaders in the Ancient Synagogue: Inscriptional Evidence and Background Issues,* Brown Judaic Studies, 36 (Chico, Calif.: Scholars Press, 1982), by Bernadette Brooten.

Philo's *Questions on Genesis* is quoted from the translation by Ralph Marcus in the Loeb Classical Library edition of Philo's works (Supplement I, 1953).

Commentaries on I Corinthians are given at the end of chapter 2. I have quoted the Latin dictum on page 87 above according to the translation provided in the English edition of Conzelmann's commentary, page 246, note 57. A number of interesting texts on women's hairstyles and head coverings in antiquity are gathered together on pages 185-86 of the same volume.

Commentaries on Romans are given at the end of chapter 3.

There are excellent commentaries on the Pastoral Epistles: M. Dibelius, rev. H. Conzelmann, trans. P. Buttolph and A. Yarbro for Hermeneia (Philadelphia: Fortress Press, 1972); C. K. Barrett in the New Clarendon Bible series (Oxford: At the Clarendon Press, 1963); A. T. Hanson in the Cambridge Bible Commentary on the New English Bible series (Cambridge: At the University Press, 1966), and, more recently, in the New Century Bible Commentary (Grand Rapids: Wm. B. Eerdmans, 1982). The best commentary on Colossians is Eduard Lohse's, trans. W. R. Poehlmann and R. J. Karris for Hermeneia (1971); a more recent and less technical one is Eduard Schweizer's *Letter to the Colossians: A Commentary,* trans. A. Chester (Minneapolis: Augsburg Publishing House, 1982). For Ephesians, F. W. Beare's exegesis in *The Interpreter's Bible,* Vol. 10 (1953), is still useful.

V

CHRISTIANS AND THE GOVERNING AUTHORITIES

The topics examined so far have kept our attention fixed primarily upon the Christian community itself and on problems of personal, family, and ecclesiastical morality. None of these spheres of moral concern is separable from the others, of course. Moreover, we have been reminded in various ways that Paul's moral instructions and advice were given and received in the still broader context of the Christian's life in "the world." It is appropriate, then, that our final probe of Paul's teaching should attempt to assess this dimension of his moral concern. We can do this best by posing the specific question of the Christian's obligations to the governing authorities. The passage that will have to claim our closest attention is Romans 13:1-7. These verses would certainly stand high on anyone's list of problem texts in Paul's ethical teaching. A consideration of them will afford an excellent opportunity to close this book as it opened—by emphasizing that Paul's moral instruction should not be regarded either as a sacred cow or as a white elephant.

The Pauline Principle

As in the case of the role of women in the church, so in the matter of the Christian's relation to "the world" and its various kinds of claims, Paul's principle would seem clear. Three famous texts express it in different ways, but the underlying conception is the same in each instance.

He reminds the Philippians that the "state" (RSV translates "commonwealth") to which Christians belong "is in heaven," whence they "await a Savior," their one true "Lord Jesus Christ" (Phil. 3:20). Christians are thus distinguished from those who have their "minds set on earthly things" (3:19).

We have already seen how Paul wrote to the Corinthians that "the form of this world is passing away," and that they should therefore regard all worldly institutions and claims as provisional only:

> From now on, let those who have wives live as though they had none, and those who mourn as though they were not mourning, and those who rejoice as though they were not rejoicing, and those who buy as though they had no goods, and those who deal with the world as though they had no dealings with it. (I Cor. 7:29-31)

The third text is one of the most fundamental of the Apostle's exhortations and serves to link the theological argumentation of the first eleven chapters of Romans to the ethical teaching of chapters 12 and 13.

> Therefore, my brothers, I implore you by God's mercy to offer your very selves to him: a living sacrifice dedicated and fit for his acceptance, the worship offered by mind and heart. Adapt yourselves no longer to the pattern of this present world, but let your minds be remade and your whole nature thus transformed. Then you will be able to discern the will of God, and to know what is good, acceptable, and perfect. (Rom. 12:1-2 NEB)

This text, like those from Philippians and I Corinthians, is written with a keen sense that history is drawing to a close and that Christ's return is imminent. Elsewhere Paul says of "the end" that Christ "delivers the kingdom to God the Father after destroying every rule and every authority and power" (I Cor. 15:24), and that he "will change our lowly body to be like his glorious body, by the power which enables him even to subject all things to himself" (Phil. 3:21). Can there be any question, then, about the implications of this for one's obligations to earthly rulers? Christians belong to another world, to the one Ruler above all earthly rulers, to the One to whom all earthly powers shall be put in subjection. Does not Paul himself show us what kinds of practical consequences follow from this when he tells the Corinthians not to take their disputes to the secular courts (I Cor. 6:1-6)? It would seem so—until one reads Romans 13:1-7 with its explicit admonition to "be subject to the governing authorities." Is this not a monumental contradiction of what seems, from other texts, to be a fundamental Pauline principle?

Romans 13:1-7

There have been times in the history of Christianity when this passage has been the victim of the sacred-cow approach to Paul's moral instruction. Thus, some Christians in Hitler's Germany appealed to it as the decisive biblical warrant for obedience to the Nazi regime. More recently, many American Christians invoked this text against those who refused to support their government's policies and actions in Vietnam. Indeed, as J. C. O'Neill has written, "These seven verses have caused more unhappiness and misery in the Christian East and West than any other seven verses in the New Testament" because of the support they have seemed to require for even tyrannical governments and unjust policies.

On the other side, what some have used as a sacred cow others have discarded as a white elephant. Paul has often been called naïve on this point; or else, granting its pertinence for his own time, the admonition of Romans 13:1-7 has been dismissed as outmoded for ours. There have even been some scholarly attempts to ease us out of this problem passage by denying that Paul ever wrote it. The claim is that we have here another late interpolation into the text of a Pauline letter, a passage that not only interrupts the context but contradicts

Paul's own conviction that the Christian's sole allegiance is to God. In another instance, I Corinthians 14:33*b*-36, we have seen good evidence of a later addition to a Pauline letter. There is no real evidence for a similar theory about Romans 13:1-7, however; the arguments rest entirely on conjecture and a strong feeling that Paul simply would not have required such obedience to political rulers. The vast majority of commentators are agreed that this passage must be considered part of Paul's own moral instruction, whether we like it or not.

We shall be aided in our analysis of the form and content of Romans 13:1-7 if we consider first the historical-social context from within which Paul approaches the matter, and then the literary-theological context of the passage in which his instructions are given.

1. The Historical-Social Context

Paul, born and reared a Jew, was influenced in various ways by the traditions, values, and teachings of Hellenistic Judaism in particular. We have seen examples of such influence in his instructions on marriage and divorce, in his attitudes toward homosexual behavior, and in his counsels about men's and women's hairstyles. It is not unreasonable to suppose that his ideas about allegiance to political authorities will also show signs of his religious background in Judaism.

The Jews were no strangers to political crisis and to the potential conflict between allegiance to God and allegiance to earthly rulers. As a people they had experienced exile, persecution, political oppression, and the indignities, intrigues, and terrors of life under puppet governments. In 200 B.C. Antiochus III, one of the Seleucid successors to Alexander the Great, had wrested the control of Palestine away from the Ptolemies of Egypt, who had exploited both the land and its people. The Jews not unnaturally supported Antiochus against the Ptolemies, and in return the new government lessened the burden of taxation that had so vexed the Jews. In 190 B.C., however, Antiochus himself suffered a military defeat at the hands of the Romans in Asia Minor, and the Seleucids were forced to pay exorbitant reparations to Rome. To help, they imposed additional taxes on the Jews and even attempted—but failed—to appropriate the temple treasury in Jerusalem. The infamous Antiochus IV (Epiphanes) deposed the Jewish high priest in 175 B.C. and twice in succession sold the office to the highest bidder. When he sought to turn Jerusalem itself into a Hellenistic city, the Maccabees, a group of Jewish "freedom fighters," revolted (167 B.C.); and by 141 B.C. the Jews had their independence under the Hasmoneans, a new dynasty of high priests.

Roman control of Palestine dates from 63 B.C., when the Roman general Pompey intervened in a dispute between rival factions of the Hasmonean house. After several months of siege, Jerusalem fell, and all of Palestine was subsequently brought under Roman jurisdiction. A measure of independence was granted to the Jews by Augustus in 47 B.C., but under Herod, Rome's puppet-king in Palestine (37–4 B.C.), the Jews experienced a merciless despotism, which included the confiscation of property and the imposition of heavy taxes. The Herodian royal house retained some power in Palestine until A.D. 94, but always in uneasy tandem with imperial Rome, whose officers, like Pontius Pilate, who served in Judea from A.D. 26 to 36, were responsible directly to the emperor.

In 6 B.C. Judea was officially declared a Roman province, and over the next twelve years a group of Jewish revolutionaries, the Zealots, came into being. Zealotism was rooted in a zealous determination to adhere firmly and without compromise to the Jewish law. The movement as such took shape, however, when Judas the Galilean departed from Pharisaism in general and proposed that the first of the Ten Commandments had a directly political application. "No other gods before me," he insisted, precluded any foreign rule over Israel. For example, if one pays taxes to the king, one breaks the law of God. From small-scale guerrilla operations against Roman military units in Palestine, Zealot activities escalated into a full-scale revolt in A.D. 66. Zealot forces freed Jerusalem from the occupying Romans and made sure to destroy the Roman archives there, including the tax records. Now the full might of Roman military force was felt in Palestine. It was all-out war. Then in A.D. 70 a Roman army under Titus recaptured the city after a bloody siege, killed many of its inhabitants, and burned the temple. The last Zealot forces retreated to the fortress at Masada, where in A.D. 73/74 they chose suicide over the alternative of surrender to the Romans.

Not all Jews shared the religious zeal and political objectives of the Zealots, however. Jewish scripture and tradition had generally taught that the governing authorities deserved respect. Jeremiah's letter to the exiles in Babylon laid upon them as God's own command the charge to "seek the welfare of the city where I have sent you into exile, and pray to the Lord in its behalf, for in its welfare you will find your welfare" (Jer. 29:7). One sees an emphasis on the importance of respect for earthly rulers in the Wisdom literature especially. Wisdom herself teaches, "By me kings reign, and rulers decree what is just; by me princes rule, and nobles govern the earth" (Prov. 8:15-16). Another proverb counsels, "My son, fear the Lord and the king, and do not disobey either of them" (Prov. 24:21).

The Wisdom of Solomon, an apocryphal book of the first century B.C., has already helped us follow Paul's thought in Romans 1:18-32. It can help us also on the subject of allegiance to governing authorities. The "kings," "judges," and "rulers" of the earth (Wisd. 6:1-2) are reminded, "Your dominion was given you from the Lord, and your sovereignty from the Most High" (6:3). However, because "as servants of his kingdom [they] did not rule rightly, nor keep the law [of God]," swift and terrible judgment will come down upon them (6:4-8). All earthly rulers are warned, therefore, to "learn wisdom and not transgress" and to be instructed in holiness (6:9-11). Another document of Hellenistic Judaism of about the same date affirms that "it is God who bestows on all kings glory and great wealth, and no one is king by his own power" (*Aristeas* 224).

The Jewish Essene sect was a closed community devoted to the strict observance of the Mosaic Law, but did not draw the same political conclusions from it that their contemporaries, the Zealots, did. Rather, as Josephus tells us, every new member of the sect pledged to "forever keep faith with all men, especially with the powers that be, since no ruler attains his office save by the will of God" (*The Jewish War*, II, 140). From various sources we learn that even under Roman rule the Jews in general continued to offer sacrifices to God for the emperors and that in their synagogues most Jews continued to pray for the rulers and their welfare (for example, Philo's *Against Flaccus*, 48, 49; *Embassy to Gaius*, 279-80, 301, 305). And about the time that the Zealot party openly revolted against Rome, Rabbi Hanina was teaching his disciples, "Pray for the welfare of the government, for were it not for the fear of the government, a man would swallow up his neighbor alive."

A final example of Jewish custom in this matter is in a sense the most remarkable of all. Shortly after the accession of Gaius (Caligula) to the imperial throne in A.D. 37, a vicious pogrom was launched against the Jews of Alexandria, a city in the Roman province of Egypt. Philo, the distinguished philosopher of that city, in the year 39 headed a delegation of Jews to go to Rome and plead with the Emperor for relief. Philo's essay, *Embassy to Gaius*, tells us about this mission and the events leading up to it. Philo was certainly not naïve about the injustice and evil that could be perpetrated by earthly rulers, especially by a madman like Gaius. But even as he tells about his mission to the imperial court, he continues to stress the point that the Jews "had a twofold motive, respectful fear of the emperor and loyalty to the consecrated laws" (236). The former was demonstrated when, as Philo tells it, he and his delegation were presented to the emperor: "The moment we saw him we bowed our heads to the ground with all respect and timidity and saluted him addressing him as Emperor Augustus" (352). The latter was demonstrated by the fact that the Jews offered sacrifices *for* Gaius at his accession but not *to* him. The distinction was a crucial one to the Jews, and that point was not lost on the emperor who therefore judged the sacrifices to be an inadequate sign of obeisance (356-57).

The apostle Paul could not have been a Christian very long when Philo was in Rome on his "embassy to Gaius"—his missionary travels in Asia Minor and Greece were still in the future. Christianity was still a largely Palestinian and Jewish movement, probably regarded as an eccentric Jewish sect by any Gentile who happened to encounter or hear of it at all. Even with the establishment of Pauline congregations in such important cities as Ephesus, Miletus, Troas, Philippi, Thessalonica, and Corinth, the Christian church had an extremely low profile in the Greco-Roman world. The movement is barely mentioned in the non-Christian literature of the first century; if even known, it was dismissed as unimportant. And so it was, from a political point of view.

Occasionally, Christian evangelists and leaders had confrontations with Roman authorities at the local level, but this was not because of any active governmental program of repression or persecution. Not until the disastrous fire of Rome in the summer of A.D. 64, which Nero sought to blame on the Christians, was there concerted persecution of Christians (Paul himself was probably one of the victims), and even then it was local and temporary. The persecutions under Domitian some thirty years later were more serious, but Christianity as a movement was not outlawed until the edict of Diocletian in A.D. 303. Before then, Christians generally were safe from governmental interference unless accused of specific crimes; they were more the victims of informers than of the state itself. This is important to remember as we seek to recreate the political and social setting in which Paul wrote to the Roman Christians about being subject to the governing authorities. The year was most likely 56 or 57, still early in Nero's reign (A.D. 54–68), when there was considerable confidence abroad that his administration would be just and humane. The Great Persecution of the church was still centuries off.

2. The Literary-Theological Context

Romans 13:1-7 stands in the midst of a series of concrete ethical exhortations, which begin in 12:3 and end in 13:7. These exhortations are framed by the introductory appeal of 12:1-2 and the concluding appeals of 13:8-14.

The introductory appeal is of a very fundamental nature, as we have already had occasion to note. It urges Christians to offer themselves wholly and unreservedly to the spiritual worship of God. They are not to be conformed to this present age, but are to live rather as transformed and renewed persons within it, seeking out and doing God's holy will.

The concluding appeals serve as a summary of what had preceded. God's will is love; that is how all the law's commandments are fulfilled. The urgency of this is then underscored, as it had been at the beginning, by remarking that the Christian belongs to the New Age, not to the old. Now the symbolism of "night" and "day" is employed to express this. Because "the night is far gone" and "the day is at hand," Christians must "cast off the works of darkness and put on the armor of light" which is "the Lord Jesus Christ" himself.

The specific moral injunctions that are framed by these opening and closing appeals may themselves be divided into two main groups. The first group of injunctions applies to life within the body of Christ, the second to one's relationships with those outside the church. It is not completely agreed where the boundary line is between these two. Some place it before the exhortation of 12:14 to "bless those who persecute you," but others believe it should be placed in the middle of 12:16. On this latter view a new sentence and a new paragraph would open with the words, "Do not be haughty, but associate with the lowly. . . ." The "borderline verses," in other words, are 12:14-16*a*, but our present topic does not require us to settle the questions that have been raised about them. It is enough to observe that 13:1-7 not only belongs to the second group, but constitutes the lengthiest topic within it.

What is the theological context of these appeals in Romans 12 and 13? This is indicated first of all by the way they are introduced and concluded. In each case Paul emphasizes that the Christian's present life is radically qualified by the imminence of the New Age. He does not conclude from this, however, that those who in Christ belong to the New Age no longer have any responsibilities for the present age. On the contrary, his point is that the new life in Christ places special moral requirements upon the believer. The power of the New Age is already evident in the gifts with which the members of Christ's body have been individually endowed (12:3-8): gifts to prophesy, to serve, to teach, to exhort, to aid others, and to show mercy. These gifts are not to be put on display as trophies of salvation (the Corinthian error) but are to be used for the service of God in the world. They are the means by which the believer's faith may be enacted in love.

Paul's discussion of spiritual gifts in I Corinthians 12 had led him to stress love as the fundamental claim of the new life in Christ (I Cor. 13–14:1). Now here again, in Romans 12, his description of the spiritual gifts by which Christians are summoned to obedience is followed by a summary appeal to "let love be genuine" (verse 9*a*). From this point through verse 21, the individual admonitions spell out love's requirements to those inside and outside the Christian community. Then in 13:8-10 the love command reappears in the summary appeal of the whole section.

The theological context that is provided by the letter as a whole accords with that suggested by 12:1-2 and 13:8-14. All persons ("Jew and Gentile") stand in need of God's grace. Apart from that, the Gentile is enslaved "to a base mind and to improper conduct" (1:28), and the Jew is enslaved to a law that promises righteousness but actually opens the door to sin (for example, 2:17-24; 7:7-11). But those who by faith are united with Christ in his death have been freed from bondage through God's love, which is made effective there; and they have been brought instead under the rule of grace (5:6–7:6; 8:2-4). The "base mind" is now "renewed" and "transformed" for the service of God (12:2). The one true "law" is now understood to be the "law of love" (13:8-10), which derives from God's redemptive action in Christ (5:6-11; love is thus "the law of Christ," Gal. 6:2). In summary, the admonitions of Romans 12–13 illustrate how those whose lives have been transformed in Christ are to become "instruments of righteousness" (Rom. 6:13) wherever and however long in the present age it is given them to exist.

3. The Passage Itself

What theme or concern is common to 13:1-7 and its context in chapters 12 and 13? We have noted the importance of love in this context, and it is true enough that the various admonitions in 12:9-21 are all more or less derivative from the basic appeal of 12:9*a* to "let love be genuine." But those admonitions are rounded off in 12:21, "Do not be overcome by evil, but overcome evil with good." Nothing in 13:1-7 suggests that Paul is thinking of the governing authorities as an instance of "evil" or of the Christian's subjection to them as the overcoming of evil with good (love). Rather, Paul describes the governing authority as "God's servant for your good" (13:4), and he identifies "conscience," not the love command, as the basic reason to "be subject" (13:5).

What does link 13:1-7 with its context in chapters 12 and 13 is the concern to show how, even in the "secular" sphere, the Christian must seek to do what is "good" according to God's will. This is articulated in the introductory appeal of 12:2 ("to discern the will of God, and to know what is good" NEB); it resurfaces in 12:9*b* ("hate what is evil, hold fast to what is good"), again in 12:17, 21 ("Repay no one evil for evil, . . . but overcome evil with good"), and yet again in the midst of 13:1-7 ("do what is good," 13:3*b*).

As we shall see, the topic in 13:1-7 is *not* "the state," and the main appeal of these verses is *not* to "be subject" to it. The admonition to "be subject" does open the paragraph (verse 1), and it is repeated in verse 5. But these verses are preliminary to the main appeal, which is to pay whatever kinds of taxes one owes (verses 6, 7). Once this chief point has been made, Paul is ready to summarize all the preceding instructions. He does this by generalizing the appeal of 13:6-7 in such a way as to return to the importance of love: "Owe no one anything, except to love one another" (13:8).

Now we are able to examine this passage itself more closely. In order to clarify the structure and progression of Paul's argument, the seven verses may be subdivided into four groups. In verses 1 and 2 Paul is saying that the authority of the governing authorities has been granted to them by God. The next thought, verses 3-4, is that earthly rulers function as servants of God to employ the authority granted them for the common good. Verse 5 advances a third point, and in doing so repeats the opening admonition: one should "be subject" not only for fear of punishment, but "for the sake of conscience." Finally, in verses 6-7, it is said that in the specific instance of taxes, one should comply with the demands of the governing authorities.

Here we have the gist of the passage, but obviously all of the really interesting and difficult questions remain to be answered. How does this accord with Paul's fundamental principle that one lives in the world but should not be of the world? Does Paul regard the Roman Empire as divine? Does he leave no room for "civil disobedience"? To get at these questions, we must examine in turn each of the four phases of the argument.

> Let every person be subject to the governing authorities. For there is no authority except from God, and those that exist have been instituted by God. Therefore he who resists the authorities resists what God has appointed, and those who resist will incur judgment. (13:1-2)

One should observe, first of all, that neither here nor elsewhere in this passage does Paul speak of "obeying" or "disobeying" the governing authorities. Instead, and in line with the tradition in which he stands, he speaks of being "subject" to them, the opposite of which is "resisting" them. Both words imply the existence of an orderly structure, in this case a political structure. The opposite of "subjection" is not so much "disobedience" as "disruption." To "be subject" means to acknowledge the reality of the political structure under which one stands, and to respect it. One might, for example, "disobey" a law of the state and still "be subject" to the political structure, namely, to the due processes and penalties administered in cases of disobedience.

In the second place, it should be carefully noted that there is nothing distinctively Pauline, or even distinctively Christian, in these first two verses. Two interrelated points are being made. First, earthly rulers have no authority except what God has given them; and second, whoever resists them is resisting God's authority and is liable to judgment. Paul has inherited both of these ideas from the traditions of Hellenistic Judaism, as a comparison with the various passages we have examined earlier will show. There is, for instance, the statement of Josephus when commenting on the Essene pledge that "no ruler attains his office save by the will of God." And the advice, "My son, fear the Lord and the king, and do not disobey either of them" (Prov. 24:21, distinctly echoed in a later Christian text, I Peter 2:17). It is crucial to realize that this same tradition held the earthly ruler accountable to God and emphasized that he himself was liable to God's judgment. For those who do not "walk according to the purpose of God," the judgment will be swift and severe, and it does not matter that they are among the high and the mighty; "a strict inquiry is in store for the mighty" (Wisd. 6:4-8). Their possession of authority is not to be construed as a sign of their inherent goodness and wisdom. Rather, it lays upon them the *responsibility* to "learn wisdom and not transgress," and to long for divine instruction in the ways of holiness (Wisd. 6:9-11).

> For rulers are not a terror to good conduct but to bad. Would you have no fear of him who is in authority? Then do what is good, and you will receive his approval, for he is God's servant for your good. But if you do wrong, be afraid, for he does not bear the sword in vain; he is the servant of God to execute his wrath on the wrongdoer. (13:34)

The first point to notice in these verses is that Paul describes the governing authorities as God's *servants*. Neither here nor in verse 6, where he uses the synonymous expression, "ministers of God," does he imply that earthly rulers are the divine representatives of God on earth. They are here to *serve*, and the authority they hold is to be recognized not because it is theirs, but because it but has been given them by God. Both points are in accord with the presumption of the tradition in which Paul stands on this matter, that earthly rulers are responsible for governing wisely and justly.

The other important point in these verses is Paul's specification of the proper functions of the governing authorities. They are to support what is good, thereby assuring the welfare of the whole society. They are the administrators of civil justice (Paul isn't thinking about disputes within the church, as he is in I Cor. 6:1-6), not only punishing those who do wrong, but supporting those who work for what is good. Thus, the governing authorities are set here "for your good," Paul writes. If we are to believe the picture drawn for us by Acts, Paul had more than once been the beneficiary of the law and order that Roman civil and military authority had made a reality throughout the Mediterranean world, even though he had also been its victim. His own continuing confidence in the political system of his day was demonstrated when, sometime after the writing of this letter to the Roman Christians, having been arrested in Jerusalem and imprisoned in Caesarea, he appealed his case, as a Roman citizen, to the emperor (Nero) himself. World traveler that he was, Paul was doubtless more aware than the average person of the social, economic, and political stability that Roman rule had made possible even in the farthest reaches of the Empire. His thought in this passage is similar to that expressed by Rabbi Hanina (about A.D. 66), which was quoted earlier. "Were it not for the fear of the government, a man would swallow up his neighbor alive."

There has been much debate about the exact meaning of the reference here to the one who "does not bear the sword in vain." Is this a reference to the administration, in certain cases of capital punishment by Roman tribunals? Or rather to the military power of Rome, which Paul well knew was capable of putting down rebellion, keeping the sea lanes free of pirates and the highways free of brigands? The reference may be more specific than either of these, but further comment is best reserved until we have looked at the remaining verses, especially the last two.

> Therefore one must be subject, not only to avoid God's wrath but also for the sake of conscience. (13:5)

The appeal to "be subject" with which this paragraph had opened (verse 1) is now repeated. But an important idea is also added in this verse. Until now, Paul's prime argument for being subject to the governing authorities has been that they are God's servants for the maintenance of law and order and the administration of justice. Now he says it is not only for this reason, but "for the sake of conscience" that one must be subject. "Conscience" is a term Paul seems to have picked up from the Corinthians, among whom it was popular. It was not a term that had currency in Hellenistic Judaism, and the appeal to conscience was therefore not a part of the tradition about subjection to earthly rulers on which Paul is otherwise dependent in this passage. Paul ordinarily thinks of one's conscience as that facility for engaging in the critical assessment of a course of action already taken or the critical reflection upon a course of action about to be taken. In this particular passage it seems to refer to one's capacity to reflect critically upon what is appropriate given the realities of existence in the world. Here Paul does not regard conscience as the mediator of any special "Christian truth." He means simply that if one thinks reasonably and carefully about the matter at hand, subjection to the ruling authorities will commend itself as the wise and prudent way. But what, after all, *is* "the matter at hand"? If it were the abstract question of whether a Christian ought to "be subject" to the governing authorities, the proper climax of this passage would have been reached here in the fifth verse: the charge is repeated, the power of rulers to enforce subjection is summarized, and there is a final appeal to one's "conscience." This verse does not conclude the discussion, however. It only sums it up to this point. The conclusion and the real point of the paragraph come in the next two verses.

> For the same reason you also pay taxes, for the authorities are ministers of God, attending to this very thing. Pay all of them their dues, taxes to whom taxes are due, revenue to whom revenue is due, respect to whom respect is due, honor to whom honor is due. (13:6-7)

Everything Paul has been saying in verses 1-5 has been leading up to the specific topic of "taxes," which emerges finally in these two verses. Paul has reminded his readers of their obligation to "be subject to the governing authorities" and of the reasons for that. In verse 6 he points out a specific way in which they are now fulfilling that obligation: by paying taxes. Finally, in verse 7, he indicates what they *should* do to fulfill their obligation. Some interpreters believe that there is an allusion here to the famous saying of Jesus that we know from the Synoptic Gospels and that Paul perhaps knew from the oral tradition: "Render to Caesar the things that are Caesar's, and to God the things that are God's" (Mark 12:17). We might have expected some explicit appeal to "the Lord's" authority, if that is what Paul is invoking (compare I Cor. 7:10), though it could be argued that Paul presumes his readers would be familiar enough with the saying to recognize it at once. More seriously, however, the potential *conflict* between the claims of God and the claims of earthly rulers is not the point under discussion in Romans 13:1-7, and the saying of Jesus is not sufficient for explaining the content of the exhortation in verse 7 or its relation to the statement in verse 6.

It could be argued, and many commentators have, that the exhortation to pay one's taxes as evidence of one's respectful subjection to the governing authorities has no particular problem in mind. Paul certainly did not have the kind of knowledge about the Roman congregation that he had about the one in Corinth. He had not founded the Roman church and had not yet been in Rome when he wrote this letter. The preceding exhortations in this section (12:3-21) are quite nonspecific and would be applicable to Christians anywhere. There are, in fact, similar admonitions in Paul's other letters.

(A few examples: compare Rom. 12:3 with I Cor. 4:6, Rom. 12:10 with Phil. 2:3, Rom. 12:11-12 with I Thess. 5:16-19, Rom. 12:17 with I Thess. 5:15.) Must we not conclude, therefore, that the admonition to pay taxes is one more of these general illustrations of what it means to do God's will in one's daily life? Perhaps, but in this case there are two special points to consider. First, this is the *only* extant Pauline letter where the matter of taxes is raised. The payment of taxes is not a standard topic of Paul's moral instruction so far as our evidence allows us to judge. Second, the way this admonition is worded suggests that Paul does have a specific issue in mind, and one that he could have at least *supposed,* if he did not actually *know,* to be of concern to the Christians in Rome.

The distinctive wording of verse 7 is apparent as soon as we compare it with verse 6. One distinctive feature is of course the imperative mood; verse 7 is clearly an admonition, verse 6 is not. In the second place, verse 7 uses two different words to refer to taxes due, whereas verse 6 had used only one. One of these words (*phoros* in Greek) appears in both verses and is translated each time by "taxes" in the RSV. The second word (*telos* in Greek) appears only in verse 7, where the RSV has translated it as "revenue." Third, two different verbs are used in the two verses, although the RSV has used the same English word in each case. The distinction that is present in Greek is reflected in the NEB, however, where "pay" is used in verse 6 and "discharge" is used in verse 7. Finally, one is struck by the appearance of the word "all" in verse 7, where Paul charges his readers to hand over to *all* what is owed them.

What is the significance of these features of verse 7? The verb that NEB translates as "discharge" happens to be the same that is usually translated as "render" in Jesus' saying about Caesar and God. This has seemed to some a good indication that Paul is actually alluding to Jesus' saying in verse 7, but we have noted some reason to doubt this. There may be no special significance to the change of verbs. The other points, however, would be explained quite nicely if a recent suggestion by a team of German scholars can be accepted. Their whole argument need not be reproduced here, but in what follows I am dependent upon some important clues and conclusions they have presented.

In Paul's day the Roman government levied two main types of taxes, *direct* and *indirect*. It cannot be accidental that the two different words Paul uses for taxes in the passage before us are the Greek equivalents of the official Latin terms for those two types. The direct taxes (Latin: *tributa;* Greek: *phoros;* RSV: "taxes") were collected by government officials. The indirect taxes (Latin: *portoria;* Greek: *telos;* RSV: "revenue") were chiefly harbor fees and *ad valorem* duties on exports and imports. These were collected by companies of Roman knights, infamous for their abuse of the responsibility and their exploitation of the public. From the Roman historian Tacitus, we know that the public outrage at the corrupt practices of these citizen collectors of "revenues" reached a climax in A.D. 58. Tacitus reports that Nero, alarmed by the widespread unrest, seriously considered abolishing the indirect taxes altogether, as mindful as modern legislators that his popularity with the people would surely be increased! "His impulse, however," Tacitus goes on,

> after much preliminary praise of his magnanimity, was checked by his older advisers, who pointed out that the dissolution of the empire was certain if the revenues on which the state subsisted were to be curtailed:—"For, the moment the duties on imports were removed, the logical sequel would be a demand for the abrogation of the direct taxes." (*Annals,* Book XIII, 50)

Nero did institute major reforms, however, issuing new regulations to govern the collection of the indirect taxes and waiving the right to trial of any collector caught abusing his office (Tacitus, *Annals,* Book XIII, 51).

Paul's letter to the Romans was sent from Corinth in A.D. 56 or 57, before Nero's tax reforms and during the period when public pressure was building against the abuses of the revenue collectors. Paul could not have been ignorant of this situation, since Corinth was not only a Roman colony, but also a busy commercial and trade center. Indeed, his mention in 13:4 of the one who "does not bear the sword in vain" might be a reference to special military police who were responsible for enforcing the collections of tax officials; the phrase Paul has employed matches the description of such police found in other ancient sources. Recent sociological studies of the Pauline congregations have demonstrated the probability that a significant number of the Apostle's own converts were persons of some means. These certainly did not constitute the majority in his congregations, but those congregations were not made up exclusively of the poor either. There were among them tradespeople, merchants, and others with substantial resources. These persons of the commercial class would have been exactly those most affected by the revenue abuses of the middle fifties.

If, now, we put together what is known about tax collections and tax problems in the early years of Nero's reign and what is known about the sociological makeup of Paul's congregations, we are able to read the injunction of Romans 13:7 with new appreciation. Paul would be urging his readers in Rome to pay all the taxes for which they were obligated (see "all of them" in verse 7). This would mean not only the direct taxes (*tributa*), which he could presume they would be paying anyway (verse 6), but also the controversial indirect ones (*portoria*). The Christians of Rome were in a strategic—and therefore sensitive—position. That had been proved some years earlier when their activity among the Jews of that city had precipitated the edict of Claudius (see above, page 104). We may suppose that one of the reasons Paul himself was eager to get to Rome (see, for example, Rom. 15:22-29) was his recognition of the importance for his own mission such a visit would have, indeed the specific help the Christians of Rome could give him in getting on to Spain (Rom. 15:24, 28). The factors that lie behind the admonition of 13:7 would then be as follows: (1) the present rising controversy about the justice of the revenue system of taxation; (2) the strategic location of the Christian congregation to whom Paul is writing; (3) the

Apostle's own impending visit to the city, which he hopes will be beneficial to his ministry. In the meantime, Paul urges, pay whatever taxes are levied, without complaint. On the one hand, this will keep you safe from the punishment that, as God's servants, the government officials are authorized to administer and are known to administer through the "tax police." On the other hand, it is the wise and reasonable thing to do as a sign of your respect for law and order.

4. Summary

Our analysis of Romans 13:1-7, including the traditional views that are incorporated here, the literary-theological context in which it stands, and the specific issue to which it seems to be addressed, may be summed up as follows.

(1) The admonition to "be subject to the governing authorities" (verses 1 and 5) is secondary and preliminary to the main point of the passage, which is only disclosed in verses 6-7 (one should pay one's taxes in both kinds).

(2) Paul's view that the governing authorities have been appointed by God is not of his origination but is deeply rooted in the Jewish (particularly Hellenistic-Jewish) tradition in which he stands.

(3) The traditional view includes the idea that earthly rulers function as God's servants, and that because the authority they hold comes from God alone they are accountable to him for ruling wisely and benevolently.

(4) In Paul's day there had not yet been any fundamental confrontation between Rome and the church; the Empire could still be hailed as the one political force capable of creating and maintaining political, economic, and social stability in the world; and the young Nero (only nineteen or twenty years of age when Paul wrote this letter) showed promise of being a just emperor.

(5) Paul does not believe the tax issue is one in which the Christians of Rome should become embroiled; they should demonstrate their support of the rule of law by paying whatever taxes are levied.

Conclusion

Our examination of Romans 13:1-7 was prompted by the question whether this passage does not in fact contradict the otherwise clear Pauline principle that Christians are in the world but not of it. As we have analyzed the passage, its special pertinence for Paul and his readers has become increasingly evident. This requires us to pose a second question, however: To the extent that we are able to affirm the particular relevance of Romans 13:1-7 for Paul and the Roman Christians in A.D. 56–57, are we not simultaneously diminishing its relevance for Christians two thousand years later, facing immensely different and more complex political realities? In answer to the first question, we may respond that Romans 13:1-7 is not only compatible with Paul's own principle but, read in its context and against the background we have sketched, actually illustrates that principle. The considerations that allow us to arrive at this conclusion may be formulated in several points, which, taken together, constitute a response to the second question as well: There are some fundamental ways in which this passage may still speak to us today.

1. *Authority is not to be considered an intrinsic property of those by whom it is exercised.* Paul's way of saying this is that "there is no authority except from God" (13:1*b*). The authority of the governing powers is something with which they have been entrusted. It is surprising that this point, basic to the whole argument of the passage, has so often been overlooked. The authors of the American Declaration of Independence were called revolutionaries for claiming something similar, although, to be sure, they approached the matter rather differently. Governments derive "their just powers from the consent of the governed," they wrote; and, thus authorized, the government has a duty to secure for its citizens those "unalienable rights" with which all people "are endowed by their Creator." Paul does not and could not speak of "the consent of the governed." Whether he *would* have spoken this way had the political realities of his day been

different is moot. However, the conviction that he shares with his religious tradition and that he affirms in Romans 13:1-7 is in its own way a "declaration of independence" from any earthly power that would claim to exercise a self-generated and self-validating authority. That the practical political consequences of this are nowhere indicated by the Apostle may be due in part to the relatively favorable political situation that obtained during his ministry. It is due most of all, however, to his belief that all earthly institutions are in the process of "passing away."

2. *The governing authorities are accountable to God.* If Romans 13:1-7 may be seen as a Christian "declaration of independence" from all tyrannical governments, it may also be seen as a declaration of the dependence of all earthly rulers upon God. Since their authority has been given to them, they are dependent upon and accountable to the One from whom it has come. Paul here specifically describes the government authorities as the "servants" and "ministers" of God. The authority they exercise has its basis in this relationship, and from this belief it is but a step to the conclusion that when they no longer exercise authority in God's service it is no longer the authority of God. But what is their proper function? Paul is explicit about this.

3. *The governing authorities exist to serve "the good" of those who are governed.* They can be said to be exercising the authority given them by God when they support those who do good and restrain those who do evil (Rom. 13:3-4*a*). They are responsible for the rule of law in society, for the administration of justice. One may describe this function according to the context of Romans 12 and 13 as: the maintenance of an ordered society wherein God's will may be sought out and obeyed. It is important to observe that Paul does *not* regard the governing authorities as agents of "salvation." He envisions no Utopia, no perfect society, no theocracy, no "Christian government." The function of the governing authorities is important, but it is not all-embracing; and it belongs still and only to the old age, which is passing away. The Roman Empire, no matter how chastened, will not become God's

kingdom; no Caesar, however noble, will be God's Messiah. Just as Paul declines to regard authority as an intrinsic property of government, so also he declines to regard the governing authorities as inherently either good or evil. They are appointed to *support* the good, but they are not themselves the arbiters of what is good.

4. *The Christian's "subjection" to the governing authorities is secondary to his or her obedience to the will of God.* The whole context within which Romans 13:1-7 stands, as well as what the passage itself says about the authority, accountability, and specific function of the governing authorities, points to this conclusion. The opening appeal in Romans 12:1-2 reminds the readers that their lives are not to be patterned after this present age; as transformed persons they are to seek God's will and do what is acceptable in his sight. Similarly, the closing summary and appeals remind the readers that they stand finally only under the "law" of love (13:8-10) and that they belong not to the "night" of this present age, but finally only to the "day" (13:11-13). Their Lord is not Caesar, but Jesus Christ (13:14). Here we are in touch with the fundamental Pauline principle that Christians belong to another "commonwealth" and that their ultimate allegiance is to God. This point is not repealed or compromised by anything Paul says in Romans 13:1-7. He does not say or imply that Christians belong to their rulers in any ultimate sense. He makes it clear that those rulers are themselves dependent upon God and exist to serve what may be reckoned good according to God's will. His reference to the role of "conscience," verse 5, is crucial. Not only the external restraints and sanctions of the governing authorities, but also one's own critical reflection and judgment about what is "good" come into play. There is no need for Paul to develop the point, of course, because in the case before him he sees no conflict between the Christian's conscience and the law's requirements.

Neither Romans 13:1-7 nor the other problem texts we have examined should be used as sacred cows or discarded as white elephants. Their special pertinence to the conditions and needs of the first century precludes the first, whereas the fundamental theological and moral concerns that lie behind them preclude the second. In summarizing and concluding the admonitions of Romans 12 and 13, Paul reminds us that those who are committed to finding and doing God's will should have only one debt, but it is a constant one—to love. In effect, the concrete ethical teaching of Paul requires us to reformulate every question about our life in the world into the question about our common life before God. It requires us to understand that faith is not faith until it is enacted in love. And it requires us to find out what this means concretely, given the realities of our own place and time, and to do it.

For Further Reading

On the general topic of this chapter see the article, "Rome, Early Christian Attitudes Toward," by Gerhard Krodel in *The Interpreter's Dictionary of the Bible,* Vol. 5, which has a brief bibliography. Two essays by Ernst Käsemann provide an excellent orientation to the context and underlying issues of Romans 13:1-7, "Worship and Everyday Life: A Note on Romans 12," and "Principles of the Interpretation of Romans 13," both in *New Testament Questions of Today* (Philadelphia: Fortress Press, 1969).

In the present chapter, I have relied on several of the basic insights of an article coauthored by three German scholars, Johannes Friedrich, Wolfgang Pöhlmann, and Peter Stuhlmacher. This is an exceedingly thorough study of the historical situation and intention of Romans 13:1-7, but it is so far available only in German, in the *Zeitschrift für Theologie und Kirche,* 73, 1976, pages 131-66. Abraham J. Malherbe's *Social Aspects of Early Christianity,* 2nd ed., enlarged (Philadelphia: Fortress Press, 1983) provides an introduction to some recent social-historical analyses of the Pauline congregations, and makes the point that there were some persons of considerable means within them. If so, then the possibility is increased that Romans 13:1-7 reflects the controversies about the revenue system known to have occurred under Nero.

The Loeb Classical Library has again been used where possible to quote ancient sources: Josephus, *The Jewish War,* trans. H. St. J. Thackeray (1927); Philo, *On the Embassy to Gaius,* trans. F. H. Colson (1962); Tacitus, *Annals,* trans. John Jackson (1937). The *Letter of Aristeas* is quoted from the translation of H. T. Andrews in R. H. Charles, *The Apocrypha and Pseudepigrapha of the Old Testament in English,* Vol. II (Oxford: At the Clarendon Press, 1913). The saying of Rabbi Hanina is cited by G. F. Moore in his discussion of "Duties to Rulers," pages 112-18 in *Judaism in the First Centuries of the Christian Era,* Vol. II (Cambridge: Harvard University Press, 1932).

J. C. O'Neill is quoted from his commentary, *Paul's Letter to the Romans* (Baltimore: Penguin Books, 1975), p. 209. O'Neill himself believes that Romans 13:1-7 is not Pauline, and he makes similar judgments (unpersuasive to most) about large portions of Romans. In addition to the commentaries on Romans mentioned at the end of chapter 3, one may profitably consult the treatment of Romans 13:1-7 in J. H. Yoder, *The Politics of Jesus* (Grand Rapids: Eerdmans, 1972), chapter 10.

INDEX OF SCRIPTURE PASSAGES
(Selected)

ECOLOGICAL INTELLIGENCE

THE HIDDEN IMPACTS
OF WHAT WE BUY

DANIEL GOLEMAN

BROADWAY BOOKS

New York

For all the grandchildren,

And their grandchildren's grandchildren

BROADWAY

Copyright © 2009, 2010 by Daniel Goleman

Published in the United States by Broadway Books, an imprint of
the Crown Publishing Group, a division of Random House, Inc.,
New York.
www.crownpublishing.com

BROADWAY BOOKS and the Broadway Books colophon are
trademarks of Random House, Inc.

Originally published in hardcover in slightly different form in the
United States by Broadway Books, an imprint of the Crown Publishing
Group, a division of Random House, Inc., New York, in 2009.

Library of Congress Cataloging-in-Publication Data
Goleman, Daniel.
Ecological intelligence : the hidden impacts of what we buy / Daniel
Goleman. — 1st pbk ed.
p. cm.
Originally published in 2009 as: Ecological Intelligence: how knowing
the hidden impacts of what we buy can change everything.
1. Environmentalism—Economic aspects. 2. Consumer behavior—
Environmental aspects. 3. Environmental responsibility—Economic
aspects. 4. Industries—Environmental aspects. I. Title.
HC79.E5G635 2010
333.7—dc22

ISBN 978-0-385-52783-5

First Paperback Edition

146064513

CONTENTS

FOREWORD

Back when I was writing this book, the vision I sketched regarding our efforts to make ourselves more ecologically intelligent seemed hopeful, but a long way off in terms of coming to fruition. This book's original subtitle, *How Knowing the Hidden Impacts of What We Buy Can Change Everything,* sums up that vision. For the first time, information systems, coupled with life-cycle analysis of products, could begin to capture all the ecological impacts of a given product—from the potentially toxic chemicals in shampoos to the greenhouse gases emitted while making a solar panel—and sum up the damage done in a single rating.

I argue that if that data were displayed for us on the store shelves as we shop, you and I could shift our purchases toward more virtuous products. And as such individual buying decisions begin to shift market share, competitive advantage will go to those companies that can continually innovate ways to make the stuff we buy truly more green—not just "greenwashed" with green-sounding PR.

In 2009, when this book was launched, the world was at the peak of distraction with the economic meltdown and the specter of a swine flu pandemic. Business media had little-to-no interest in what must have seemed, to some eyes, a naively optimistic notion.

Then, just months after the publication of *Ecological Intelligence,* there came a seismic shift in the business landscape. Wal-Mart, the world's largest retailer, announced it was actively pursuing, in essence, the path I propose here. As one executive there told me, "We're doing your book."

The giant retailer—the 900-pound gorilla of stores—has begun working with an independent academic consortium to design a sustainability index that will use life-cycle-analysis-type data to rate all the products on the store's shelves. Shoppers will see those ratings just as readily as they can see prices today—not just at Wal-Mart, but at any retailer that decides to use the index.

Perhaps most important: the chain's 100,000-plus suppliers have been put on notice that they will be evaluated on their ecological transparency and impacts: this information will matter for the orders the retailer places with them (or whether it places any order at all). The announcement has transformed what once seemed merely an intriguing idea into a market reality, one that companies will have to deal with not just in tomorrow's strategic plans but in today's logistics and operations. This sharpens our understanding of the now common wisdom that "the next business model must be green."

The initivative creates a new lens through which to see the formerly hidden impacts of a product's supply chain. Pilot experiments with the sustainability index have already led to changes, ranging from putting methane digesters on dairy farms in order to lower greenhouse gases, to finding printing companies with the capacity to print colored labels on recycled paper (rather than virgin paperboard) for pizza boxes.

The Wal-Mart initiative had been in the planning stages long before this book came out—but by the time the public announcement was made, *Ecological Intelligence,* I'm told, was being passed around the company's executive offices. (I'm also happy to report the book making the rounds at organizations like Greenpeace, the EPA, and People4Earth, a not-for-profit that helps investors manage sustainability risk.)

As you'll read in Chapter 7, I was present the day the shoppers' eco-rating system, GoodGuide, launched its beta version to a group of eco-moms to try out. GoodGuide aggregates hundreds of databases to render a simple score, on a ten-point scale, of a product's ecological impacts. Back when I witnessed the beta release, it seemed that users would have to click their cell-phone camera on a product bar code in order to pull up the rating—an effort relatively few people would likely bother to make.

Since then, GoodGuide has set aside the bar-code step and developed a streamlined app for the iPhone and Google's phone—and GoodGuide.com has become an immensely popular website (three million visitors in the first year). Perhaps most exciting, some online and national retailers (Wal-Mart and Safeway among them) are discussing putting GoodGuide ratings right on products or next to price tags—lowering to zero the "effort cost" required from shoppers to get a product's eco-rating.

At this writing, GoodGuide rates more than 70,000 products, adding about 1,000 each week, mainly food, toys, household cleansers, and personal care products. Next: pet food, fast food, electronics, and apparel. And the rating system has begun to go global, with plans to launch product ratings in the U.K. in late 2010.

Dara O'Rourke, GoodGuide's founder, has found himself invited to speak at a succession of business and industry meetings to explain the new ecological transparency systems. "My message to them is: This is coming. In the last two months we've been getting more and more calls from big retailers wanting us to let them put our ratings on their products."

GoodGuide complements Earthster (profiled in Chapter 14), an open-source information system that analyzes a product's supply chain to render a precise diagnosis of its negative environmental impacts—data that companies can use to spot where ecological upgrades will improve a product's rating. Earthster, another independent, not-for-profit group, has teamed with Wal-Mart (among others) to pilot analyses of seven products to see how the data can help suppliers become more sustainable in their operations.

Suppliers for the seven house brands are feeding Earthster product-data on nonrenewable resources consumed, climate change gases, and impacts on local ecosystems and on human health. This marks a leap forward from where Earthster was when I first wrote about it in this book. At that point there had been just a handful of pilot trials with companies assessing their own manufacturing impacts and where they can make ecological improvements.

Since then, Earthster founder Gregory Norris tells me, interest from companies—and even from an American city—in using Earthster has been growing exponentially. By 2010 he expects Earthster to be tested with fifty to a hundred products, and is actively developing Earthster 2.0, which will take the system to scale. At that point, Norris says, "Any company can use Earthster to calculate its sustainability footprint in cradle-to-gate analyses of environmental, health, and social impacts."

Going to scale also means going global; Norris hopes to translate Earthster into Spanish and Chinese in the near future. As systems like GoodGuide and Earthster grow in their usage, it becomes ever more likely that one day every item in the aisles of stores will have trustworthy, simple-to-read ecological impact ratings. One intriguing possibility: a system like Earthster might feed audited ecological data from companies directly into a rating system like GoodGuide, making the resulting product ratings more precise, trustworthy, and current than any available today.

Progressive companies like Johnson & Johnson are already rethinking their product-development process to build in perpetual ecological upgrades that will continually improve the ecological footprint—and eco-ratings—of their brands.

As retailers start to view the products they choose to sell through the lens of sustainability, suppliers are incentivized to reduce ecological impacts. When shoppers use GoodGuide to decide what brand to buy, or when retailers tell their suppliers that they are being evaluated in part on their eco-transparency and their products' ecological footprints, this triggers a virtuous cycle, where a market shift based on open information creates a business imperative to do the right thing.

Historically there has always been a vast information asymmetry between consumers and manufacturers, with consumers knowing next to nothing about the true ecological impacts of what they buy. Ecological transparency hands that once-hidden data to shoppers. The new information systems fostering ecological transparency in the marketplace are disruptive technologies, promising to be a game changer both for business and for environmental, public health, and social activists.

But, as the saying goes, the devil is in the details. Will the emerging sustainability index for products be independent and transparent, and credible to shoppers? Will it cover the entire range of environmental, health, and social impacts of a product?

Will the ratings be simple to grasp and easy to see—for instance, a single number or symbol or color code posted on a product or next to its price tag? Will manufacturers and suppliers rise to the challenge and allow enough transparency about their activities to make the ratings meaningful? And will a host of retailers adopt the same standard?

To the extent these questions are answered with a "Yes," the ecological transparency initiative will let shoppers perceive products in a bold new way: not just the item itself and its price, but also its ecological impacts with all *those* costs to our planet, as well as to ourselves and our families.

Such a change in how we perceive products should, in theory, shift market share, creating a never-before-seen market reality: a true top-line premium for businesses that stay ahead of the curve by exploring a multitude of ways to upgrade the environmental impacts of the products they make. This virtuous cycle should vastly accelerate the exploration of more ecologically sound industrial methods, platforms, and chemicals. Such an economic incentive should unleash a bonanza of entrepreneurial innovations, expanding the green economy far beyond energy savings to include improvements in any and all ecological impacts.

The essential reinvention of everything industrial has begun to get traction. Take the lowly brick. The basic method for making bricks—baking clay for twenty-four hours at 2,000°F, has been used for three thousand years. But some Silicon Valley entrepreneurs have done the R&D that re-imagines brickmaking.

For one, these new-style bricks are baked at only 212°F in an innovative process that takes just ten hours from start to finish, compared to an entire week for ordinary bricks. The recipe (a carefully calibrated chemical mix) uses large amounts of fly ash, the powdery residue from coal burned at power plants that would otherwise be a pollutant. This process emits around 80 percent less greenhouse gases and consumes up to 90 percent less energy than conventional methods. Energy savings mean these neo-bricks sell for the same price as those made the ancient way.*

One driver of the necessary wave of reinvention for ecological improvements will be, no doubt, the emerging market force unleashed by these transparency systems. Much can be done by governments acting where the free market cannot reach, for example, incentivizing companies to find ecological upgrades—rewarding smart innovations like the lower-impact brick—and by making sound product-related ecological impact data more easily available.

The need to review standard manufacturing practices through the lens of ecological impacts should trigger a fresh tide of such reinvention and rethinking. This wave of market-driven ecological innovation could well become one driver of a much-needed surge in economic growth.

Such innovation can be both grand and simple. One approach starts with fresh thoughts on industrial design that induce cascading improvements from the ground up. Here, small changes can have rippling impacts; reducing package sizes for prosaic products like detergents has meant cost and material reductions, fewer trucks on the road and less fuel used, greater efficiencies in distribution centers, more detergents on the shelf of stores and less in store rooms, less wast for consumers—and on and on.

Such innovative reinventions of the basics of industry and commerce are more than business solutions. They can also raise the bar beyond mere "sustainability," (to the degree the term

*David Lawsky, "Silicon Valley reinvents the lowly brick," Reuters, September 21,2009.

means just maintaining the status quo of a diseased planet). Instead of simply maintaining things as they are and calling that "sustainable," we should reach further.

Some voices predict that unless we change direction, we are on course for a planetary extinction akin to the death of the dinosaurs—except the extinction this time would be of the ecosystems that mankind and countless other species depend upon. So, beyond sustainability, we need to seek ways to replenish our depleted world and reinvigorate weakened ecosystems.

Ecological Intelligence maps one route forward to a more promising future, an alternative to the predicted planetary disasters due to our present slow-motion depletion and pollution of our world. The success of this approach depends on all of us—you and me as mindful consumers, making choices for that better future, along with anyone who makes or sells goods of any kind.

The big question: Will the likes of GoodGuide or the Sustainability Index be used by enough shoppers and big buyers to matter? Some survey data suggests that those born from the 1980s on are far more motivated than past generations to make buying decisions that will lead to a better planet. Many companies are already anticipating this market trend, and changing their practices and purchases for better ecological profiles.

But can these disruptive information technologies actually catalyze a critical mass of marketplace awareness of ecological impacts? Years ago when the Internet first launched, I was at the *New York Times*. Back then it was a laughable notion that an upstart technology—the Web—could ever threaten a newspaper's economic viability.

Time will tell.

THE HIDDEN PRICE OF WHAT WE BUY

A while ago I made an impulse buy: a small, bright yellow wooden racing car, with a green ball for the driver's head and four black discs pasted on its sides for wheels. The toy cost just 99 cents. I bought it for my eighteen-month-old grandson, who I thought would love it.

After I came home with that little wooden racer, I happened to read that because lead in paint makes colors (particularly yellow and red) look brighter and last longer—and costs less than alternatives—cheaper toys are more likely to contain it. Then I came across a news item reporting that a test of twelve hundred toys taken from the shelves of stores—including the chain where I bought that car—revealed a large percentage contained various levels of lead.

I have no idea if the sparkling yellow paint on this toy car harbors lead or not—but I am dead certain that once it was in the hands of my grandson his mouth would be the first place it would go. Now, months later, that toy car still sits atop my desk; I never gave it to my grandson.

Our world of material abundance comes with a hidden price tag. We cannot see the extent to which the things we buy and use daily have other kinds of costs—their toll on the planet, on consumer health, and on the people whose labor provides us our comforts and necessities. We go through our daily life awash in a sea of things we buy, use, and throw away, waste, or save. Each of those things has its own history and its own future, backstories and endings largely hidden from our eyes, a web of impacts left along the way from the initial extraction or concoction of its ingredients, during its manufacture and transport, through the subtle consequences of its use in our homes and workplaces, to the day we dispose of it. And yet these unseen impacts of all that stuff may be their most important aspect.

Our manufacturing technologies and the chemistry they deploy were largely chosen in a more innocent time, one when shoppers and industrial engineers alike had the luxury of paying little or no attention to the adverse impacts of what was made. Instead they were understandably pleased by the benefits: electricity generated by burning coal, with enough to last for centuries; cheap and malleable plastics made from a seemingly endless sea of petroleum; a treasure chest of synthetic chemical compounds; cheap lead powder to add luster and life to paints. They were oblivious to the costs of these well-meaning choices to our planet and its people.

Though the composition and impacts of things we buy and use

daily are for the most part the outcome of decisions made long ago, they still determine daily practice in manufacturing design and industrial chemistry—and end up in our homes, schools, hospitals, and workplaces. The material legacy left to us by the once wonder-inducing inventions of the industrial age that ran through the twentieth century has made life immeasurably more convenient than the life our great-grandparents knew. Ingenious combinations of molecules, never before seen in nature, concoct a stream of everyday miracles. As utilized in yesterday's business environment, today's industrial chemicals and processes made utter sense, but all too many make little sense going forward. Consumers and businesses alike can no longer afford to leave invisible decisions about those chemicals and processes—and their ecological consequences—unexamined.

In my past work I've explored what it means to be intelligent about our emotions and, more recently, about our social lives. Here I look into the sense in which we can, together, become more intelligent about the ecological impacts of how we live— and how ecological intelligence, combined with marketplace transparency, can create a mechanism for positive change.

In the interest of full disclosure, when it comes to ecological intelligence I am as clueless as most of us. But in researching and writing this book I've been fortunate enough to stumble upon a virtual network of people—executives and scientists alike—who excel in one or another subset of the skills we urgently need to build the human store of shared ecological intelligence, and to let that knowledge guide our decisions in better directions. In sketching the possibilities of this vision I've drawn on my background as a psychologist and science journalist to delve into the world of commerce and manufacturing, and to explore cutting-edge ideas in fields like neuroeconomics and information science, and particularly an emerging discipline, industrial ecology.

This journey continues one I began more than two decades ago, when I wrote in a book on self-deception that our habits of consumption on a worldwide scale are creating an ecological deficit at a rate unparalleled in history, as I put it, "simply by our heedlessness of the links between the decisions we make daily—for instance to buy this item rather than that—and the toll those decisions have."

Back then I imagined that one day we would somehow be able to gauge with accuracy the ecological damage from a given act of manufacturing or the packaging, shipping, and disposal of a given product and sum it up in some handy unit. Knowing that metric about a TV set or box of aluminum foil, I reasoned, we could take more responsibility for the impact on the planet of our individual choices. But I ran out of steam, conceding "there is no such information available, and even the most ecologically concerned among us do not really know the net effect on the planet of how we live. And so our obliviousness lets us slip into a grand self-deception that the small and large decisions in our material lives are of no great consequence."

All those years ago I had never heard of industrial ecology, the discipline that routinely does the very impact analyses I dreamed of. Industrial ecology exists at the cusp where chemistry, physics, and engineering meet ecology, and integrates those fields to quantify the impacts on nature of manmade things. Back when I was wishing for this field to exist, that still-obscure discipline was just gathering itself. In the 1990s a working group of the National

Academy of Engineering spawned the field, and the very first issue of the *Journal of Industrial Ecology* appeared in 1997, well over a decade after I had wished for its existence.

Industrial ecology had its roots in the insight that industrial systems parallel natural ones in many ways: the streams of manufactured stuff running between companies, extracted from the earth and emitted in new combinations, can be measured in terms of inputs and outputs regulated by a metabolism of sorts. In this sense industry, too, can be seen as a kind of ecosystem, one that has profound effects on every other ecological system. The field includes topics as diverse as estimating CO_2 emissions from every industrial process or analyzing the global flow of phosphorus, to how electronic tagging might streamline the recycling of garbage and the ecological consequences of a boom in fancy bathrooms in Denmark.

I see industrial ecologists—along with those at the cutting edge of fields like environmental health—as the vanguard of a dawning awareness, one that may well add a crucial missing piece in our collective efforts to protect our planet and its people. Imagine what might happen if the knowledge now sequestered among specialists like industrial ecologists were made available to the rest of us: taught to kids in school, easily accessible on the Web, boiled down into evaluations of the things we buy and do, and summarized as we were about to make a purchase.

Whether we are a single consumer, an organization's purchasing agent, or an executive managing a brand, if we knew the hidden impacts of what we buy, sell, or make with the precision of an industrial ecologist, we could become shapers of a more positive future by making our decisions better align with our values.

All the methods for making that data known to us are already in the pipeline. As this vital knowledge arrives in our hands, we will enter an era of what I call *radical transparency*.

Radical transparency converts the chains that link every product and its multiple impacts—carbon footprints, chemicals of concern, treatment of workers, and the like—into systematic forces that count in sales. Radical transparency leverages a coming generation of tech applications, where software manipulates massive collections of data and displays them as a simple readout for making decisions. Once we know the true impacts of our shopping choices, we can use that information to accelerate incremental changes for the better.

To be sure, we already have a mélange of eco-labels based on high-quality data assessing pockets of products. But the next wave in ecological transparency will be far more radical—more inclusive and detailed—and come in a flood. To make that mass of information usable, radical transparency must reveal what has been hidden from us in ways far more comprehensive and better organized than the sometimes haphazard product ratings we have now. With the right, targeted data, a continuous cascade of consumer-driven shifts would ripple through the world of commerce, from the most distant factory to the neighborhood power grid, opening a new front in the battle for market share.

Radical transparency will introduce an openness about the consequences of the things we make, sell, buy, and discard that goes beyond the current comfort zones of most businesses. It will reshape the marketing environment to ensure a better reception for the enormous variety of greener, cleaner technologies and products now in the pipeline—creating a far greater incentive for us all to make the switch to them.

Such full ecological disclosure presents an untried economic path: applying to the ecological impacts of the things we buy the high standards for transparency required, say, in financial statements. It would hand shoppers information for their choices akin to what stock analysts apply in weighing the profits and losses of companies. It would give senior management greater clarity in carrying out their company's mandates to be more socially responsible and sustainable, as well as anticipate where markets will shift.

This book tracks my personal journey into this realm, beginning with my speaking to industrial ecologists about the enormous complexity in making even the simplest product, and about this new science that tracks the environmental, health, and social impacts at every step. Then I explore the reasons this information remains largely concealed from us, and why the remedy lies in boosting our ecological intelligence, a collective understanding of hidden ecological impacts and the resolve to improve them.

I show how we could boost our ecological intelligence by making this data on impacts available to shoppers—and visit the inventors of a technology about to make such radical transparency a reality. Next, I look at evidence suggesting how this could shift market share to a point where companies would see more clearly the competitive advantage in ecological improvements far wider-ranging than what is typical now. I examine a case in point: controversies about industrial chemicals, as viewed through the lens of brain researchers examining purchase decisions, reveal why consumers' emotional reactions to products' ecological impacts can matter for sales.

Finally, I shift from the psychology of buyers to the strategies of sellers, and talk to a widening circle of businesspeople who are ahead of this coming wave and who already have changed the way they manage their company's supply chains to upgrade impacts, thus positioning their businesses to thrive in a radically transparent marketplace. These executives realize that at the emotional level, good business means good relationships, and that by demonstrating their ecological concern in these ways, they make their customers feel cared for, too. My mission here is to alert businesses to a coming wave, one that will wash over any company that markets a man-made product.

We hear much about helping the planet by changing what we *do*—bike, don't drive; use the new, energy-saving fluorescent bulbs; recycle our bottles; and other ready fixes. All such changes in ecological habits are laudable; if more of us made these efforts they would have great benefits.

But we can go further. The true impacts of what we *buy* have been ignored for the majority of goods. Surfacing the myriad hidden ecological impacts during a product's life cycle, from manufacturing to disposal of those bikes, bulbs, and bottles, as well as the rest of the materials in the room, opens a floodgate of effective action. Using a deeper understanding of the impacts of the things we use to guide our buying decisions can give us added leverage that ripples widely through the worlds of commerce and industry.

That opens the door to a vast opportunity for benefiting our future. For shoppers, this singular mechanism can add potent forcefulness to our collective will to protect the planet and its people from the unintended harms done by commerce. For business, this more powerful alignment of consumers' values with their purchasing choices will foster a hot new arena for competitive advantage—

a financial opportunity sounder and more promising than our present-day "green" marketing. We may not be able to shop our way out of the current crisis, but radical transparency offers one more avenue to essential change.

We have been besieged by messages about the dire threats of global warming and toxins in everyday objects and demands that we must somehow change before it's too late. One version of this litany is all too familiar: ever-warmer temperatures, fiercer hurricanes, fiery droughts, and rampant desertification in some places and relentless rains in others. Some predict escalating global scarcity of food and water within the next decade or so, or—with Hurricane Katrina in the Gulf of Mexico the harbinger—the evacuation of more cities around the globe because of environmental collapse.

Another chorus, growing stronger by the day, tells us that man-made chemicals in everyday items are slowly poisoning us and our children. This creeping toxicity goes far beyond lead in toys. These voices warn that compounds used to harden and soften plastics leach carcinogens into everything from IV bags in hospitals to water wings; chemical softeners in lipstick pose other dangers to health; our computer terminals off-gas one toxin, while their printers ooze a cloud of another. The manufactured world, it seems, is creating a chemical soup that is slowly polluting the ecosystem that is our body.

All such warnings implicate the same culprits: you and me. Human activity has become the main driver of this burgeoning crisis, one that gravely threatens, well, you and me.

We are collectively enmeshed in activities that inexorably endanger the ecological niche that houses human life. The continued momentum from our past actions will unfold over decades or centuries; toxic chemicals that permeate our water and soil, and the buildup of greenhouse gases, will take their toll for years to come.

That catastrophic scenario can readily lead to feelings of hopelessness, even despair. After all, how can any of us turn back the vast tsunami of human activity?

The sooner we can stop adding to that tidal wave, the less drastic the damages will be. And if we examine more carefully our part in fouling our niche on this planet, we can find points of leverage where simple, gradual changes might halt or even reverse our contribution to this cataclysm.

As individual shoppers we are trapped in making choices among an arbitrary range of product options, a range determined by the decisions of industrial engineers, chemists, and inventors of all stripes, at some distant remove in time and space. We have the illusion of choice, but only on the terms dictated by those invisible hands.

On the other hand, as we are able to make choices based on full information, power transfers from those who sell to those who buy, whether a mom at the local market, a purchasing agent for a vendor or institution, or a brand manager. We become the shapers of our destiny rather than passive victims. Just by going to the store, we will vote with our dollars.

By doing so we will create an entirely new competitive advantage for companies that offer the kinds of products our collective future needs. Those informed choices will shape new mandates for today's engineers, chemists, and inventors. I would argue that this market force will drive a demand for a wave of innovations, each of them an entrepreneurial opportunity. In this way, upgrading our ecological intelligence will prime a boom that will alter for the better the industrial processes used to make everything we buy. Global shocks like skyrocketing oil prices create a synergism with the search for ecological upgrades by radically shifting cost equations, boosting the urgency of finding advantageous alternatives.

As control of data shifts from sellers to buyers, companies would do well to prepare ahead for this informational sea change. The business rule of thumb in the last century—cheaper is better—is being supplemented by a new mantra for success: sustainable is better, healthier is better, and humane is better, too. Now we can know with greater precision how to implement that mantra.

"GREEN" IS A MIRAGE

The *Visudhimagga,* a fifth-century Indian text, poses a riddle: "Precisely where is what we call a 'chariot' located? Is it in the axles, the wheels, the frame? Is it in the poles that connect to the horse?"

The answer: Nowhere. What we mean by the term "chariot" refers to the temporary arrangement of its component parts. It's an illusion.

The ancient text uses that insight to illustrate the elusive nature of the self, which resides neither in our memories nor in our thoughts, perceptions, sensations, or actions (an analysis that anticipated modern philosophy's deconstruction of the self by fifteen hundred years). But this insight applies as well to a Game Boy, a blender, or any manufactured thing. Every such object breaks down into the multitude of its parts and the constituent processes that made them.

An industrial engineer's version of the deconstruction of stuff is called Life Cycle Assessment, or LCA, a method that allows us to systematically tear apart any manufactured item into its components and their subsidiary industrial processes, and measure with near-surgical precision their impacts on nature from the beginning of their production through their final disposal.

LCAs had a prosaic start; one of the very first such studies was commissioned by Coca-Cola back in the 1960s to determine the relative merits of plastic and glass bottles and quantify the benefits of recycling. The method slowly spread to other industrial questions; by now a large and growing band of companies with national or international brands deploys the method somewhere along the way to make choices in product design or manufacturing—and many governments use LCAs to regulate those industries.

Life Cycle Assessment was created by a loose confederation of physicists and chemical and industrial engineers documenting the minutiae of manufacturing—what materials are used and how much energy, what kinds of pollution are generated and toxins exuded, and in what amounts—at each basic unit in a very long chain. In that dusty text the Riddle of the Chariot names a handful of components; today the LCA for a Mini Cooper breaks down into thousands of components—like the electronic modules that regulate electrical systems. These electronic modules deconstruct—like the chariot into its main parts—into printed wiring board, various cables, plastics, and metals; the chain leading to each of these in turn leads to a trail of extraction, manufacture, transport, and so on. These modules run dashboard systems, regulate the radiator fan, wipers, lights, and ignition, and manage the engine—and for each of these parts in turn the analysis can run into a thousand or more discrete industrial processes. In total, that petite car's LCA entails hundreds of thousands of distinct units.

My guide in this terrain is Gregory Norris, an industrial ecologist at the Harvard School of Public Health. With degrees in mechanical engineering from MIT and aerospace engineering from Purdue and several years in the air force as an astronautical engineer helping build better space structures, Norris has impeccable credentials. But he readily concedes, "For LCA you don't need to be a rocket scientist—I know, I was one. It's mainly data tracking."

That meticulous analysis yields metrics for harmful impacts over an auto's life cycle, from manufacture to junked car, for the raw materials consumed; energy and water depleted; photochemical ozone created; contribution to global warming; air and water toxicity; and production of hazardous wastes—to name but a few. An LCA reveals that in terms of global warming effluents, for example, everything in the car's life cycle from manufacture to getting scrapped pales when compared to the emissions while it is driven.

Another apt metaphor for the nature of industrial processes comes from an eighth-century Chinese treatise that describes a supernatural net belonging to the god Indra. In the heaven where Indra dwells, the text tells us, a miraculous net stretches in every direction. In each eye of the webbing glitters a magnificent jewel, cut so cleverly that its facets reflect all the other jewels in that net, in an endless web of interconnection. Any single jewel in that web bears a reflection of every other.

Indra's net offers a handy image for the endless interconnections within and between systems in nature, as well as in manmade systems like the supply chain. When Norris walked me through a Life Cycle Assessment for glass packaging, like that for jams or pasta sauce, we ended up in a maze of interdependent linkages in a seemingly endless chain of material, transportation, and energy demands. Manufacturing bottles for jams (or anything in a glass container for that matter) requires getting stuff from dozens of suppliers—including silica sand, caustic soda, limestone, and a variety of inorganic chemicals, to name but a few—as well as the services of suppliers of fuels like natural gas and electricity. Each one of the suppliers makes purchases from or otherwise utilizes dozens of its own suppliers.

The basics for making glass have changed little since the time of ancient Rome. Today, natural gas-powered furnaces burn at up to 2,000 degrees Fahrenheit for twenty-four hours to melt sand into glass for windows, containers, or the monitor on your cell phone. But there's far more to it than that. A chart showing the thirteen most important processes deployed to make glass jars revealed a system stitching together 1,959 distinct "unit processes." Each unit process along the chain itself represents an aggregate of innumerable subsidiary processes, themselves the outcome of hundreds of others, in what can appear an infinite regression.

I asked Norris for some detail. "For example, let's trace the production of caustic soda. That requires inputs of sodium chloride, limestone, liquid ammonia, a variety of fuels and electricity, and transport of those inputs to the site. Sodium chloride production in turn involves mining and water use, and inputs of materials, equipment, energy, and transport."

Because "everything connects to everything," Norris says, "we need to think in a new way."

Another insight: the supply chain for a glass jar may consist of seemingly endless links, but these eventually hook back onto earlier links. As Norris explained, "If you go beyond the total 1,959 links in the glass jar's supply chain, you loop into repeats—the chain goes on forever, but asymptotically."

Norris gave a simple example of such repetitive loops. "It takes electricity to make steel, and it takes steel to make and maintain an electric power plant," he explained. "You could truly say that the chain goes on forever—but it's also true that the extra impacts of the upstream processes get smaller and smaller as you trace them farther and farther back."

The industrial version of Indra's net meets its limits in something like the Ouroboros, the mythic serpent that swallows its own tail. That tail-devouring beast symbolizes repetitive cycles or renewal in the sense of something constantly repeating and reinventing itself.

In industrial processing, the Ouroboros can also symbolize an ideal detailed in the "cradle to cradle" notion that everything used in a product should be designed so that on disposal it all biodegrades into compounds nature can use or becomes a manufacturing nutrient, recycled into other products. This contrasts with the current mode of cradle to grave, where a discarded item's ingredients simply add to the pile in a landfill, leach toxins, or create molecular or other nightmares.

These images of the chariot, the net, and the snake came to mind as Gregory Norris and I were in a virtual meeting where we talked by phone while my computer screen in Massachusetts displayed what was on his in Maine. Through the lens of an LCA every one of the nearly two thousand links in the glass jar's supply chain becomes a window on its impacts on human health, ecosystems, climate change, and resource depletion.

Making a glass jar requires the use of hundreds of substances somewhere upstream in the supply chain, each one with its own profile of impacts. There are around one hundred substances released into water and fifty or so into soil along the way. Among the 220 different kinds of emissions into the air, for instance, caustic soda at a glass factory accounts for 3 percent of the jar's potential harm to health and 6 percent of its danger to ecosystems.

Another ecosystem threat, accounting for 16 percent of glassmaking's negative impact, results from the energy for the furnace. Twenty percent of the negatives specifically for climate change are attributed to the generation of electricity for the factory that makes the glass. Overall, half the emissions from making a glass jar that contribute to global warming occur at the glass factory, the other half in other parts of the supply chain. The list of chemicals released into the air from the glass factory runs from carbon dioxide and nitrogen oxides at relatively high levels through trace amounts of heavy metals like cadmium and lead.

When you analyze the inventory of materials needed to make one kilogram of packaging glass, you get a list of 659 different ingredients used at various stages of production. These range from chromium, silver, and gold to exotic chemicals like krypton and isocyanic acid to eight different molecular structures for ethane.

The details are overwhelming. "That's why we use impact assessment, where we can sum it all up into a few informative indicators," says Norris. For instance, if you want to know what carcinogens are involved in glassmaking, an LCA tells you the main culprit is aromatic hydrocarbons, the best known being VOCs, the volatile organic compounds that make the smell of fresh paint or a vinyl shower curtain a matter of concern. For glassmaking, these compounds account for about 70 percent of the process's cancer-causing impact.

However, none of these are released directly from glassmaking at the factory; they are all somewhere else in the supply chain. Each one of the units of analysis in the glass jar's LCA offers a point for analyzing impacts. Drilling down into the LCA reveals that 8 percent of the cancer-causing impacts come from releases of volatile organic compounds associated with constructing and maintaining the factory, 16 percent from producing the natural gas the factory uses to heat its furnaces, and 31 percent from making HDPE, high-density polyethylene for the plastic the glass is wrapped in for shipping.

Does this mean we should stop using glass jars for foods? Of course not. Glass, unlike some plastics, does not leach questionable chemicals into fluids and remains endlessly recyclable.

But as Norris took me through the highlights of that glass jar's LCA, it hit me: all this was for a glass jar that is 60 percent *recycled*.

Exactly what, I asked Norris, is gained by that 60 percent? For one, he answered, the amount of new glass replaced by the recycled content saves about that proportion of weight in raw materials extracted, processed, and transported. "Of course you still need to process and transport post-consumer glass, but the net impact of glass recycling is still beneficial," he reassured me, adding an example: "Every twenty-eight percent of recycled content saves five hundred gallons of water per ton of glass produced and avoids emissions of twenty pounds of CO_2 to the atmosphere."

And yet all those other impacts remain, despite the recycling. This transforms our notions of "green" from what seems a binary judgment—green or not—into a far more sophisticated arena of fine distinctions, each showing relatively better or worse impacts along myriad dimensions. Never before have we had the methodology at hand to track, organize, and display the complex interrelationships among all the steps from extraction and manufacture of goods through their use to their disposal—and summarize how each step matters for ecosystems, whether in the environment or in our body.

In this light, consider the tote bags British fashion designer Anya Hindmarch put out in a limited edition of twenty thousand. Hindmarch's inspiration came when she was approached by a charity called "We Are What We Do"—what Hindmarch decided to do was use her fashion platform to raise public awareness about refusing plastic bags in stores. And that it did.

Priced at $15, the bags were sold in supermarkets rather than the pricey boutiques where Hindmarch's handbags are usually to be found. Eager buyers lined up at the selected stores throughout England as early as 2 a.m.—and by 9 a.m. not one remained. When they later went on sale at Whole Foods' flagship market on Columbus Circle in Manhattan, the bags were snapped up within thirty minutes. When the bags were made available in Hong Kong and Taiwan, shoppers were injured in stampedes—so the bag's release in Beijing and several other cities was canceled. And in Britain the bags were repeatedly mentioned in nationwide discussions about higher standards for recycling.

Hindmarch's eco-chic suggests one way smart habits and products can nudge us to change our ways. And change we must. Those little plastic bags we carry our purchases home in are an ecological disaster. In the United States alone 88 billion are used each year; their abundant cousins are blowing in the breeze from São Paulo to New Delhi, caught in shrubbery, filling gutters, and killing animals that eat or get caught in them. The biggest curse: they take an estimated five hundred to one thousand years to decompose.

Not that paper bags are necessarily better. The EPA estimates that it takes more energy and pollutes more water to make paper bags than plastic ones. There are pros and cons on both sides of the paper-versus-plastic debate. Plastic bags, for instance, are 100 percent recyclable—though in the United States only about one in a hundred actually gets recycled.

One of the pioneering LCA studies, published in *Science* back in 1991, was an analysis of the merits of paper versus plastic as the ingredient in hot-drink cups, which highlighted the complexities of such comparisons. A paper cup consumes 33 grams of wood, while a polystyrene one uses about 4 grams of fuel oil or natural gas; both require a slew of chemicals (the analysis neglects their health impacts). Making the paper cup consumes thirty-six times as much electricity and 580 times the volume of wastewater, which contains some level of contaminants like chlorine; on the other hand, making the plastic cup produces pentane, a gas that increases ozone and greenhouse gas. But then there are the methane releases of paper cups left to biodegrade in a landfill. When the analysis shifts from the environment to impacts on human health, the math gets yet more complex.

Still, the smart answer to "Paper or plastic?" is "Neither—I brought my own bag." This is already standard practice throughout many parts of the world, where customers have to pay stores for shopping bags or bring their own; the practice has been spreading through stores in the United States. But LCA raises the question, what are the impacts of that virtuous bag?

Hindmarch's company went to great lengths to make her bags ecologically correct: they were manufactured in factories certified to offer fair wages with no child labor, carbon offsets were purchased to cover the impacts of manufacture and transport, and they were sold at cost. Hindmarch even tried to use fair trade cotton, bought directly from small growers, but could not find enough and so settled for organically grown.

And yet you have to wonder what an LCA of that exemplary bag might reveal about all the ways it harms the environment—and thus all the ways it could become even more virtuous.

"GREEN" IS NOT WHAT IT SEEMS

That Hindmarch canvas tote was emblazoned with the slogan "I'm NOT a plastic bag," a play on the 1929 painting by the Belgian surrealist René Magritte depicting a pipe, below which were the words *Ceci n'est pas une pipe*—"This is not a pipe." The painting's title, *The Treachery of Images,* underscores Magritte's point that the image is not the thing and things are not what they seem.

The other day I bought a T-shirt that hung in a prominent spot in a department store. My T-shirt bears the proud label "100% Organic Cotton: It Makes a World of Difference."

That claim is both right and wrong.

First, what's right: the benefits of forgoing pesticides in cotton. Cotton crops alone account for about 10 percent of the world's use of pesticides. To prepare soil so that fragile young cotton plants can grow, workers spray the soil with organophosphates (linked to central nervous system damage in humans), which kill off any plant that might compete with the cotton or any insect that might eat it.

Once soil has been so treated, it can take up to five pesticide-free years before even earthworms return, a vital step in recovering soil health. Then there's the paraquat sprayed by crop dusters on cotton just before it's harvested. About half this defoliant typically misses the cotton and ends up in streams and fields nearby. Given the damage done by pesticides, there's little question about the intrinsic environmental goodness of organic cotton—so far as it goes.

Then there are the downsides. For example, cotton has a prodigious thirst. It takes about 2,700 liters of water to grow the cotton for one T-shirt; the Aral Sea evaporated into desert largely because of the irrigation demands of regional cotton farms. Simply tilling the soil has its own ecosystem impact, releasing carbon dioxide.

The organic T-shirt I bought was dyed a dark blue. Cotton yarn gets bleached, dyed, and finished with industrial chemicals that include chromium, chlorine, and formaldehyde, each toxic in its own way. What's worse, cotton resists absorbing dye, and a large amount rinses off into factory wastewater, which can end up in local rivers or groundwater. Some commonly used textile dyes harbor carcinogens—epidemiologists have long known that workers in dye plants have unusually high rates of leukemia.

That label on my T-shirt exemplifies "greenwashing," the selective display of one or two virtuous attributes of a product meant to impart goodness to the whole thing. The more complete analysis of its hidden impacts reveals multiple ways in which the T-shirt may not be so green after all. Although an organic shirt is all to the good, when the adverse impacts of a product stay hidden, the "organic" part at best marks the first step toward a business becoming more socially responsible or sustainable; at worst, it is a marketing ploy.

When the fast-food chain Dunkin' Donuts announced that its doughnuts, croissants, muffins, and cookies would henceforth be "trans fat free," the company joined most other major players in its industry in making its foods a bit healthier. But the operative phrase is *a bit:* all those "zero trans fat" pastries remain an unhealthy mix of fat, sugar, and white flour. When nutritionists analyzed ingredients in tens of thousands of supermarket items, they found—no surprise—a vast number of foods marketed as "healthy" choices were not.

From a marketing perspective, spotlighting the organic cotton in a T-shirt or the absence of trans fats in a doughnut imbues that product with the sheen of virtue. Advertisers, of course, tout one or two positive qualities of a product to shine up its market appeal. Playing up the sizzle, not the steak, has always been standard operating procedure.

But that attentional bait and switch directs shoppers' focus away from whatever negatives a given product may still have. The T-shirt's dyes are as dangerous as ever, just as a "zero trans fats" doughnut still harbors fats and sugars that drive insulin levels sky high. But so long as we stay focused on that thin slice of virtue in the T-shirt or the doughnut, we can buy it feeling good enough about our choice.

So greenwashing merely creates the illusion that we are buying something virtuous. Such products are *greenish*—they are draped with the mere appearance of ecological merit.

Every small step toward green helps, to be sure. But our craze for all things green represents a transitional stage, a dawning of awareness of ecological impact but one that lacks precision, depth of understanding, and clarity. Much of what's touted as "green" in reality represents fantasy or simple hype. We are past the day when one or two virtuous qualities of a product qualify it as green. To tout a product as green on the basis of a single attribute—while ignoring numerous negative impacts—parallels a magician's sleight of hand.

That quasi-green T-shirt is not alone; consider a study of 1,753 environmental claims made for over a thousand different products plucked from the aisles of big-box stores. Some paper brands, for instance, focus on a narrow set of features, like having some recycled fiber content or chlorine-free bleaching, while ignoring other significant environmental issues for paper mills, such as whether the pulp comes from sustainable forestry or whether the massive amounts of water used are properly cleansed before return to a river. Or there's the office printer that proclaims its energy efficiency but ignores its impact on the quality of indoor air or its incompatibility with recycled printer cartridges or recycled paper. In other words, it was not *designed* to be green from cradle to grave, but only engineered to tackle a single problem.

To be sure, there are *relatively* virtuous products, building materials, and energy sources. We can buy detergent without phosphates, install carpeting that exudes fewer toxins or flooring of sustainable bamboo, or sign up for energy that comes mainly from wind, solar, or other renewable sources. And all that can make us feel we have made a virtuous decision.

But those green choices, helpful as they are, too often lull us to more readily ignore the way that what we now think of as "green" is a bare beginning, a narrow slice of goodness among the myriad unfortunate impacts of all manufactured objects. Today's standards for greenness will be seen tomorrow as eco-myopia.

"Very few green products have been systematically assessed for how much good they actually do," says Gregory Norris. "First you have to do an LCA, and that's rare." Maybe thousands of products of any kind have gone through these rigorous impact evaluations, he adds, "but that's a tiny fraction—millions are sold. Plus, consumers don't realize how interconnected industrial processes are," let alone their myriad consequences.

"The bar is too low for green products," Norris concludes. Our current fixation on a single dimension of "green" ignores the multitude of adverse impacts that shadow even the most seemingly virtuous of items. As Life Cycle Assessment of just about anything shows, virtually everything manufactured is linked to at least trace quantities of environmental toxins of one kind or another, somewhere back in the vast recesses of the industrial supply chain. Everything made has innumerable consequences; to focus on one problem in isolation leaves all the other consequences unchanged.

A publisher (not mine) wanted to make a book as "green" as possible. He found paper that had been whitened by an eco-friendly oxygenation method rather than with tons of chlorine, and he bought energy offsets—investments like wind farms on

Native American reservations—to compensate for the energy used to produce the book. But there were obstacles. "One big problem was with the ink," he told me. "Ink used to print books has been made from synthetic chemicals that are toxic. When a print run for a book finishes, the printers needed to wash their rollers; they used to just wash the ink off their rollers into water runoff from their plants. Now they try to capture the excess ink. If the ink is water based, then they can do this—but if oil based, they need to wash their rollers with a solvent, many of which are also toxic. Soy-based ink has become fashionable as a green alternative, but 'soy' ink in fact has just eight to ten percent soy; the rest is just as bad as ever. I tried to use soy ink, but I need a four-color ink process for the graphics, and only three of the inks met the standard for soy—the fourth was a bit short of the eight percent requirement. So I couldn't make that claim."

Indeed, nothing made industrially can be utterly green, only relatively more so; Indra's net reminds us that every manufacturing process has adverse impacts on natural systems somewhere along the way. As one industrial ecologist confided, "The term 'eco-friendly' should not ever be used. Anything manufactured is only relatively so."

This shadow side of industry has been overlooked in the value chain concept, which gauges how each step in a product's life, from extracting materials and manufacture through distribution, adds to its worth. But the notion of a value chain misses a crucial part of the equation: while it tracks the value added at each step of the way, it ignores the value *subtracted* by negative impacts. Seen through the lens of a product's Life Cycle Assessment, that same chain tracks a product's ecological negatives, quantifying its environmental and public health downsides at each link. This window on a company or product's negative ecological footprint might be called the *"de*value chain."

Such information has strategic importance. Every negative value in an LCA offers a potential for upgrading and so improving the item's overall ecological impacts. Assessing the pluses and minuses throughout a product's value chain offers a metric for business decisions that will boost the pluses and lessen the minuses.

In a day when major players in every industry, and more and more consumers, are pressing for green, we would do well to understand the implication of improving impacts all along the supply chain and throughout a product's life cycle. Green is a process, not a status—we need to think of "green" as a verb, not an adjective. That semantic shift might help us focus better on green*ing.*

WHAT WE DON'T KNOW

Try this mind experiment. Imagine an old-fashioned two-tray balance scale, like that held by the classic image of a blindfolded goddess of justice. On one of the trays put the total benefits that accrue from all the recycling, use of green products, and other environmental, public health–minded, and socially concerned activities you engage in over a typical month. Now on the other tray place what an industrial ecologist might assess as the harmful impacts of everything else you buy and do over the same month—all the miles you drive in a car, the hidden consequences of producing, transporting, and discarding your groceries, the printer paper you use, and everything else.

Unfortunately, for any of us but the most incredibly virtuous, the harmful impacts are enormously greater than the benefits. As Life Cycle Assessment data reveals, in today's marketplace it's almost impossible to come out well in this balance.

Among the few people I know whose scale might drop to the better side is a band of freegans who make exceptional efforts: they try never to buy anything new; they walk or bike instead of using cars; they barter, comb giveaway bins, even Dumpster dive. Such extreme enviro-asceticism is for the few. A middle way might appeal to a wider swath of enthusiasts: a combination of consuming less and shopping with more precision for beneficial environmental impacts. Buy less, but when you do shop, buy smart.

As we saw in the last chapter, almost all of us go shopping oblivious to the true impacts of our purchases and our habits. The main barrier comes down to a lack of crucial information, a gap that leaves us in the dark. The old saying has it that "What we don't know can't hurt us." But the truth today is just the reverse: what we do not know about what goes on backstage, out of sight, harms us, others, and the planet. Look behind the light switch to glimpse the environmental cost of electric power; swoop down to the molecular level to assess the chemicals off-gassed by everyday products and absorbed by our bodies; burrow down through the supply chain to grasp the human cost of the goods we enjoy.

In the world of commerce, we are collective victims of a sleight of hand: the marketplace comes arranged as though by an illusionist working a trick in our perception. We don't know the true impacts of what we buy and don't realize that we don't know. Failing to know what we do not notice is the essence of self-deception.

We are at cause for a wide range of perils in large part because the web of connection between what we buy and do and the resulting adverse impacts remains hidden from us. Even as some of these consequences grow ever more dire, we can blithely continue habits that intensify these very perils. A fundamental disconnect resides within our awareness, between what we do and how it matters.

An example: The Swiss Federal Institute for Snow and Avalanche Research documents warming that leads mountain slopes below 5,000 feet to get 20 percent less snow than was true in earlier decades. Too little snowfall means that resorts have to manufacture the stuff, using machines that require enormous amounts of energy—and so worsen climate heating. Yet even in balmy weather, come the season skiers blithely expect to hit the slopes no matter what. So resorts concoct the man-made fluff with energy-hungry snowmaking equipment.

Another example: Industrial ecologists did a careful analysis of a green housing project in Vienna where residents gave up cars and used the money saved by not building garages to build solar energy collectors and the like. When it came to energy use and getting around, these households were far lower in their carbon emissions than conventional households. But when it came to everything else—food, travel beyond Vienna, and the overall basket of goods they bought—these households were no better than any others.

A third: Common ingredients in sunscreen turn out to prime the growth of a virus in the algae that live inside coral reefs. Researchers estimate between 4,000 and 6,000 metric tons of sunscreen wash off swimmers each year worldwide, threatening to turn about 10 percent of coral reefs into bleached skeletons. The dangers are greatest, of course, where the most swimmers are drawn to the beauty of these reefs.

Our inability to instinctively recognize the connections between our actions and the problems that result from them leaves us wide open to creating the dangers we decry. Somehow it's as though our commutes and carpools, our coal-burning power plants and overheated offices, the toxic mix of molecules that float around inside our homes have nothing to do with *us*. There remains a disconnect between our collective role in generating all those harmful particles and the damage they do.

We suffer a vast, shared blind spot. The millennia since the dawn of civilization have seen the slow but steady emergence of novel varieties of threats, so that today our species faces danger from forces that elude our built-in perceptual alarms. Because such shifts befuddle the brain's alarm system, we must make a pointed effort to bring subliminal dangers into awareness, beginning by understanding our perceptual dilemma.

Our brains are exquisitely attuned to pinpoint and instantly react to a fixed range of dangers, those that fit within nature's periscope. Nature hard wired the brain's alarm circuitry to spot and recoil immediately from objects hurtling toward us, threatening facial expressions, snarling animals, and like dangers in our immediate physical surroundings. That wiring helped us to survive to the present.

But nothing in our evolutionary past has shaped our brain for spotting less palpable threats like the slow heating of the planet, the insidious spread of destructive chemical particulates into the air we breathe and things we eat, or the inexorable destruction of vast swaths of flora and fauna on our planet. We can spot a menacing stranger's sinister face and immediately start walking in the other direction. But when it comes to global warming, we shrug.

Our brain excels at handling threats in the moment but falters at managing those coming at us in some indefinite future.

The human perceptual apparatus contains imperceptible limits, thresholds below which we do not notice what goes on. We are limited in what we sense by boundaries that themselves stay forever beyond our perception. Our range of perception was carved out in nature by fierce weeding out by predators, poisons, and the multitude of other threats to life our species encountered. Back in those tooth-and-claw days the human life span was a mere thirty years or so; evolutionary "success" meant you lived long enough to have children who lived long enough to have children themselves. But today we live long enough to die of cancer, which in itself can take three or more decades to develop.

We have invented industrial processes and fallen into habits of living that cumulatively may slowly erode the narrow niche of temperature, oxygen, exposure to sunlight, and so on that nurtures human life. But the changes that might result in a higher rate of cancers, or in the steady march to a warmer planet, fall beyond the threshold of our sensory perception. Our perceptual system misses the signals of danger when the threat comes in the form of gradual rises in planetary temperature or minuscule chemicals that build up in our body over time. Our brain has no built-in warning radar for these.

Our brains have been finely tuned to be hypervigilant at spotting dangers in a world we no longer inhabit, while the world we live in today presents us with abundant dangers we do not see, hear, taste, or smell. The brain's threat response system is buffaloed time after time.

Although the human brain is extremely alert to threats it can sense, our brain is unsuited for the ones we face on the ecological front: these are dangers that come gradually, or at the microscopic level, or globally. Our brain has been exquisitely tuned to notice changes in light, sound, pressure, and the like within a narrow range—the zone of perception that tigers and reckless drivers come in. These trigger our get-out-of-the-way system to react in milliseconds; we sense these familiar threats as clearly as we see a match light up a dark room. Ecological dangers, though, we notice as poorly as we see the difference that a lit match makes in a well-lit room.

Psychophysicists use the term "just noticeable difference" to describe the merest amount of shift our senses can detect in sensory signals like pressure or volume. The ecological changes that signal impending danger are sub-threshold, too subtle to register in our sensory systems at all. We have no ready-made detectors for, nor instinctive response to, these hazy sources of harm. The human brain adapted to spot dangers within its sensory field. But to survive today we must perceive threats that are beyond our thresholds for perception. We must make the invisible visible.

As Harvard psychologist Daniel Gilbert puts it, "Scientists lament the fact that global warming is happening so fast, but the fact is it's not happening fast enough. Because we barely notice changes that happen gradually we accept things we would not allow if they happened suddenly. The impurity of our air, our water, our food has increased dramatically in our lifetimes, but it happened one day at a time, transforming our world into an ecological nightmare that our grandparents never would have tolerated."

VITAL LIES, SIMPLE TRUTHS

The Norwegian playwright Henrik Ibsen coined the phrase "vital lie" for the comforting story we tell ourselves that hides a more painful truth. When it comes to the full costs of ecological ignorance in the marketplace, we endorse the vital lie *what we don't know or can't see does not matter.* In fact, our indifference to the consequences of the sum total of what we buy and do, and our unexamined habits as consumers, drive a vast number of threats to the environment and to health.

Every vital lie requires cover stories that paper over the simple truth. Take recycling. We tell ourselves, "Well, I recycle my newspapers and bottles. Plus I bring my own bags to the store" and feel a bit better for having done our part. As virtuous as such recycling may be—and it is certainly better than nothing—it is nowhere near enough to remedy things. And recycling can feed our self-deception by creating a momentary green bubble that offers the illusion that our individual efforts are solving the problem.

"Recycling," as industrial designer William McDonough puts it, "simply says we are going to recycle our toxins." The reason: too many of the chemicals routinely used in manufacturing the stuff we use become destructive when leached into the environment. When we send our junk to the dump, we are doing our part in making our local landfill a minor-league toxic site. As the saying goes, "When you throw something away, there is no away." It remains here, on planet Earth.

When it comes to recycling, we can do far better. One day, as McDonough proposes in his groundbreaking book *Cradle to Cradle,* we'll have total recycling, where all parts of a product can be completely reused in new products or broken down completely into molecules nature can absorb well. But for now we make what seems a good enough choice given the options—while we fail to perceive that we are offered only an arbitrary and very narrow range of options in the first place.

In this sense, recycling contributes to the vital lie that we are *already* doing what matters, when in fact what we are doing barely dents the vast tidal wave of collateral damage done to people and the planet by the things we buy and use. In this light, "green" labels and recycling programs may do harm as well as good; they lull us into the illusion that we are doing enough, while ignoring the remaining adverse impacts of what we buy and do. Humanity can no longer afford these comforting cover stories.

Vikram Soni and Sanjay Parikh decry how in their native India and other parts of the developing world the very term "development" can hide the extinguishing of vast swaths of nature by huge dams or enormous construction projects. A careful choice of terms disguises a more grim reality; for instance, real estate developers deploy the term "water harvesting" when they overdraw from an aquifer or pave over a floodplain. By the same token, Soni and Parikh question the term "sustainable" forestry when the word disguises the replacement of natural forest preserves by a monocrop; even planting two trees for every one lost in a clear-cut first-growth forest can fail to replace the richness of that vanished biodiversity.

Such vital lies create a collusion among us all not to look squarely at the hidden impacts of our choices. There are four rules of attention in any group, from a family to a company, to society as a whole. These govern our ratio of information to ignorance, and so have great consequences.

The first two determine what information we hold in common. Number one: *Here's what we notice.* When it comes to a product, what we notice is largely what's in it for us. For a corporation it's the bottom line; for the consumer, price and value. The second rule: *Here's what we call it.* In economic terms, to a company a product's price might be a "competitive advantage"; to a consumer, a "bargain."

The second pair of rules determines our level of ignorance. Number three: *Here's what we don't notice.* What we haven't noticed about the free market has been the hidden costs to our planet and its people of the things we make, sell, and buy. The fourth rule: *Here's how we talk about that,* or what we say to keep the blind spot hidden. In terms of commerce, that has been some version of "only price matters, and little else counts."

These four rules can be restated in terms of economic theory: in the marketplace, what we see and name represents the information we have about a product. Those aspects of the product that go unseen, and so unnamed, represent our ignorance. These attentional rules explain why, unfortunately, harmful product impacts go unpunished by buyers and virtuous ones go unrewarded.

In the lore of Alcoholics Anonymous, the collusion of friends and family to ignore the fact that someone has become an alcoholic and needs help is called the "elephant in the room." We are ignoring another variety of elephant in the room: the room itself and the unrecognized impacts of everything in it.

Much of the world's focus on ecological improvements has pinpointed what individuals do—upgrading the impacts of our habits in terms of driving, home energy use, and the like. But seen through the lens of an LCA, what we do with the stuff we own represents only one stage in the life cycle of products. And that stage may have little or nothing to do with a given product's worst ecological effects. Focusing solely on how we behave ignores a vast, promising arena for change.

Certain theorists hold that we are all helpless victims of what amounts to a conspiracy. In the eyes of some, faceless corporations are handy villains to blame our predicament on, a convenient Evil Other. Seen from within some corporations, the forces of unreason are embodied in activists who push for changes that make no business sense. Within companies this same bent of mind takes the form of shifting the burden, making difficult decisions someone else's responsibility—an engineer, specialist, consultant, the government. Finding other people to blame has always been a favored ploy of the human psyche. Psychoanalysts call this "projection," the casting out of our own failings and pasting them on someone—or something—other than ourselves.

Such scapegoating may simply reflect how our self-deception channels our sense of helplessness. Scapegoating offers too easy an out: each of us is both victim and villain. As individuals our own habits and consumption—the things each of us buy and do— drive the very effects we bemoan. When I flip on a light switch or fire up the microwave powered by a coal plant, I subsidize the addition of a tiny amount of greenhouse gases to the atmosphere. When you do likewise, the same happens. When tens of millions or billions of us do it day in and day out over the course of decades or centuries, we get global warming.

By imagining some disembodied power that has victimized us—"those greedy corporations," say—we avoid having to examine our own impacts. It's a convenient arrangement, one that lets us deflect our discomfort at facing the ways in which we add to the onslaught against the natural world. But in the current crisis, there are no backroom villains, no hidden cabal of evil plotters; we are all enmeshed in systems of commerce and manufacturing that perpetuate our problems. The sad truth is that our roles as victims and villains are due to the collective habits and technologies that we have inherited from a more innocent time, when life could more readily be lived without regard for the ecological impacts of our own activity.

Businesses respond to consumers' desires; the free market—at least in theory—provides us what we want to buy. But this means that all of us, at every step, can become *active agents* for the broadscale, incremental improvements we desperately need. The intelligence that might save us from ourselves requires a shared awareness by and coordinated efforts from all of us—as shoppers, as businesspeople, as citizens.

ECOLOGICAL INTELLIGENCE

For over a thousand years Sher, a tiny village in Tibet, has clung to its existence despite its dire location, perched on a narrow shelf along a steep mountainside. This site on the dry Tibetan plateau gets just three inches of precipitation a year. But every drop is gathered into an ancient irrigation system. Annual temperatures average near freezing, and from December through February the mercury can hover below that mark by 10 to 20 degrees Fahrenheit. The region's sheep have extra-thick wool that holds heat remarkably well; locally spun and woven wool makes clothes and blankets that help villagers endure the excruciatingly cold winters with little heating other than a fire in the hearth.

The stone-and-wattle houses need to be reroofed every ten years, and willow trees planted along the irrigation canals provide the roofing. Whenever a branch is cut for roofing, a new one is grafted to the tree. A willow tree lasts around four hundred years, and when one dies a new one is planted. Human waste is recycled as fertilizer for herbs, vegetables, and fields of barley—the source of the local staple, *tsampa*—and for root vegetables to store for the winter.

For centuries Sher's population has stayed the same, around three hundred people. Jonathan Rose, a founder of the movement for housing that is both green and affordable and a builder himself, finds instructive lessons in the clever ways native peoples have found to survive in perilous niches like Sher. Says Rose, "That is true sustainability, when a village can survive in its ecosystem for a thousand years."

Tibetans, of course, are not unique in their remarkable ability to find simple solutions to the daunting challenge of surviving, even thriving, in the most dire of environmental surrounds. From the Arctic Circle to the Sahara Desert, native peoples everywhere have survived only by understanding and exquisitely attuning themselves to the natural systems that surround them and designing ways of living that best interact with those systems. The tiny hamlet of Sher depends on three forces for its survival: sunlight, rainwater, and the wisdom to use nature's resources well.

Modern life diminishes such skills and wisdom; at the beginning of the twenty-first century, society has lost touch with what may be the singular sensibility crucial to our survival as a species. The routines of our daily lives go on completely disconnected from their adverse impacts on the world around us; our collective mind harbors blind spots that disconnect our everyday activities from the crises those same activities create in natural systems. Yet at the same time the global reach of industry and commerce means that the impacts of how we live extend to the far corners of the planet. Our species threatens to consume and befoul the natural world at a rate that far exceeds our planet's carrying capacity.

I think of the brand of wisdom that has kept that tiny Himalayan village alive for these centuries as "ecological intelligence," our ability to adapt to our ecological niche. *Ecological* refers to an understanding of organisms and their ecosystems, and *intelligence* connotes the capacity to learn from experience and deal effectively with our environment. Ecological intelligence lets us apply what we learn about how human activity impinges on ecosystems so as to do less harm and once again to live sustainably in our niche—these days the entire planet.

Today's threats demand that we hone a new sensibility, the capacity to recognize the hidden web of connections between human activity and nature's systems and the subtle complexities of their intersections. This awakening to new possibilities must result in a collective eye opening, a shift in our most basic assumptions and perceptions, one that will drive changes in commerce and industry as well as in our individual actions and behaviors.

The Harvard psychologist Howard Gardner reinvented the way we think about IQ by arguing that there are several other varieties of intelligence besides the ones that help us do well in school, and that these other intelligences also allow us to do well in life. Gardner enumerated seven kinds, from the spatial abilities of an architect to the interpersonal aptitudes that make teachers or leaders great. Each of these intelligences, he argues, involves a unique talent or ability that helped us adapt to the challenges we faced as a species and that continues to benefit our lives.

The uniquely human ability to adapt our way of living to virtually any of the extremes of climate and geology the earth offers would certainly qualify. Pattern recognition of any kind, Gardner suggests, may have its roots in the primal act of understanding how nature operates, such as classifying what goes in which natural grouping. Such talents have been displayed by every native culture in adapting to its particular environment.

The contemporary expression of ecological intelligence extends the native naturalist's ability to categorize and recognize patterns to sciences like chemistry, physics, and ecology (among many others), applying the lenses of these disciplines to dynamic systems wherever they operate at any scale, from the molecular to the global. This knowledge about how things and nature work includes recognizing and understanding the countless ways man-made systems interact with natural ones, or what I think of as ecological intelligence. Only such an all-encompassing sensibility can let us see the interconnections between our actions and their hidden impacts on the planet, our health, and our social systems.

Ecological intelligence melds these cognitive skills with empathy for all life. Just as social and emotional intelligence build on the abilities to take other people's perspective, feel with them, and show our concern, ecological intelligence extends this capacity to all natural systems. We display such empathy whenever we feel distress at a sign of the "pain" of the planet or resolve to make things better. This expanded empathy adds to a rational analysis of cause and effect the motivation to help.

To tap into this intelligence, we need to get beyond the thinking that puts mankind outside nature; the fact is we live enmeshed in ecological systems and impact them for better or worse—and they us. We need to discover and share among our-selves all the ways this intimate interconnectedness operates, to see the hidden patterns that connect human activity to the larger flow of nature, to understand our true impact on it, and to learn how to do better.

We face an evolutionary impasse: the ways of thinking that in the ancient past guided our innate ecological intelligence were well suited to the harsh realities of prehistory. It was enough that we had a natural urge to gobble as many sugars and fats as we could find to fatten ourselves against the next famine, sufficient that our olfactory brain would ensure that toxins triggered nau-sea and disgust in response to spoiled food, and that our neural alarm circuits made us run from predators. That hardwired savvy brought our species to the threshold of civilization.

But ensuing centuries have blunted the survival skills of the billions of individuals who live amid modern technologies. Career pressures drive us to master hyperspecialized expertise and in turn to depend on other specialists for tasks beyond our realm. Any of us may excel in a narrow range, but we all depend on the skills of experts—farmers, software engineers, nutritionists, mechanics—to make life work for us. We no longer can rely on our astute attunement to our natural world nor the passing on through generations of the local wisdom that lets native peoples find ways to live in harmony with their patch of the planet.

Ecologists tell us that natural systems operate on multiple scales. At the macro level there are global biogeochemical cycles, like that for the flow of carbon, where shifts in the ratios of elements can be measured not just over the years but over cen-turies and geologic ages. The ecosystem of a forest balances the entwined interplay of plant, animal, and insect species, down to the bacteria in soil, each finding an ecological niche to exploit, their genes evolving together. At the micro level cycles run their course on a scale of millimeters or microns, in just seconds.

How we perceive and understand all this makes the crucial difference. "The tree which moves some to tears of joy is in the eyes of others only a green thing which stands in the way," wrote the poet William Blake two centuries ago. "Some see Nature all ridicule and deformity, and some scarce see Nature at all. But to the eyes of the man of imagination, Nature is Imagination itself. As a man is, so he sees."

When it comes to seeing nature, these differences in perception have huge consequences. A polar bear stranded on an ice drift or a vanishing glacier offer powerful symbols of the perils we face from global warming. But the inconvenient truths don't stop there—only our collective ability to perceive them does. We need to sharpen the resolution and broaden the range of our lens on nature, to see how synthetic chemicals disrupt the cells of an endocrine system as well as the slow rising of ocean levels.

We have no sensors nor any innate brain system designed to warn us of the innumerable ways that human activity corrodes our planetary niche. We have to acquire a new sensitivity to an unfamiliar range of threats, beyond those our nervous system's alarm radar picks up—and learn what to do about them. That's where ecological intelligence enters the picture.

The neocortex, the thinking brain, evolved as our most versatile neural tool for survival—what the hardwired reflexive circuits of our brain cannot help us understand, the neocortex can discover, comprehend, and marshal as needed. We can learn the now-hidden consequences of what we do, and what to do about them—and so cultivate an acquired ability to compensate for the weakness of our preprogrammed ways of perceiving and thinking.

The variety of ecological intelligence humanity so urgently needs demands that this generalist zone work along with the brain's prededicated modules for alarm, fear, and disgust. Nature designed the olfactory cortex to navigate a natural universe of odors we rarely encounter today; the amygdala's neural web for alarm innately recognizes with effectiveness only a limited—and largely antiquated—range of danger. Those hardwired areas are not easily reprogrammed, if at all. But our neocortex—through what we intentionally learn—can compensate for our natural blind spots.

Smells are just combinations of volatile molecules wafting from some object and reaching our nose. Our olfactory brain assigns a positive or negative valence, separating the desirable from the repulsive, the putrified meat from the fresh bread. But life now requires learning that the scent of newly applied paint or that distinctive aroma in a just-bought car comes from volatile, man-made chemical compounds, which act like low-grade toxins in our body and should be avoided. Likewise we need to acquire a learned early warning system for toys laden with lead and gases that pollute the air we breathe, and to dread toxic chemicals in our foods that we cannot taste or see. But we can "know" these are dangers only indirectly, through scientific findings—a different order of knowing. What may eventually become a learned emotional reaction must begin with intellectual comprehension.

Ecological intelligence allows us to comprehend systems in all their complexity, as well as the interplay between the natural and man-made worlds. But that understanding demands a vast store of knowledge, one so huge that no single brain can store it all. Each one of us needs the help of others to navigate the complexities of ecological intelligence. We need to collaborate.

Psychologists conventionally view intelligence as residing within an individual. But the ecological abilities we need in order to survive today must be a *collective* intelligence, one that we learn and master as a species, and that resides in a distributed fashion among far-flung networks of people. The challenges we face are too varied, too subtle, and too complicated to be understood and overcome by a single person; their recognition and solution require intense efforts by a vastly diverse range of experts, businesspeople, activists—by all of us. As a group we need to learn what dangers we face, what their causes are, and how to render them harmless, on the one hand, and, on the other, to see the new opportunities these solutions offer—and we need the collective determination to do all this.

Evolutionary anthropologists recognize the cognitive abilities required for shared intelligence as a distinctly human ability, one that has been crucial to helping our species survive its earliest phases. The most recent addition to the human brain includes our circuitry for social intelligence, which allowed early humans to use complex collaboration to hunt, parent, and survive. Today we need to make the most of these same capacities for sharing cognition to survive a new set of challenges to our survival.

A collective, distributed intelligence spreads awareness, whether among friends or family, within a company, or through an entire culture. Whenever one person grasps part of this complex web of cause and effect and tells others, that insight becomes part of the group memory, to be called on as needed by any single member. Such shared intelligence grows through the contributions of individuals who advance that understanding and spread it among the rest of us. And so we need scouts, explorers who alert us to ecological truths we have either lost touch with or newly discover.

Large organizations embody such a distributed intelligence. In a hospital a lab technician does one set of jobs well, a surgical nurse another, and a radiologist still another; coordinating all these skills and knowledge allows patients to receive sound care. In a company the sales, marketing, finance, and strategic planning departments each represent unique expertise, the parts operating as a whole via a coordinated, shared understanding.

The shared nature of ecological intelligence makes it synergistic with social intelligence, which gives us the capacity to coordinate and harmonize our efforts. The art of working together effectively, as mastered by a star performing team, combines abilities like empathy and perspective taking, candor and cooperation, to create person-to-person links that let information gain added value as it travels. Collaboration and the exchange of information are vital to amassing the essential ecological insights and necessary database that allow us to act for the greater good.

The way insects swarm suggests another sense in which ecological intelligence can be distributed among us. In an ant colony no single ant grasps the big picture or leads the other ants (the queen just lays eggs); instead each ant follows simple rules of thumb that work together in countless ways to achieve self-organizing goals. Ants find the shortest route to a food source with simple hardwired rules such as following the strongest pheromone trail. Swarm intelligence allows a larger goal to be met by having large numbers of actors follow simple principles. None of the actors needs to direct the group's efforts to achieve the overall goal, nor is there any need for a centralized director.

When it comes to our collective ecological goals, the swarm rules might boil down to:

1. Know your impacts.
2. Favor improvements.
3. Share what you learn.

Such a swarm intelligence would result in an ongoing upgrade to our ecological intelligence through mindfulness of the true consequences of what we do and buy, the resolve to change for the better, and the spreading of what we know so others can do the same. If each of us in the human swarm follows those three simple rules, then together we might create a force that improves our human systems. No one of us needs to have a master plan or grasp all the essential knowledge. All of us will be pushing toward a continuous improvement of the human impact on nature.

Signs of the dawning of this shift in collective consciousness are amply visible globally, from executive teams working to make their companies' operations more sustainable to neighborhood activists distributing reusable cloth shopping bags to replace plastic ones—wherever people are engaged in creating a way of interacting with nature that transforms our propensities for short-term trade-offs into a long-term, saner relationship. High-profile investigations into the innumerable dangers human activity poses to our planet's ecosystems, like the growing study of global warming, are a bare beginning. Such efforts help raise our sense of urgency. But we can't stop there. We need to gather the on-the-ground, detailed, and sophisticated data that can guide our actions. That takes a thorough and ongoing analysis, determined discipline—and the pursuit of ecological intelligence.

THE NEW MATH

Buy a snack-sized bag of Walkers Salt & Vinegar Flavour Potato Crisps—the British version of potato chips—and its label tells you its carbon footprint, 75 grams of carbon emissions (by comparison a full jumbo jet flying from Frankfurt to New York City emits 713,000 grams per passenger). The bag proclaims that Walkers has been working with an outfit called the Carbon Trust since 2005 to analyze the carbon footprints of its products and to find ways to reduce them.

To calculate that 75 grams took enormous effort. For starters, researchers from the Carbon Trust calculated how much energy was used when the seeds for its two ingredients, potatoes and sunflower oil, were planted. Then they added in the carbon emitted by the diesel tractors that harvest the potatoes, as well as during their cleaning and chopping, frying and bagging, storing and shipping. They also threw in the greenhouse gases emitted when the bags were printed and the potato crisps packaged. Finally, the carbon accountants factored in what happens when the empty bag gets tossed into a garbage can, including collection and trucking to the dump and burying in a landfill.

The produce in the typical American supermarket travels an average fifteen hundred miles from field to bin—but food miles do not necessarily equate directly to carbon footprints. For instance, shipping by sea produces about one-sixtieth the emissions of shipping by air, and about one-fifth that of trucking. For someone in Boston, it turns out, a bottle of Bordeaux that came from its French vineyard by ship will have a smaller carbon footprint than a bottle of California Chardonnay brought by truck (the geographic point where wines from California and those from France reach equivalence in their carbon costs lies somewhere near Columbus, Ohio).

Beyond shipping distance, there are a great number of other carbon variables involved in producing food, from harvesting methods to the type of fertilizer used and the fuel consumed to make the packaging. That's why environmental scientists at Lincoln University in Christchurch, New Zealand, calculate that lamb from New Zealand shipped to Britain has a carbon footprint just one-fourth that of British lamb—in part because most electricity in New Zealand comes from renewable sources, and ample rain and sun means pastures need less fertilizer there than in cloudy Britain. (On the other hand, ships use the most heavily polluting fuel, "black yogurt," the otherwise unusable sludge left from processing petroleum into oil; because of the pollutants they give off, ships in some harbors are required to plug into land-based electricity rather than idle their engines while sitting in port.)

How much of a difference does it make to stop taking plastic bags at the local store to bring our groceries home in, turn down the thermostat by four or five degrees, or switch off the lights whenever we leave a room? To switch from using incandescent bulbs to energy-saving neon ones? The answers get us into a zone of complexity that can create small moral quandaries throughout the day.

We need to master a new kind of math to answer these questions, one that spells out the consequences of our everyday choices and purchases more deeply than ever before. The answers can be surprising. A carbon footprint analysis done at Cranfield University in Britain zeroed in on a life-cycle assessment for twelve thousand long-stemmed roses for sale in London during the wintry days of February, some from the Netherlands, some from Kenya. It turns out that the Dutch roses—because they grow in greenhouses—have a carbon footprint six times greater than the Kenyan variety.

Kenya's steamy climate, combined with small farms, a scarcity of tractors, and use of natural manure rather than chemical fertilizer, reduced its roses' carbon costs, compared to the costs of factory farming in greenhouses—even when the CO_2 emissions from flying roses all the way from Nairobi get factored in. That's why it would be greener for Britons to buy roses air-freighted from Kenya rather than those grown just over the Channel in the Netherlands.

The benefits of shopping for local produce and products are not in doubt—protecting the community's economy through jobs and wages, for one; generally lower carbon footprints (despite the odd exception) for another. But Life Cycle Assessment raises the question, what exactly do we mean by "local"? A Montreal-based industrial ecologist tracked the geography of the life cycles of tomatoes grown in greenhouses near Montreal. As she told me, "Not much local was in the 'local' product. While the tomato R&D was conducted in France, the seeds were grown in China and transported back to France, where they were treated and shipped to Ontario, where the seedbeds are sprouted. Finally these seedbeds are trucked to Quebec, where the final plant is cultivated and the fruit harvested. Even a 'local' tomato has a global past."

Another thing to keep in mind is that any intervention in a complex system has unintended side effects. Solutions over here can create new problems out there. A classic case of unintended consequences may be the boom in corn farming as a subsidized source for ethanol in biofuel. Farmers, of course, also rely on corn as a livestock feed staple so hogs get fat, cows make milk, and hens lay eggs. Corn syrup sweetens soft drinks and a host of processed foods. So the booming demand for corn as a fuel source stirs a ripple of unforeseen consequences. As subsidized farmers chase the bonanza—corn as the answer to petroleum!—its scarcity raises prices for corn-reliant items like beef, tortillas, and breakfast cereal.

Of course the rise in food prices is driven by more than just the scarcity of corn, as my guide to industrial ecology, Gregory Norris, points out. "When you put pressure on farmland, food prices escalate, but that impact may account for a small share of the rise in food prices," says Norris. "We can't blame biofuels alone for price rises; we also need to consider the rising oil prices and the increasing affluence in Asia, where people are shifting toward more meat in their diets. But if folks in a poor rural area can find ways to grow biofuel on marginal land that has not been farmed and is not forest, there is a huge positive impact, a source of income where there was none before."

Which simply shows that systems are complex. We need systematic metrics for sorting out the myriad impacts of the things we produce. Industrial ecology is the discipline that seeks to master this new math. At best, our thinking about hazards like toxins in toys, threats like global warming, and the impacts of the stuff we manufacture, grow, distribute, consume, and discard has been one-dimensional, focusing on a single problem in isolation from everything else. The flood of guides to living a greener life too often offers such blindered details.

For example, objections to the carbon footprint of bottled water led many restaurants to stop offering it and some people to refill the plastic bottles their water had come in. But this ecologically correct response to the bottles' environmental impacts overlooked another downside: the plastic in the bottles posed potential adverse health impacts from chemicals leaching into the bottled water. The suspected endocrine disrupter BPA (bisphenol A, a basic chemical building block of many plastics) spreads into fluids fifty-five times faster than normal if the bottles are filled with boiling hot liquid—a common practice among climbers in cold climates and routine with parents putting formula in plastic baby bottles.

One way to boost our collective ecological intelligence is to become familiar with a wider range of ways to classify and think about impacts from products. Ideally, we want to understand an item's adverse consequences in three interlocking realms:

- the *geosphere* (including soil, air, water, and, of course, climate)
- the *biosphere* (our bodies, those of other species, and plant life)
- the *sociosphere* (human concerns such as conditions for workers)

57

THE GEOSPHERE

Global warming is the poster child for harm to the geosphere, with the details of CO_2 emissions and their damage to the earth's carbon cycle capturing the popular imagination and the attention of policy wonks alike. It is a grave problem, but a small part of a far larger picture. By focusing solely on carbon-driven warming, we ignore the huge range of other ways in which human activities interfere in natural cycles essential to keeping our soil, air, and water healthy. "Healthy" here means able to sustain life—more particularly, the band of sustainability where humans, among other species, thrive (there are, after all, organisms, like those thriving in torrid vents from hot springs in the deepest ocean bed, that can survive in environments where we would not).

Carbon footprints, while the celebrity of environmental measures, are just one of a host of ways to vet a product's impact on the carbon cycle (the vehicle for continual exchanges among living things), the geosphere, and earth's atmosphere. The carbon cycle itself is just one process affected by human activity. Among the myriad other measures is *embedded carbon*, which represents the CO_2 per kilogram released in manufacturing, transport, use, and disposal of a product. Calculating the embedded carbon in a bottle of shampoo, say, requires evaluating the CO_2 shed over the product's life cycle for each separate ingredient (there can be fifty or more ingredients in a bottle of shampoo), as well as for the type of plastic in the bottle.

Let's look at *eutrophication*, one measure of our impact on water. When nutrients like nitrogen and phosphorous enter water, often from chemical fertilizers, they create explosive algae growth that in turn depletes oxygen in the water, choking other species; common sources include sewage effluent and runoff from fertilizers used on lawns and in farming. About half of the lakes in Asia, Europe, and North America suffer from eutrophication; the enormous dead zone encompassing much of the Gulf of Mexico testifies to the fertilizer runoff streaming down the Mississippi River.

Despite the threat from global warming, some argue there is even greater urgency from the razing of forests, depletion of aquifers, species extinction, and other losses of or damage to our planet's natural reserves. Global warming operates over decades or centuries; through concerted human effort we may be able to slow or perhaps eventually reverse it. But when human activity destroys natural resources that took aeons to create—a rain forest that is leveled and eliminated from the earth, an aquifer depleted, a mineral used up—the loss is both immediate and irreversible. By measuring a product's *resource burden* we can see how much raw material was consumed and what kind of contamination resulted or value was destroyed. A product's debt to nature's commons can be calculated as the sum of nonrenewable resources depleted, plus its total "load" or impact on the commons, such as pollutants emitted into air, toxins dumped into water, or contaminants buried in landfills during manufacture.

When we toss something out that ends up in our local landfill, we engage nature's eternal campaign to retrieve molecules from one form for use in a multitude of others. Soil contains an enormous number of enzymes and the like whose sole task is to catalyze reactions that break down chemical compounds, whether they be knit to last night's T-bone or the packing the steak came in. Biology degrades into component parts that get reused by bacteria, plants, insects, and higher animals. *Biodegradability* has become a scientific field of study in itself. Of the tens of thousands of chemical compounds used in man-made products today, only a small portion has been assessed for whether or not microorganisms will eventually be able to break them down into forms useful in nature.

As the industrial designer William McDonough likes to say, "All waste equals food for another system." The end products of industry can, ideally, all be seen as *industrial nutrients*, man-made substances that at the end of their useful life—if they cannot be left to biodegrade—can be used once again to make something else.

These are but a few of the hundreds of metrics for assessing the impact of human activity on the geosphere. Others include water consumption, adverse changes in land use, acidification of soils and lakes, depletion of the stratosphere's ozone layer; there is no fixed limit to the ways human activity can befoul—just to the ways we measure.

THE BIOSPHERE

Our bodies, like the earth itself, consist of interlocking ecosystems. In ecology, an environment's "carrying capacity" refers to the maximum number of people (or any other species) that a given environment can support before damage occurs. Just as the earth's systems have a limit they can sustain before they begin to degrade and finally collapse, the systems within our body have limits on the accumulating foreign compounds they can sustain before they break down into disease.

The ecosystem within our bodies involves immensely complicated interactions between our genes and the everyday industrial chemicals we take in through what we eat, breathe, and touch. These are so complex we rarely can trace specific links between single suspected chemicals and a specific biological outcome. With some exceptions, the precise biological consequence on the human body of day-to-day exposure to even tiny amounts of synthetic chemicals is unknown.

The main drawback of exposing ourselves to thousands of synthesized chemicals stems from the fact that nature economizes, reusing a given molecular structure in many different ways for multiple purposes. An alkaloid resin secreted from the ovary of a poppy bud mimics endorphins in the human opioid system to create a state of benumbed bliss. An industrial chemist may prize a molecular compound that keeps pans from sticking or kills crabgrass in the backyard, while nature will find other uses for that same compound once it enters the inordinately complex chemical factory that is the human body.

Nor does this take into account what happens when these chemicals are absorbed by the bodies of other species. The man-made compounds that end up in soil, water, and air do not disappear; they mix with the complex ecosystems of nature that animals depend on. We have made a panoply of discoveries about the havoc man-made chemicals, from pesticides to Prozac, create in the natural systems they invade. Even tiny doses of certain chemicals can have side effects no one ever anticipated. Our better living through chemistry can become nature's nightmare.

Take, for example, all those pills in our medicine cabinets. Pharmaceuticals are purposely designed to initiate a precise biological reaction at extremely low doses. Such designer chemicals can become something like biological bullets when they end up in nature, whether through sewage or seepage from dumps. Tiny doses of a synthetic form of estrogen found in birth control pills "feminize" male fish; scientists who put a bit of the compound into a Canadian lake found that male minnows stopped making sperm and instead produced eggs. Within three years the minnows had virtually disappeared, and the lake trout that feed on them had declined by close to 30 percent.

As science progresses in its ability to detect ever more subtle dangers from side effects of man-made substances, the list grows longer. Geneticists who study bacteria from soil and lakes tell us that the massive use of antibiotics inadvertently breeds germs that resist those very antibiotics—and that the more we use, the more widespread those antibiotic-resistant bacteria become throughout nature. Though antibiotics kill specific bacteria, they also favor the spread of DNA combinations immune to their effects; these resistant strains end up swapping their genes with other bacteria, which gain their immunity. The 25 million pounds of antibiotics used annually by farm factories to help fatten sheep and cows quickly—making it cheaper to bring them to market sooner—end up breeding enormous amounts of bacteria that resist those very animal antibiotics. Any of us who takes antibiotics or uses antibiotic soaps add to this problem.

That's just one of countless ways industrial chemicals interfere with nature. Here's a casual list from the much lengthier inventory of Life Cycle Assessment evaluations of how chemicals impact our health or that of the biosphere:

- *Cancer impact* assesses an industrial process or chemical in terms of the expected pathways of carcinogens put into the environment, their persistence once there, the probability of human exposure to them, the cancer potency of each chemical, and just where in the supply chain all those cancer impacts come from. For example, environmental scientists can calculate how many excess cancer cases were caused over the year by the entire U.S. industrial output for highly toxic chemicals released into the air from industrial processes. Of the 116 cancer-causing chemicals, the two worst culprits were polycyclic aromatic compounds released from making aluminum and dioxins released by cement plants.

- *Disability adjusted life years* (DALY) measure the amount of healthy life lost due to impacts from particulate emissions, toxins, carcinogens, risks on the job, and so on. This can be calculated for even tiny amounts of a substance and translated into its contribution to increased rates of childhood cancer or emphysema for those affected. The basic unit, one DALY, represents the loss of a year of full health.

- *Loss of biodiversity* refers to the degree of species extinction caused by a given process or substance. Technically measured in terms of a "potentially damaged fraction," this allows a calculation of how much the release of, say, a given chemical might diminish an ecosystem by speeding the decline of plants or animals.

- *Embodied toxicity* calculates how many problematic chemicals are deployed into nature over a product's life cycle. For a polyvinyl chloride (or PVC) shower curtain, one has to calculate the petroleum oil extracted and processed and the chlorine added to make the polyvinyl chloride—high in carcinogens—the shower curtain is made from. Then when we use the curtain, there's the off-gassing of phthalates that were mixed in to make the curtain soft as their molecules leach into the air. When a shower curtain finally ends its days in a dump, it slowly exudes chlorine gas. But a shower curtain's greatest danger to human life may be to workers during manufacture or from the chlorine gas released if it is incinerated at a dump. The curtain's overall embodied toxicity takes all these hidden factors over the product's life cycle into account. Embodied toxicity recasts what have long been thought of as "occupational hazards"—like welders' heightened risk of Parkinson's disease from inhaling manganese fumes—as consumer issues.

Gregory Norris warns us against all-or-none thinking about such impacts, reminding us that "everything is connected." We need to realize, he points out, "that *every* product's life cycle is linked to the release of at least trace quantities of pollutants somewhere far back in the supply chain." So the telling question becomes quantitative: how much of which pollutants are released, and how can we most effectively reduce those releases? Because every supply chain has so many impacts, we can no longer ignore climate change, habitat destruction, toxic chemicals released or embedded, or workers' conditions—nor can we take any one of these as our exclusive focus anymore.

THE SOCIOSPHERE

Recently the news carried the tale of a Brazilian ethanol company that raises sugarcane for biofuel. On-site inspections revealed its 133 workers were suffering from hunger and cold, living in over-crowded rooms with terribly unsanitary conditions. In this kind of predicament, how can we weigh any environmental pluses from ethanol production against the human minuses?

That is the sort of question that has sparked a movement to add a social dimension to products' LCAs. Human concerns like work-ing conditions, forced labor or child labor, fair wages, health ben-efits, and the like are of increasing concern to companies that embrace ethical standards and take corporate social responsibility seriously.

"Social impacts have been long neglected in Life Cycle Assess-ment, but you see the demand now," says Norris. "Governments and companies are asking for these methods. You see it in the bio-fuel debate. A major international company that has been re-viewing biofuels to decide how they might play into their business strategy has been asking me for an analysis of the social impacts. They want all the pluses and minuses. We can't think of the environmental impacts to the exclusion of the social."

Norris did an LCA of the health consequences in the global supply chain from generating electricity in the Netherlands, com-paring the harms from pollution with benefits due to increased economic activity. By converting the two scores to a common unit of analysis—disability adjusted life years, or DALY—Norris could compare the pluses and negatives with regard for health, drawing in part on a World Bank data set that was used to calculate the increase or decrease in years of life that results from every $1 million increase in GNP. The main adverse environmental effects turn out to be electricity power plants' particulate emissions, as well as their contribution to global warming.

But around 10 percent of the economic activity related to Dutch power occurred in developing countries. Some were poverty stricken, with many people lacking access to basic sanitation, clean water, and education. In such poorer countries the health benefits from added wealth can have a hugely positive impact if that wealth is invested in health and education infrastructure like clinics, hospitals, and schools. Doing the math in terms of DALY, Norris concludes that those benefits to the poor can dwarf the minuses in the rest of the world—economic boosts in the world's poorest regions result in an immense health payoff.

On the other hand, when a Dutch agency analyzed the country's total environmental impact as a result of private consumption as a whole, the picture reversed. The negative toll of Dutch shopping, in the form of environmental stressors like resource depletion, pesticides, and such, fell heavily on developing countries. That may be true for any developed country, though few countries have been so conscientious in calculating these impacts as the Dutch.

Current thinking on sustainability recognizes that saving the environment or creating safer products should include maintaining or improving people's well-being. All three systems—the geosphere, biosphere, and sociosphere—need to be weighed in the equation for improvements. That's why the United Nations Environmental Program (UNEP) has been grappling with the trade-offs between environmental considerations and human needs, seeking to use LCA methods to find points in supply chains where the greatest benefits could be found for the environment, as well as for the people in a given region. I spoke with Catherine Benoit, a Montreal-based social scientist, just after she returned from a meeting in Freiburg, Germany, with a UNEP Life Cycle Initiative task force that was drafting a code of practice for assessing socio-economic impacts of a product's life cycle from cradle to grave.

"If you really want to change things for the better, a social LCA will give you the picture of where things are good and where they need to improve," Benoit told me. "The social dimension talks about positive human impacts, as well as negative. If a company has a high level of involvement in the local community, empowers women, is philanthropic at the local level, pays living wages, or is involved in international movements to improve working conditions, all these are positive impacts." On the other hand, the social scales also track the cruelty of sweatshops where underpaid workers are faced with overly long hours under dangerous conditions, are emotionally or physically abused, lack safe drinking water, and the like.

Sometimes using LCA methodology to quantify human conditions makes sense, sometimes not. For example, researchers at the University of Stuttgart calculated the rate of accidents workers suffered throughout the supply chain while making different kinds of packaging materials. The number of lethal accidents (though relatively rare) was highest for wooden boxes, followed by cardboard boxes, and finally for plastic crates. Such an analysis yields actionable data. But social LCAs can become overly precise, out of touch with the human reality. For instance, Benoit argues, it makes no sense to tie human conditions to overly precise measures like benefit from units of work done in terms of "working seconds per process," as has been proposed. Instead she favors calculating the percentage of a product's supply chain where, say, child labor is involved, or fair trade certification, or health insurance provided to workers.

Assessing social impacts represents unique challenges, because numbers alone can distort the human situation. "You can try to come up with a number for how many children a company hires," Benoit said, "but in many countries child labor is illegal, so nobody will tell you. It is impossible to get the correct number for hours of child labor found in a supply chain. It's more to the point just to ask 'Is there child labor, and why?'"

Benoit adds, "You might want to use generic data to identify hot spots, where the risk of child labor is greatest. For textiles in India, for example, the risk of child labor is high—but even within India there will be higher- and lower-risk regions. Generally the hot spots for child labor are where there's lots of poverty, wages are low, and employers do not respect human rights. Identifying hot spots gives you valuable information when you want to improve the social conditions over a product's life cycle."

Gregory Norris argues, "The paradigm LCA has worked from is that the analyst knows best. We can sit in a university lab and say CO_2 release matters, we can set performance thresholds and say, 'We don't care how you do it, but get your toxin release and CO_2 emissions below this level.' That makes sense, but when you factor in social impact, with its possible magnitude of health benefits from economic development, it's better to empower producers and people where they operate to tell buyers, 'These are the benefits we care about. Help us achieve and report them.' Going bottom up gets new voices into the conversation between buyers and sellers and expands the dialogue about the impacts that matter."

"The very best method for spotting say, child labor, somewhere in the supply chain is still to visit the work site and get in touch with local organizations, but that's costly and time-consuming when you need to do it for the whole life cycle," Catherine Benoit points out. "So you need to do that where it matters the most to you: where there's most value added in the product life cycle, where you find hot spots, or where you can act to improve conditions. Those three things are not necessarily the same. If you're an IT company making cell phones and the ore for one component is mined in Africa, that's a hot spot for both forced and child labor. But that component may be a very small piece of your phone, representing very few work hours in the product's life cycle. So if you're looking for where you can act, you may not have much power in that situation, if you're a relatively small customer for that supplier. But you could collaborate with other IT companies to apply pressure."

Expanding LCAs to include their social impact can reveal pluses for companies that operate in the world's zones of poverty. But the picture is not always that clear. Norris points to the case of ecotourism. If that term refers to an impoverished rural village that now attracts more spending from visitors so locally owned businesses do better and some profits are reinvested to improve local schools, clean up water, and improve sanitation and medical care, it's all to the good.

On the other hand, if the tourism is "eco" only in the sense that water and energy are conserved and buildings use green materials, other questions arise. Have locals lost access to land or water formerly held in common that has now been used for development? Do all profits go to a company based somewhere else, with none used to improve local conditions? Do tourism-related jobs for locals pay enough to improve their standard of living? Or has the cost of living, but not wages, gone up because of the development, increasing local poverty and crime or worsening health? In other words, does what looks like "sustainable" development hold up on closer inspection of its impacts on local populations?

Norris questions the green maxim that "less is always better." While that clearly applies, say, when it means fewer pollutants per widget made, he points out positive results in the social sphere from industrial production, starting with "your salary, my salary, taxes for teacher's salaries and malaria clinics. Not all impacts of product life cycles are bad. The positive social impacts of companies that operate in zones of poverty can be great."

Instead of all-or-none thinking, Norris calls for a more nuanced approach: How much of which impacts does a product's life cycle spawn, and how can we get to a desired outcome with the least overall harm? And how can everyone, from shoppers to manufacturers, play a role in reducing that harm?

And, I would add, why can't we know the actual impacts of everything we buy as we are deciding whether to purchase it? And how would our knowing this transform our world?

THE INFORMATION GAP

An industrial engineer I was talking with, pointing to my tape recorder, posed some questions: "I'm sure you got a great deal on that. But how did they make it so cheap? What corners did they cut in the manufacturing of the metals, plastics, and chemicals that went into the recorder's body, the LED display, the circuit boards? What did they dump in a local river? What emissions went into the air? What did they just bury somewhere? And what was the impact on the neighbors, or the workers in those factories?"

Consider our present predicament. If you want to buy a given product that's best for the environment, for your health, and for the well-being of those who made it, it's largely impossible to get sound comparative information. The data we need to compare these impacts has for the most part gone missing. We can check cost and, usually, quality. But apart from organic or "eco" brands and labels, shoppers can rarely express a preference for less toxic or more environmentally sound alternatives.

Price is one thing we understand, so costs become the singular driving force in how things are made and marketed. The big factor in supply chains has been the "China price"—the lowest cost for manufacturing. If I'm a supplier operating a factory in Vietnam or Bangladesh, say, and I'm competing with other suppliers for orders from a manufacturer, it pays to lower my costs any way I can. I may resort to questionable savings: kids will work for less than adults; safety measures add expense; I can use the cheapest ingredients no matter their hazards, dump wastes in the local river rather than having them properly disposed of.

As retailers sound the drumbeat of faster, cheaper, and more, they create a powerful downward pressure on suppliers that rewards rock-bottom wages, long hours, and hazardous working conditions, as well as toxic materials and dangerous pollutants in local rivers and landfills. Such cost-cutting measures are reinforced in the marketplace, where price alone drives most of consumers' buying decisions, while they ignore the hidden impacts of the steps taken along the way to keep prices low.

A maxim in economics holds that healthy markets communicate information openly. But when keeping information secret or hidden makes a producer more money, there is little if any incentive to divulge it. When it comes to the environmental or health impacts of a product, manufacturers and suppliers may know the answers, but they rarely go out of their way to offer up such data unless compelled to by government fiat. This lack of available information on the hidden consequences of what we buy insulates companies from this portion of the supply–demand pressures central to a healthy, competitive market. We as consumers lack a sound way to know the harm or good a product might do, and let that sway our preferences. Instead, the companies that make stuff most cheaply—and shun the expense of environmental or other virtues—can capture more of the market or achieve more profitable margins. Too often, they are in a race to the bottom.

When the ecological impact of goods remains invisible, merit goes unrewarded. To be sure, we can find a scattering of eco-labels here and there, each helping us to identify relatively better choices. But the overall lack of authoritative indicators to alert shoppers to the hidden impacts of what they buy means there is only sporadic or paltry marketplace reward for products that are ecologically sound, and so there is weak competitive pressure to improve products along these lines. Sellers have little reason to share information that would help buyers make better ecological choices.

This inequality between consumers and companies in terms of access to key data has been dubbed "information asymmetry" by Joseph Stiglitz, who won a Nobel Prize in economics for his theory of how information shapes the operation of markets. Stiglitz sees any data gap between buyers and sellers as a major market flaw: ignorance cripples market efficiency, while sound data lets buyers make smarter choices. When sellers know something consumers do not—in other words, *always,* as Stiglitz wryly notes—the information inequity hampers market fairness and efficiency.

Information itself has value; knowledge translates into market power. The essence of transparency lies in conveying information from the informed to the uninformed. Making once-hidden data available to all remedies the unfair advantage of sellers over buyers. Economists have thought about this mainly in terms of price. But expanding the domain of value for an item beyond price and quality to include its harmful or beneficial consequences converts the once-hidden ecological impacts into a market force.

Consider the implications of greenwashing in this light. Take the claims that can't be supported, such as household lamps that trumpet "energy efficiency" on their packaging without the least shred of supporting evidence. Or claims that are simply too vague, like "eco-conscious" shampoo, or poorly defined, like "chemical-free" insecticide (no product is free of chemicals altogether, so what kinds of chemicals does this label refer to?). Another type of marketing sleight of hand takes the form of irrelevant environmental claims that distract shoppers from making brand comparisons that count: the aerosol can of insecticide that trumpets, "No CFCs!" (the ozone-depleting chlorofluorocarbons banned in the 1970s) draws attention away from its remaining toxic ingredients.

Greenwashing pollutes the data available to consumers, gumming up marketplace efficiency by pawning off misleading information to get us to buy things that do not deliver on their promise. This squanders the benefits of our purchases. Because greenwashing undermines consumer trust, it devalues sound data, instilling doubts and cynicism in customers who might want to put their dollars to good use by supporting true green innovations. Greenwashing steals market share from products that genuinely have more benefits and hampers the success and market penetration of better innovations.

Sound product information has been a perennial need in commerce. Olive oil was perhaps the biggest cash crop in the Roman Empire; it was the petroleum of its day. Some estimates put per-capita consumption in the first century A.D. at 50 liters a year; producing and selling olive oil made many Roman Empire merchants and growers immensely wealthy. The sheer volume of olive oil imported to Rome literally altered the landscape; today a hill 50 meters high marks the spot where the clay amphorae used to transport the oil were discarded. That ancient landfill to this day bears the name Monte Testaccio—Mount Potsherd.

Archaeologists who study these potsherds tell us they were part of an ancient system for point-of-purchase transparency. Whether from Andalusia in southern Spain or the hills of Tripoli in what is now Libya, the pots holding olive oil were each sealed with a painted detailing of the exact weight of its oil, the name of the farm where the oil was pressed, and the identities of the merchant who shipped it and the Roman official who verified all this information. David Mattingly, an archaeologist at the University of Leicester and expert on the Roman olive oil trade, concludes that even then the explicit labeling of these goods was designed to protect consumers. Those painted seals were insurance against one of the scams of the day, switching to inferior oil, or stealing some of the precious fluid en route.

"Sunlight," wrote Louis D. Brandeis in 1913, "is the best of disinfectants." Brandeis, later a Supreme Court justice, was writing to propose new laws that would force public companies to reveal their profits and losses. Insider trading represents a classic case of information asymmetry; Brandeis saw "sunlight" as a way to foil the flood of seamy deals that were cheating investors of his day.

The long history of economic transparency documents a

continuing pressure for information symmetry—for giving buyers a fair break by ensuring that sellers tell them the truth. In the current chapter of this story, some consumers want far more finely detailed explicitness about the things they buy: How were the olives grown—without fertilizer or pesticides? How well were the farm workers paid and treated? What was the carbon cost of transporting all that olive oil? Was the mill where it was pressed run on fossil fuels or alternatives? Are there any additives or preservatives that could affect our health?

Late one night at a London corner store I bought a bag of hard candy, a rainbow of brightly colored discs. A look at their ingredients list revealed that the candies were packed with "E numbers," which alert shoppers to a junk food treat that harbors flavorings and colorings that can drive a four-year-old into a bout of hyperactive frenzy. Those candies, I learned by following an asterisk through the fine print of ingredients, contain E104, E110, E120, E122, E124, E132, E133, and E171.

It took me a good deal of time, and the help of a young friend whose eyes could make out the teeny print, to decipher those E numbers. And, truth to tell, I did not bother to track down the website that translates the E number code into the actual ingredients they stand for. So just how useful are these right-on-the-candy revelations?

The question of precisely what makes a label most useful to—and used by—shoppers has preoccupied scores of economists for years. The issue, while seemingly trivial, actually matters greatly as an influence on what customers buy; the tiny patch of real estate on product labels is one of the most hotly contested in the world of commerce. There are weighty books of regulations for companies to follow in labeling their foods and countless studies of how one or another word, graphic, or phrase impacts sales.

For economists, the fight over label design translates into a lofty question: how can labeling move shoppers to buy in a way that maximizes social benefit? The first assumption that goes out the window is that the information on a product's label captures shoppers' awareness; studies find that label-induced market changes can take months or years, because it takes many shoppers that long to notice the change in the first place, let alone do anything about it.

That troublesome fact has led to detailed studies of just what makes a label work as intended. For instance, "green" certification programs are found in products ranging from plywood to tea. But market researchers find a notable number of shoppers are wary of these eco-labels, doubting their veracity or seeing them as a marketing gimmick. Skeptical shoppers put more credence in labels that give specific details and let them use their own judgment. They crave information.

George Stigler, also a winner of a Nobel Prize in economics and a founder of the influential Chicago School of Economics, pointed out that information has its price: the "cost" of searching for it, whether reckoned in time, effort, or cognitive demands. As Stigler notes, "the assimilation of information is not an easy or pleasant task for most people." From his perspective, the most desirable data comes "cheap," in a user-friendly form.

The multiplication of consumer choices, and decay of brand loyalty, has only whet consumers' appetites for more and better information on which to make their choices. Tide detergent, which came in a single variety in my childhood, now offers thirty-nine varieties, from Tide with Bleach and Tide with Bleach Alternative to Tide for use with high-efficiency washing machines. When a single brand makes a once-simple purchase decision suddenly so complex, small wonder we need help sorting it all out, given the thousands of brands of various kinds of goods and their variations.

But the human mind has its own shortcuts. When we face a complicated decision, our minds make what seems like a good enough choice, given the options at hand, the mental effort demanded by weighing every variable, the benefit to us, and how much (or, more likely, little) time we want to spend making up our minds.

Psychologist Herbert Simon (yet another Nobel winner in economics) coined the term "satisfice," a combination of "satisfy" and "suffice," for the kind of mental shortcut we go through in the supermarket aisle. He saw that all but the most obsessive among us lack the cognitive power to go through the endless computations that would make our decision-making approach optimal.

Anyway, who's got the time? So we settle for a good enough approach and get on down the aisle: I'll take whatever detergent I bought last month—it worked okay. Indeed, studies of consumer choice find that most often we as consumers just look for what we've gotten before. We settle for what's adequate rather than search for what's optimal: once we have "satisficed" a product choice, we stop looking. In other words, much of what is known in marketing circles as "brand loyalty" is really just a peculiarity of cognitive inertia.

One drawback of satisficing is that we don't see how the range of options that we are given could be far larger or the ways it could be better. By focusing on what's just good enough, we fail to see that what we are offered is only an arbitrary, narrow number of choices in the first place. This handy cognitive shortcut for quick and easy decision making feeds a self-deception, diminishing the range of what we seek and so consider.

RADICAL TRANSPARENCY

Let's say I don't just want the cheapest tape recorder I can buy; I want one that was made in ways that exposed workers to no toxins and that will do the least harm to the environment when I'm done with it. With full ecological transparency, I could know which one that is. The more systematic and comprehensive that transparency becomes, the better the choices for buyers.

Ecological transparency becomes *radical* when its analysis encompasses the entire life cycle of a product and the full range of its consequences at every stage, and presents that information to a buyer in ways that demand little effort (unlike those hard-to-decipher E numbers on that bag of candies). Radical transparency means tracking every substantial impact of an item from manufacture to disposal—not just its carbon footprint and other environmental costs but its biological risks, as well as its consequences for those who labored to make it—and summarizing those impacts for shoppers as they are deciding what to purchase.

In economic theory, transparency's power comes from providing key information that changes consumers' choices, which in turn creates new incentives for businesses to align their practices with the public's priorities. Radical transparency would alert shoppers to, say, which piece of clothing was manufactured in a model factory, which in a horrific sweatshop. Bringing such information to the surface at the point of purchase puts into competitive play these otherwise hidden dimensions. Suddenly we could make choices that would shift market share on the basis of a range of ecological virtues, in addition to price and quality. In such a market, virtuous products and companies would be rewarded with more sales—and bottom feeders would lose.

Radical transparency brings to the neighborhood shopping mall the same full disclosure now imperative in corporate financial statements. At the moment of truth—the point of purchase—shoppers could learn the true ecological impact of their dollars and so spend them more pointedly. Companies could track how specific improvements in the environmental or health impact of their products affect sales and market share, and so respond by making changes in manufacturing design and the like that a radically transparent marketplace demands.

The remedy for a vital lie is always to face the truth it obscures. In our consumer purchases, that truth takes the form of the countless hidden impacts that the things we buy have during their manufacture, their use, and their disposal. At present, we are largely blind to those consequences.

We typically have little or no idea what chemicals, for instance, we are bringing into our homes with what we get at the store (let alone what molecules the stuff already there might be off-gassing into household air). Radical transparency would give us a clear picture of these hidden consequences of what we are buying. Just as opaqueness in the stock market lets insiders take advantage of outsiders, so opaqueness in the marketplace lets companies take advantage of our ignorance of the ecological impacts of their products. In both cases, transparency levels the playing field.

If we get better, more complete information about the true effects of an item at the moment we are deciding whether to buy it, we can make wiser decisions. Such full disclosure can make each of us an agent for small, gradual changes that, when multiplied by millions, will ripple through the industrial enterprise, from manufacturing and design through supply chains and transport to the distant ends of consumption.

As shoppers express their preference for safer, more sustainable, and humane products, they will create an added fiscal incentive for companies to examine their manufacturing methods, materials, and practices. Where there are adverse impacts, this economic force will lower the financial risk and enhance the financial upside for those companies that are developing better alternatives.

Radical transparency offers a way to unleash the latent potential of the free market to drive the changes we must make, by mobilizing consumers and executives to use data to make more virtuous decisions. An ecologically transparent marketplace lets each one of us become a far more effective agent of amelioration, giving shoppers a role as crucial as that of executives.

Such a marketplace incentive could reverse the momentum begun at the dawn of the industrial revolution, when manufacturing technologies began to come into use without full understanding or regard for how they affect ecosystems. The world of commerce is rife with processes and technologies in need of reinvention—business opportunities that may drive the next decade or more of value creation through innovation. We need steady, incremental improvements across the entire range of industrial enterprise methods—not a revolution per se but an evolution, in the Darwinian sense of survival of the fittest, where a process or product's survival comes about as a result of its ecological fitness.

For companies, radical transparency can create a vibrant new competitive playing ground, one where doing the right thing also means doing better. Rewards will go to companies that innovate most quickly, upgrading qualities such as sustainability that consumers are using to compare products and brands. The greatest penalties in lost sales will go to companies that dig in their heels and resist change, even as customers insist upon it.

Radical transparency has the power to reinvent the marketplace as an arena for optimal information and decision making, one that works with powerful efficiency to reward those who merit it and penalize the rest.

Perhaps, one day. But first we need to upgrade a marketplace rife with informational black holes.

FULL DISCLOSURE

Radical transparency launched its seminal application at 3:43 on the afternoon of April 1, 2008, in what had once been a laser cosmetologist's office above a sushi restaurant on a well-worn stretch of Shattuck Avenue, Berkeley's main commercial thoroughfare. That office building, faced in attractive cobalt blue and green tile, houses GoodGuide, Inc. Its mission is to build tools that "transform how people see and interact with products and companies by delivering comprehensive and rigorous information at the point of purchase," as its official mission statement puts it.

GoodGuide is a "for-benefit" corporation, with a charter that states its mission is to benefit not just shareholders but stakeholders—in other words, the shopping public. Fittingly, the only other tenant sharing the floor is the Union of Concerned Scientists, just a few steps down the hall.

I had come to town to chat with Dara O'Rourke, an industrial ecologist and the visionary behind this project to bring radical transparency to the marketplace in the form of a software innovation, GoodGuide.

"We're in the Dark Ages now," O'Rourke told me. "We know brand and price, and think we know quality. But no one knows what's behind the label, what the product actually does to us or the planet. We want to pull back the veil of brand and go far beyond what the company tells you. What ingredients are health concerns? How far did it travel? How were workers treated?"

GoodGuide can summarize the bottom line of all that information and present you the answer in the time it takes to exhale. "This is what consumers care about," says O'Rourke. "People want simple information to help live their lives better—'Just tell me in a few seconds.'"

GoodGuide integrates hundreds of complex databases that evaluate everything from, say, Unilever's policy on animal testing to the carbon emissions in its supply chain to the specific chemicals of concern in its products by drawing on roughly 80 million bits (and growing) of data on products and companies. "This is distributed knowledge," says O'Rourke. "No one person can know all this at one time, but together we can bring the best knowledge on product and company impacts to people in a form that lets them make better choices."

In other words, GoodGuide surfaces a product's backstory. It can calculate the specific environmental impacts of a product during manufacture, transport, use, and disposal. It can perform this calculation down to a single chemical among a batch of ingredients. On a macro level, it can rate how well a given company stacks up against others in its field on environmental, health, or social performance, as well as determine which brand or company has been getting better over time. GoodGuide can evaluate a company's policies, its disclosure of key information on products, and ultimately a company's impacts on consumers, workers, communities, and the environment.

The afternoon I dropped by, the company was launching its beta release, the very first trial by shoppers of its system for revealing how a product's impacts fit their values. This initial release covers somewhere skyward of fifty thousand brands of personal care products and household cleaners. Subsequent releases will add categories such as food, electronics, and apparel.

This closed beta version allowed tests of the site by about one hundred people, most of whom were concerned parents whom O'Rourke calls eco-moms. "Having a child triggers you to think about the health or environmental impacts of products. Before you have a kid, you buy just any shampoo or dishwashing detergent. But once you're a mom, you start to think twice about what you put all over your baby's skin, or have second thoughts about what's coating your child's plate. Eco-moms are the tip of the wave of concerned consumers.

"When they find out that Dad's hair darkener is full of lead acetate, they'll tell him to stop using it. Should they find phthalates in their own shampoo, and if they still like what that shampoo does to their hair, they might e-mail the maker to ask them to drop phthalates from its ingredients. And if they learn that their baby's sunscreen contains oxybenzone, a carcinogen activated by exposure to the sun, they'll pass on that info with e-mails to other moms. Or they might post it on a social network for mothers, like

Cafemom.com, and it could spread from one trustworthy mom to hundreds or thousands of others."

O'Rourke's credentials in industrial ecology are impeccable. He is currently a professor in the Department of Environmental Science, Policy, and Management at the University of California at Berkeley. He previously taught at MIT, where he had studied mechanical engineering as an undergrad. His doctorate was done at Berkeley's Energy and Resources Group, where his interest was in the design not just of the processes used to make products, but the environmental impacts of those processes. For a time he was a consultant working with international agencies like the United Nations Development Programme and the World Bank, advising factories on how to improve their operations in countries from Vietnam and China to El Salvador.

"I was focused on the technical issues at first," he recalls, "but I eventually realized that the real impediments were never the technology, but decisions about product and process design—and the inertia in organizations."

O'Rourke's career odyssey began with an interest in workplace health and safety in global supply chains, including issues like air quality on the factory floor and the number of accidents workers suffered at a plant. But that led him to ask questions about why, for example, these accidents were happening at all.

"In a clothing factory, all these girls were losing fingers to cutting devices. When? Around two a.m. Why are they working that late? Because American retailers were pressuring the factories for delivery dates that meant operating eighteen hours a day. My research was getting at the root causes that drive these problems. It comes down to the competition among retailers in pricing, delivery times, and rapid changes in styles, which in turn drives facto-ries to the risky practices that lead to workers getting hurt. And what drives that? It's we consumers, who want the hottest, newest styles as quickly as we can and at the lowest cost. It comes down to us, to you and me."

That's where O'Rourke's efforts focus now: creating a method that lets shoppers—you and me—learn the true impacts of what we buy and make more ethical choices based on that information.

O'Rourke's passion to improve workers' health and safety led him to his fifteen minutes of fame, the Nike campaign. He was studying shoe factories in Vietnam working with nongovernmental groups. He worked with, although not for, companies like Nike and Adidas to help them develop better ways to monitor their supply chain.

"I went to Nike's country headquarters in Ho Chi Minh City and told them they had all these problems. Workers were being exposed to illegal levels of air toxins. They were working way be-yond legal limits. They were complaining of physical and verbal abuse. Nike said, 'We'll fix it.' But they never did. So then I con-tacted Nike headquarters in Beaverton, Oregon, and said, 'You've got problems in your factories.' They said, 'No, we don't.' They didn't have a clue what was really going on."

So O'Rourke went public with his data in a front-page *New York Times* story that captured world attention. The Nike brand sud-denly became linked in the public mind with the abuse of work-ers, a PR disaster. "When people from headquarters finally went to visit those factories themselves," O'Rourke tells me with a tone of satisfaction, "they found they had lots of problems. There was no incentive for the guys at the bottom of the supply chain to tell the truth to the guys at the top."

Nike has become a world leader in efforts to reform factories; O'Rourke speaks of it with admiration these days. That singular success inspired him to use the power of radical transparency for reforms in manufacturing and commerce—but this time to tackle everything, all at once. "We want to revolutionize consumption, and thereby global supply chains," says O'Rourke. "If shoppers start preferring products made from green energy, it will encourage Chinese factories to use green energy sources instead of electricity made from coal."

A hot-link feature on GoodGuide can send a message from the shopper directly to the company about a given product—giving users a miniversion of the opportunity O'Rourke had to let Nike know his opinions. In other words, GoodGuide will let customers talk directly to companies, to tell them, "I'm concerned about your ingredients," on the one hand, or "I love what you're putting in your product now" or "Please give us better data on your products."

That feature could convert a private act—a person's shift in brand preference—into marketing data for brand managers. The feature promises to open up a valuable conversation between companies and their customers, giving businesses an enormous amount of on-the-spot insight into what a shopper thinks and feels as she considers their product—the live moment that focus groups try to unpack.

GoodGuide draws on the decades of industrial ecology research that tags processes and products with precise metrics. That vast Life Cycle Assessment database has traditionally been proprietary or otherwise sequestered among specialists in manufacturing. GoodGuide offers shoppers this data mother lode in forms they can use to buy products that reflect their values. "No one," O'Rourke acknowledges, "wants the flood of raw data" offered by the two hundred or so databases crunched in the GoodGuide system. They just want the final evaluation, like a wine rating. "Just show me which item is best."

As we sat at a small table in O'Rourke's sun-filled office, he picked up my tape recorder and studied the model number for a moment. "We could tell you the energy impacts for this. It's made in China, so the factory used electricity from coal; burning the amount of coal used to make this will have a deleterious health impact through respiratory disease, which we can calculate in terms of the increase in mortality due to making this tape recorder. Granted, it's tiny. But then when you scale up to the entire production run for this model, you get a much larger figure."

The beta version of GoodGuide allows shoppers to point their cell phone's camera at the bar code of almost any consumer product and click its image to the GoodGuide server. Within seconds GoodGuide's server transforms that bar code into a three-bar rating of that very item, revealing in red, yellow, or green the relative level of virtue generated by that product's life-cycle impact in three dimensions: environmental, health, and social. If you're curious about just why the rating came back as red, you can go to GoodGuide's website and explore details of the rating.

That whole set of maneuvers is a bit cumbersome, as O'Rourke readily admits, posing a barrier that will keep many shoppers who don't want to be bothered from accessing GoodGuide judgments. But he sees the cell phone as a transitional stage. "We're building a system that can let impact ratings flow out to wherever anyone is interacting with a product. In a few years this system will be embedded, so you don't need any special device nor to do anything extra to get the information you want."

O'Rourke foresees skipping the cell-camera-to-bar-code step entirely, and instead perhaps picking up radio frequency signals from an electronic tag embedded in the product that automatically alerts your phone to display red or green. Or GoodGuide might, at your request, monitor everything you buy on your credit card, e-mailing you to suggest alternative products that would be better, given your priorities.

A regular review of purchases, with recommended upgrades, could be done for an entire household, as a service of the bank that issues your credit card. That way shoppers can come to the store with a ready-made list of better choices for the stuff they buy regularly. O'Rourke speculates, "We could put together a shopping list of the best among the categories of stuff you shop for every week or month, and continually upgrade it," according to a list of your priorities. "Just tell us what you want, and we can make the suggestions."

In a decade or two, O'Rourke conjectures, the information might be right on the product, as state and federal governments require companies to disclose it. "Our system is a baby step toward making all this information publicly available," says O'Rourke.

In whatever form people get the data on ecological impact, the clearer the better. Early versions of Life Cycle Assessment feedback have been designed by engineers and policy wonks, resulting in mystifying data such as a given product's "kilograms of acidification potential." Moreover, an LCA provides an overwhelming data flood, more than almost anyone can process at one time, especially while prowling the aisles of a store. The simple green-yellow-red rating system in GoodGuide bypasses the problem; those dedicated few who want more can navigate the website that gives the technical details behind a rating.

GoodGuide draws together over 80 million separate evaluations of the impacts of substances, components, products, and entire companies, pooling information from hundreds of separate databases. Many of the databases have been proprietary, their insights sold to companies but not accessible otherwise. For instance, consultants to socially responsible investment funds license their database for a fee to ethical investors who are evaluating stock value; by sharing those databases with GoodGuide, they are making their knowledge available to the public for the first time. The system also taps into a range of LCA databases that have until now been the exclusive domain of academics and industry.

"We're bringing this rich research to bear to answer questions for consumers that have never been asked before," says O'Rourke. "Stock analysts use it to find the best value, not to see which product is safest for me and my kids, or which causes the least pollution, or treats its workers best. We want to offer the average person enough information to make better ethical decisions while they're standing in the store aisle."

Entire companies (as well as individual products) are rated, allowing shoppers to choose to avoid firms with bad records. Personal care companies that have joined the Campaign for Safe Cosmetics, for instance, might be flagged as preferred alternatives as a shopper browsed skin creams—and the fob on her car keys might turn red or green accordingly as it passed near the various choices.

Since people vary in what issues matter most to them, GoodGuide can be tailored according to each user's priorities; it offers more than six hundred separate ways to evaluate impacts. One person could filter products through various health-focused screens, another through any of numerous ethical lenses, another evaluating products on particular environmental impacts of concern to them. GoodGuide brings precision to values shopping. A GoodGuide user can design the priorities so that animal testing gets weighted more than the chemicals in the health column. Or a concerned mother can set as her priority the safety of chemicals in what she buys.

"We want to give consumers the information they need to apply their values," O'Rourke explains. "Some people might choose as their lens on a product cruelty to animals or contribution to species extinction; others might choose the increase in childhood cancers. Some might choose toxic pollution in their vicinity, while others might care about it for the folks who live near the factories where their stuff gets made. These are each a shorthand for a more complex measure, but we can deliver these evaluations to shoppers in the form that has most emotional resonance for them."

O'Rourke adds, "We don't dictate what shoppers should care about; we just tell you what science says matters about this specific product."

GoodGuide cuts through greenwashing to the underlying facts. "If an oil company's marketing campaign brags that they planted ten thousand trees or that their headquarters was green," says O'Rourke, "we'd still show that these benefits are a minor part of their overall environmental impacts. We'll help consumers focus on what matters most in a product."

Take the ubiquitous Energy Star ratings on appliances. When it comes to evaluating a laptop, says O'Rourke, most look highly energy efficient. But that thin slice of data distorts the overall impact of a laptop; 90 percent of the environmental impact comes during manufacture and disposal, not use. "An Energy Star rating on a laptop," he notes, "means little by itself."

GoodGuide offers a credible source of comprehensive ratings on a wide swath of products, all right at the sweet spot, the point of purchase. Perhaps the most powerful psychological impact of GoodGuide may come from being able to compare products. Should GoodGuide be taken to scale, with millions of shoppers routinely consulting it, markets could churn.

When I visited, the prototype the company had developed could compare the top five products in a given category against the one a shopper was considering. O'Rourke was pondering whether to include a hot link showing where to buy the best in each class at local stores or online. If a shopper's phone sent a GPS signal along to GoodGuide, the hot link might lead to directions to another store in the vicinity with better choices—O'Rourke was in discussion with a tech outfit that has lists of every product carried by all the stores in shopping malls throughout the United States.

GoodGuide offers proof of concept, a concrete example of how radical transparency might work. GoodGuide may not be the system that eventually prevails in bringing transparency to store aisles, but it could open a competitive marketplace in which any number of companies like Google or Yahoo! or Microsoft might develop similar products themselves.

Despite its impressive database, GoodGuide's reach covers only a fraction of products available now. There remain huge gaps in data. But every tech innovation starts with a first release and, if it is to survive, must be steadily upgraded with each new release.

As O'Rourke speculates on the future of GoodGuide, I'm reminded of the program's fledgling status when a programmer interrupts us to announce that the system is ready to roll out to test users. O'Rourke goes to a desktop console where a software techie has just finished an improvised ceremonial gesture, a large red button drawn on a piece of thin cardboard placed over his computer's "Enter" key. As a dozen of the dedicated souls behind GoodGuide gather round, O'Rourke grandly hits the button, to applause and cheers.

Someone shouts, "We're launched!" At that moment a hundred eco-moms get an e-mail offering them entrée to the sea of ratings GoodGuide offers, a first step into the brave new world of radical transparency.

THE MINDFUL SHOPPER

I was daydreaming as usual while browsing the pasta sauces in my local supermarket. As I was about to reach for my favorite brand, another caught my eye. This sauce was packaged in a cloudy plastic jar that somehow intrigued me.

A closer look at the label sold me: "BPA-free container," it read. "This jar is microwavable, freezable, and reusable. Re-uses are endless."

Bisphenol-A, used to harden plastics, has a chemical structure similar to that of the hormone estrogen. That week, it so happened, I had been immersed in reading about the controversy over whether BPA leached into our food and water from plastic disrupts the endocrine system. I reached for the BPA-free sauce and pictured myself sorting through the reusable container drawer in our kitchen, throwing out our old BPA-riddled plastic containers, and replacing them with these emptied pasta sauce jars.

That moment was an exception, not the rule. As we shop, our perceptual apparatus attunes us to whatever confronts us in the immediate surround: the stylishness and cut of that outfit, the rock-bottom sales prices, or the tempting aroma wafting our way from that coffee shop. These sensory impressions drive our shopping decisions far more than some vague memory of the latest alarm over global warming, that news story about yet another toxin scare, or a grim scene of an Asian sweatshop glimpsed on some website.

In the eyes of a shopper roaming the aisles of a market, eco-campaigns and the like occur elsewhere, a dim memory in the recesses of the mind. On the floor of a store, soaked in lulling Muzak or blaring hip-hop, shoppers jostle as they navigate shelves stacked high with items begging to be bought. What's far more salient than the hidden ecological impacts of all that stuff are the immediate cues: *On Sale! Improved! Low Fat!*

That sensory clutter and cognitive fog challenge anyone trying to get shoppers to notice the impacts of what they are about to buy. Our attention, a limited capacity at best, is occupied by what we encounter; it takes a goodly added amount of cognitive effort for a tidbit stored in long-term memory to penetrate awareness.

When it comes to shopping, we operate mostly in this mindless mode, leaving our thoughts free for other, more interesting topics. This partial inattention while we shop can readily keep from awareness what matters about what we buy. Instead, half alert, we let a sale price, new packaging, or simple habit determine what we choose. We too easily fail to recall at just that moment the details of some news item or consumerist article that may have alerted us to the hidden advantages of one item over another. The act of shopping is largely guided by a fog of inertia.

GoodGuide and programs like it offer a way to pierce this fog, bringing squarely into awareness the actual impacts of what we buy—a well-timed intrusion into our attention that gives us the crucial opinion at the moment we need it. Of course there's a good possibility that the same fugue state that whisks us down a store's aisles will make us neglect GoodGuide as well. Another step is needed: making that consultation a habit, an automatic reflex we execute even within the shopper's daydream.

The moment a customer pauses, exits the shopper's trance, and pays full attention to some attribute of a product, the mental ground shifts significantly. "To be mindful," says Ellen Langer, a Harvard psychologist who has studied such attentiveness for decades, "is simply to notice new things about something."

As prosaic as that may sound, mindfulness matters immensely for marketing. The battle for consumers is, in essence, a fight for attention. Mindfulness in a shopper marks a shift in mental functioning from running on automatic, reflexively going through long-practiced routines, to an active awareness that allows new learning—and so new choice. The shift from one brand to another occurs in such bubbles of attention, as new information soaks into the mind and changes a preference.

"If you compare five products and end up buying Product A," Langer told me, "you'll feel much better about buying it than if you only looked at one. Mindful, proactive thinking increases your brand loyalty. So you'll more likely buy Product A next time you shop."

As Raina Kelley, a journalist who experimented with being a freegan for a month, observed, "I really thought that being mindful of my impact on the Earth would drive me crazy but, in the end, it was the most valuable thing I did over the whole thirty days. The more you know about where your food, clothing, entertainment, and shelter comes from, the easier it is to make buying decisions in line with your conscience."

Active attention, Langer's research shows, creates a curious benefit: it enhances your experience of whatever you're attending to. For eco-transparency systems, that means once shoppers start using GoodGuide, she says, they should enjoy shopping more. "Once it gets started, it should be self-perpetuating, because of the intrinsic pleasure of mindfulness."

Shopping becomes a game of sorts. That fits with the business rationale that led one grocery chain to put nutritional labels on its foods: it was not so much to upgrade shoppers' nutritional choices as to enhance their shopping experience (and so prolong the time spent in their stores).

The trick will be to get shoppers to use a system like GoodGuide in the first place. When I told Langer about GoodGuide, she offered some suggestions. One was to make it an actual game. A retailer seeking to enhance time in store or heighten experience could have a sign at checkout asking, "Did you find the most environmentally friendly items today?" This would prime conversations about eco-transparency while people wait in line at cash registers, making them more likely to check the system the next time they shop. Or a similar invitation could be placed at the entrance, reminding shoppers to use GoodGuide.

Such reminders, technically speaking, "prime" the mind: simply thinking of an action prepares us to perform it. Priming guides us through our daily routines: our toothbrush on the sink in the morning silently guides us to brush our teeth. Priming lets us live on automatic, not having to think much about what to do next, or how to do it. This makes room in the mind, for instance, for multitasking: we can go down the aisles of the grocery store picking out every item we always buy, all the while talking on a cell phone or daydreaming. Or, if primed, we would consult an eco-transparency system while we shopped.

Another use of ratings from a system like GoodGuide would be an inventive retailer deciding to post the product ratings right on the store shelf next to each item's price, as a service to shoppers. That way shoppers needn't go through the cell-phone-to-bar-code maneuver while wending their way down an aisle, but could get the ratings at a glance. This would lower the user effort for eco-transparency to near zero, making it far more likely to appeal to the majority of shoppers, who desire minimal information cost.

The effort demanded to open a cell phone, point the camera, and click poses an effort threshold that might well stop many shoppers from using GoodGuide. "I'm not sure how many people will do that," observed Joel Gurin, who was once an executive vice president at Consumers Union, when I briefed him about GoodGuide. "*Consumer Reports* did a similar app, where you could download our product ratings on your cell phone. If you were in Best Buy, you could go online right in the store and get the information while you were shopping. But while it was a useful service, it got only a limited number of users, far fewer than our website did."

Today, we have little to no ability to discern which products contain ingredients that raise concerns. And even if we do know about a specific hazard or two, who has the patience to read through a product list of dozens of arcane ingredients in a frozen pizza or floor polish and compare it with similar lists on an alternate choice? But, as the launch of GoodGuide shows, we are on the verge of a day when all that mental work will have already been done for us. The question remains what difference this might make.

When I discussed radical transparency with Baba Shiv, a neuromarketing researcher at Stanford Business School, his first response was a question. "If the ultimate goal is to help people choose more eco-friendly products by giving them more information, we need to know: does more information necessarily change people's consumption habits?

"Shoppers are distracted, thinking about life's preoccupations," Shiv observed. "That lowers the capacity of their working memory, what they can hold in attention. They don't have the cognitive ability they would if they were paying full attention. When we're distracted, our inhibitors for emotional impulse are weaker and we fall prey to what appeals right now, without thinking about the consequences.

"Through the years," Shiv added, "consumers have been given calorie, nutrition, and trans fat contents of food right on the label.

But sales haven't really budged on the basis of this information that much. For most of our decisions as consumers there's no clear decision matrix, where A is better than B. Product A has some bad features and some good ones, Product B the same. In a trade-off decision like that, our emotions settle it. The option that will win or lose is the one associated with the stronger emotion, negative or positive.

"But if you're a concerned mother and you never knew before which product was better for your children's safety, and suddenly a device gives you the facts about which item might have some toxic risk and which not, that emotional impact will drive your decision. It's compelling—that kind of information creates 'hot' cognition, emotionally loaded thoughts. That can drive consumer decisions to the point it shifts market share."

TWITTER AND BUZZ

In 2007 the British branch of the bank HSBC ran a promotion to recruit business from college students and recent grads by offering them checking accounts with no penalty fees for overdrafts. In August of that year, someone at the bank decided that the policy was costing the bank too much and should end. After all, the strategic thinking went, the level of effort necessary for all those new customers to switch to a new bank was too high, so the change in policy would lose the bank few accounts.

The bankers, however, failed to calculate into their decision the reaction of Wes Streeting, vice president of the student union at Cambridge University. Outraged by the bank's move, Streeting set up a site on Facebook called "Stop the Great HSBC Graduate Rip Off!" Students who saw Streeting's alarm in turn alerted their friends, in a cascading digital wave.

Within days thousands of students joined the crusade. Immediately, the students traded information on which other banks offered no penalty fees and publicly threatened to drop their business with HSBC. They started organizing protests, planned for September, in front of the headquarters of the venerable bank.

Chastened by the online customer revolt, and fearing a more public one, the bank made an about-face within mere weeks of Streeting's first post. What the bank had not seen coming was the force of such discontent when spread virally, amplified, and well coordinated.

The HSBC tale demonstrates the dual marketplace power of lowering the cost of information combined with information sharing. The multiplier effect means networks of people pooling their knowledge can diminish information asymmetry. Clay Shirky, professor of social computing at New York University, offers the HSBC tale as a seminal moment. As Shirky observes, the digital revolution catalyzes new forms of information sharing, and its networks are far larger and more widely distributed than any in human history.

Customers are no longer lone individuals, isolated and voiceless. The ability to share information freely creates a collective awareness that can trigger a coordinated reaction. Consumers can talk back to business in a far more powerful way than ever, en masse and synchronized.

Instant messaging methods like Twitter, which lets shoppers send their reactions to friends as they stroll through a store, means a customer ripple can start with a single dissatisfied (or delighted) customer. Perhaps the most powerful market force inherent in the GoodGuide system I discussed in Chapter 7—in tandem with radical transparency—may be the built-in capacity to notify your e-circle about a product's ratings in a single click. Anyone in your e-circle can spread the news to his or her own e-circle, again in one click, ad infinitum.

These digital tools threaten the standard veils that have hidden the raw facts about manufacturing processes, toxicity of ingredients, workers' conditions, and the like—for better or worse—from customers' eyes. They alter the very ecosystem of marketplace information. As Daniel Vasella, chairman and CEO of Swiss pharmaceutical giant Novartis, observes, business is being transformed by information technology that creates a "boundless world" where once there were walls. Inexorably, the Internet is shattering the walls companies have set up to keep information about products locked away, letting news spread about adverse impacts that in a former day could have been kept from the public eye.

I raised the idea of a website where consumers could go to get detailed information about a product with my friend Bill George, a professor at Harvard Business School. A former CEO of the medical device maker Medtronic and currently a member of the board of directors at Target Corporation, among other companies, Bill has long been a vocal advocate of ethical leadership and business practices. Bill posed a series of questions: "The first thing I'd want to know is, what motivates the people who rate the products? What's the motivation behind the website? What's the site's business model? Why can you trust this site?"

An executive at Wal-Mart echoed these questions, saying, "It's just a simplified scorecard—can I believe it?" He added another objection: "People don't want to know all this information—it's too complicated, too much information."

I put these questions and critiques to GoodGuide's Dara O'Rourke, who replied, "My deep motive is as a parent of a five-year-old. As a citizen and as a consumer I want this information available so parents like me can make better choices for ourselves and our families."

As for the business model, GoodGuide's remains unclear; the operation has been fueled by seed money so far. As with so many tech start-ups, the people involved have been focused on getting it up and running, not where the money will come from. "We want to give our information away to the shopping public—no charge, no subscription," said O'Rourke. "We do need to find a way to turn a profit, but not at this stage."

The tension between presenting complex information simply and respecting its complexity, O'Rourke explained, will be handled by having two levels users can access. "Our front layer will be intuitive and easy to understand; our back layer will be packed with data."

O'Rourke agrees that one of the first priorities in rolling out GoodGuide will be building credibility for the system. "We've gone overboard on this because we're academics," says O'Rourke, "but we've got to get the data right. We'll let anyone dig down to the raw data source and check that we're not just making this up. We'll be completely open about the technical details."

A website such as GoodGuide needs to be fully transparent, disclosing not only its information sources but the ways in which it reaches the ratings it displays. That was not true of a three-star nutritional rating system pioneered in Maine's Hannaford supermarkets, developed by an advisory panel of nutritionists from institutions like Dartmouth. That system is proprietary, owned by the Delhaize Group, the Belgian corporation that operates Hannaford and many other food retailers. Delhaize hopes to license the system to supermarket chains in other markets and so, presumably, make the three-star ratings a revenue source as well as a service offered to its own customers.

The Delhaize three-star ratings are derived from a complex algorithm that manipulates a food's nutrients by giving each a weight in equations that boil all the variables down to a single score for the aggregate nutritional value. Like any such algorithm, that formula contains a series of hidden judgments, such as how to interpret and value a range of scientific findings about nutrition and health. Those judgments—while no doubt benign—are, to some extent, subjective. More to the point, they are not available for inspection and questioning. As with any such for-profit information system, the rating company's competitive advantage lies in keeping secret the specifics of the algorithm for rating.

In another nutritional rating scheme being developed by Adam Drewnowski, director of the Nutritional Sciences Program at the University of Washington, the ratings can be translated into a simple score, star rating, or letter grade for any food. But Drewnowski's system will be fully transparent and not for profit: he plans to publish the details in academic journals. As a result, the assumptions underlying his ratings will be open for scrutiny by his professional colleagues—or anyone else.

While there are no apparent problems with any of these nutritional rating systems, if a group with a hidden self-interest were to control a rating system, it could undermine the credibility of all such systems' evaluations. One could argue that the best way to protect against the appearance of such conflicts is to ensure that a rating system is utterly transparent in its operation.

The website Skin Deep, which evaluates the relative safety of personal care products, provides one model of such operational transparency. For starters, the site is open about its sponsor, the advocacy organization Environmental Working Group. Skin Deep identifies the types of scientific studies on which it bases a rating of a given ingredient—for example, "one or more studies show tumor formation at high doses" or "one or more in vitro tests on mammalian cells show positive mutation results." And the site reveals how it arrives at its product ratings.

It lets visitors know the strength or weakness of a specific rating, based on how much data it actually has on a product's ingredients. So for the fifty or so ingredients in a shampoo that languishes in the bottom ten of Skin Deep's safeness rankings, the site discloses that there was "no data/high uncertainty" for 93 percent of the ingredients, no FDA review for 89 percent, no industry review for 45 percent—an aggregate data gap, as the website reports, of 80 percent. Even so, those ingredients that *have* been evaluated apparently showed high enough health hazards to rank the product so poorly that, as the site says, "100 percent of shampoos have lower concerns."

At the peak of the most recent real estate boom, a website called Zillow.com began to attract prospective American house buyers and sellers at the rate of about 4 million a month. Zillow.com used a complex artificial intelligence logarithm that scrutinized an immense amount of data on home prices, then organized it for a given zip code and zeroed in on a specific house, rendering a "zestimate," the most likely market price for that house. Zillow.com showed how information science could mix with something as complicated as real estate and render complex variables into easily understood data—in this case, an appropriate asking price.

As Zillow's creator, Rich Barton, readily concedes, any given zestimate "is only going to be as good as the information we have going in, and there are lots of holes and inaccuracies." To remedy that, Zillow.com became an open information system, one where home owners could feed in new data or correct facts about the estimates on their homes, or offer new details like the number of bathrooms that a house has, or the fact that a home has solar heating.

GoodGuide, too, welcomes such feedback. "If you find errors in our system, tell us and we'll fix them," O'Rourke says. "We want to engage companies; we welcome them telling us when they've upgraded a product we've rated. We say, 'Send us the data and we'll give you a new rating.' We'd love companies to offer data, and users to identify the issues they care about us rating. Then we can have a potential upward spiral of transparency, with better information improving over time."

Using that same principle, a group in Europe has begun development of a "sustainability Wikipedia," a version of the open-source dictionary that would focus on the backstory of everyday products. Enter "peanut butter," and it would tell you everything about its impacts on health and the environment and its social dimensions. The goal is an ever-evolving update of ecological product knowledge, fed by a stream of inputs from experts and the public at large, all managed by a dedicated cadre of skilled editors.

The principle that evaluations are dynamic, and that those who know the most about a given bit of information should have the ability to feed in fresh data, is one of the core operating rules for marketplace transparency. Of course, as open-source databases like Wikipedia recognize, such openness risks people trying to game the system by feeding in false information. Zillow.com confronts this issue daily, and Barton's view is instructive: "Once you open the information doors, it's difficult to close them. I'm of the opinion that there is no hiding, period. Everybody is a reporter, a blogger, a rater of everything. Fighting that force is like fighting gravity."

Open-source sites that allow the public to add what they know about a process, product, or company could be a boon to consumers seeking more accurate and complete information, especially about impacts a company does not want revealed. A lawyer friend tells me of a casual conversation he had with an acquaintance of his, an executive at a large manufacturing plant nearby. The executive admitted, a bit ruefully, that his factory still "dumps a lot of bad stuff" into the local river. Now, I have no idea if the charge is true, let alone what that "bad stuff" might be. But multiply that nameless executive a millionfold to approximate the numbers of industry insiders privy to such information, any of whom might potentially reveal it, to see the potential for an army of informants to add immeasurably to the public store of such knowledge.

But does such whistle-blowing serve the needs of marketplace transparency? It can, to the degree insiders can provide solid, substantial information that consumers and others can use to make better decisions on whether or not to buy a given product. But there is also a danger that such information may selectively distort the facts, serve some malicious agenda, or be tainted in some other way.

To be trustworthy, radical transparency needs to be authoritative, impartial, and comprehensive. *Authoritative* means that the parties evaluating the impacts of a product are intimately familiar with, for example, the manufacturing processes within that sector. A given industry might collectively set standards for evaluating its products, in conjunction with whoever has the expertise relevant to the question at hand—epidemiologists, toxicologists, industrial ecologists, impact auditors, and the like.

Impartiality demands that whoever does an evaluation is someone who has no personal stake in the sale of the product. At some point marketplace transparency systems might well include the post of ombudsman (or an ombudsgroup), an independent authority to whom anyone can appeal a rating that seems unfair or inaccurate.

And *comprehensive* requires that the consequences of a given product be weighed in several meaningful dimensions, examining the whole range rather than just a narrow focus. While carbon footprints are relatively easily calculated and satisfy some concerns about climate change, the scope of environmental impacts from a product goes far beyond carbon use. This means assessing a product over the full course of its life cycle, from manufacture (and even before that, to the origins of its components and extraction or creation of their ingredients) to disposal. An evaluation of a product should also cover all three spheres: it's not enough simply to claim that using solar energy sources makes a product virtuous if it off-gasses toxins or is unsafe for factory workers.

ACCELERATING BUZZ

Revolutions don't come about simply because of the advent of new technologies. They occur when those technologies result in starkly new behavior. Radical transparency will matter as a market force only to the degree it can go to scale; huge numbers of shoppers need to make a multitude of small decisions based on the information it makes available. As applications such as GoodGuide come online, the cost of getting information beyond what a seller chooses to present collapses spectacularly.

Social networking makes even a single shopper's reaction to a product into a force that can, conceivably, initiate either a boycott or a bonanza of new business. "These networks accelerate buzz in a way we've never seen before," Shirky told me. "A lot of talk-back to companies comes from user groups. The idea is that other people are as angry as I am—you're acting on behalf of hundreds of consumers. The sideways conversation about your brand on newsgroups is what hurts you. The lateral conversation among buyers wildly complaining to each other recruits new people to feel aggrieved."

Younger people are wired to each other as no previous generation and look to one another for reliable information, while deriding sources older generations had relied on. As shoppers—especially in coming generations—find themselves pleased or peeved by the cascade of revelations about products that transparency offers, they will spread the word instantaneously.

O'Rourke suspects teens, for example, may find GoodGuide a way to be cool, a prestige-boosting gadget that lets them impress their friends by knowing which skateboard or video game system is greener than others, or shock them by how "red" a favorite item turns out to be.

The possibilities here are enormous, as the remarkable success of two student projects in a viral marketing class at Stanford Business School suggests. Student teams designed two applications for Facebook: SendHotness, which lets users vote for their ten hottest Facebook friends, and KissMe, which sends a virtual kiss. Within thirty days the apps were adopted by more than a million users at a rate of around 100,000 daily; the "hotness" app reached over two million users within three months.

Dara O'Rourke sees such viral networking as one of the most effective ways to spread information about a product on GoodGuide (I can imagine twin product review apps called something like ThisSucks and ThisRules). "The apps now are pretty silly," O'Rourke admitted, "but one day they could carry this information. We're exploring how one friend can get to another friend, ad infinitum. You can go from zero to millions in a few weeks."

Shirky remains skeptical about the staying power of these viral transmissions, like a feature in GoodGuide that lets a shopper share product ughs and wows with a circle of friends. "People assume friendship circles scale up, so you go from ten to a thousand," Shirky comments. "But most information is of high value to a small group and little value to a large group; opinions from someone in a casual friendship won't travel far."

Shirky feels that radical transparency will matter more if information from sources like GoodGuide is taken up by committed groups—an eco-shoppers' club, for example—that focus on one product category at a time and broadcast the good or bad news to others who share their interests and values. "This kind of service will be more broadly effective if it's not just friend to friend but put in the hands of activists committed to a public good. A small group can digest the information and pass it on to a huge audience. They could focus on one item or category, like detergents, at a time, while other committed groups could get together, share which brands are less toxic, and act on it."

One explicit goal of GoodGuide is to serve as a catalyst for communities of people who care about the same issue and who are united in using this information to effect changes. "Activist consumers can go on YouTube and say, 'We're Moms Protesting Phthalates,'" says Dara O'Rourke. "Or a loyal customer might tell a company, 'I love your product and want to keep using it, but why does it have that suspected carcinogen in it?'"

Perhaps those most eager to take up this strategy will be the multitude of small organizations worldwide working for ecological and social justice, groups that environmental activist Paul Hawken estimates number more than a million. For many of these groups radical transparency—whether it concerns rainforest clear-cutting in Peru or a factory dumping industrial toxins in Peoria—will offer fresh ammunition that they can use to fan consumer indignation and get companies to change their practices.

In India, farmers near a Coca-Cola bottling plant were given sludge, a bottling by-product, to fertilize their fields. A band of activist groups had laboratories analyze levels of heavy metals in the sludge and posted the findings on websites. They organized protests that brought attention from media throughout India, as well as the BBC, resulting in a court-ordered shutdown of the bottling plant and a drop in Coke sales throughout India. Coca-Cola responded to this development with a series of positive steps, as we'll see in Chapter 13.

Such examples fit well with a prediction about the evolution of marketplace information made by Archon Fung, a professor at Harvard's John F. Kennedy School of Government who has pioneered studies of transparency and its impacts. In the view of the research group he leads, the first generation of transparency came about as a result of forced disclosure such as the right-to-know laws that allowed citizens to pry information out of the government. The second generation of transparency was also mandated, by rules that forced companies to disclose hard-to-detect risks or benefits, such as the safety of SUVs, CO_2 levels, or nutrients or allergens in food.

Third-generation transparency goes beyond voluntary and government-dictated disclosure to bottom-up transparency driven by vigilant, active consumers. The HSBC and Coca-Cola sagas illustrate what shared knowledge can do to trigger beneficial changes in the marketplace. Today, marketplace revelations by websites and bloggers lead a company to make such changes in response to consumer concerns surprisingly often. These consumer-driven business changes need not foster hostility; ideally, Fung argues, third-generation transparency should be more fully collaborative than any before. Progressive companies should systematically welcome this consumer feedback and incorporate these concerns in their policies by focusing their R&D or supply chain management accordingly, ending up on the same side of an issue as their customers.

Sir Terry Leahy, CEO of Tesco, the huge British supermarket

chain, may have set a best-practice standard for businesses seeking to upgrade the information cosmos. Leahy has undertaken the challenge of systematically assessing the carbon footprint of the seventy thousand products Tesco's stores stock, and labeling each with that number. In Britain suppliers of foods are under pressure from Tesco supermarkets to track and report the carbon emissions associated with a given food item—with the threat of losing a large contract if they fail to supply that data. Partly because of Tesco's move, the British government has undertaken an initiative to create a uniform measure for evaluating the carbon footprint of not just foods but a wide variety of consumer goods. Its goal: a single standard that can be adopted throughout the world.

In the phase of transparency about to come, Fung foresees consumers controlling decisions about the sorts of information disclosed and how it gets displayed. He sees GoodGuide as an early harbinger of this new phase of marketplace transparency, one that will speed up positive responses from businesses.

Some companies are already putting such pressure on other companies. A friend reached for his morning dose of Stonyfield yogurt to find this message on the foil peel-back seal: "Fight climate change at the cellular level . . . Use your cell phone to check on companies' climate practices before you purchase. Just text 'cc' and the name of the company to 30644 for an instant reply." The container also included a website address: www.climate counts.org. As the website explains, "Climate Counts is a collaborative effort to bring consumers and companies together in the fight against global climate change. We are a nonprofit organization funded by Stonyfield Farm, Inc., and launched in collaboration with Clean Air-Cool Planet."

The site had ratings for around sixty major companies spanning industries from apparel and food services to household products and electronics. Like GoodGuide's ratings, the companies are ranked in a red, yellow, and green rating system that's backed up by more detailed evaluations of a company's efforts to review and reduce emissions. On each company's score page is a link for sending consumer opinions.

What intrigues me most about the yogurt lid is that ecological transparency here is not just the result of a campaign by an activist organization but rather is promoted on a product as a value-added feature. One business uses the assessment of the ecological performance of other businesses as a competitive advantage.

Another version of this third-generation transparency might be a website that melds a populist tone and consumerist mission with highly informed posts from industry insiders—chemical and industrial engineers, industrial ecologists, systems analysts, toxicologists. They could detail improvements at the far end of the supply chain and explain what advantages they lend to the products they end up shaping. Such a website would appeal not just to individual consumers but to decision makers at every point in the retail and manufacturing world who are trying to upgrade their products. We'll explore a prototype of such a website, Earthster, in Chapter 14.

For consumers, the coming digital sources of eco-transparency will mean, as Shirky puts it, that "you can make more virtuous decisions without it inconveniencing you. If you tell me that Food Lion stores are more environmentally conscious than Kroger's, I'll change where I shop—and that will put market pressure on Kroger's to compete along those lines, too."

FAIR AND SQUARE

*These towels have been made under fair labor conditions, in a
safe and healthy working environment which is free of
discrimination, and where management has committed to
respecting the rights and dignity of workers.*

That message, printed under a logo reading FAIR AND SQUARE, was
placed on towels sold at a trendy Manhattan home furnishings
store. It proved to have remarkable sales power. Compared to ad-
jacent towels that lacked this simple information, the Fair and
Square batch showed a steady boost in sales over a five-month
period. When the labels were switched to comparable towels, the
sales advantage—a boost of 11 percent in sales—traveled right
along with the label.

Most surprising, when the price of the towels was raised, their sales increased *more* quickly. A 10 percent bump up in price brought the Fair and Square towels 20 percent more sales—and a 20 percent price rise yielded a 62 percent sales jump!

The two Harvard University political scientists who conducted the experiment, Michael Hiscox and Nicholas Smyth, conjecture that the higher price tag for the towels lent more credibility to the claim for superior labor standards. The results, they suggest, show a large untapped market for such ethical merchandise.

Of course, this happened at an upscale store; its shoppers fall within the marketing category known in some circles as "Price-Sensitive Affluents," those who equate a virtuous label with quality, and are willing to pay up to twice an item's price if it matches their concerns. But don't the vast majority of shoppers, a skeptic might argue, care more about price than goodness?

The data from less trendy venues is mixed. In an experiment by Oregon State University researchers at Home Depot stores, eco-labeled items outsold those without such labels by two to one if the prices were the same, and by slightly less than two to one when the eco-products cost 2 percent more. But at a department store in a working-class neighborhood of Detroit, the results were different. One pile of socks was labeled as having been made under "good working conditions," while an identical pile had no such sign. The prices of the two piles of socks varied. About a third of customers paid up to 40 percent more for the ethical socks. But when the socks were priced the same, the virtuous label had zero effect; again the researchers conjecture that the higher price made the claim more credible.

That eco-virtue adds perceived value finds support from recent brain studies. From her research on consumer decision making,

Caltech neuroeconomist Hilke Plassmann concludes, "Our concepts about price shape an expectation, which then biases our experience and our purchasing decisions." The brain activity when we make a decision about a brand reflects this bias, equating price with quality. A lower price lowers our expectations of a product, and a higher one raises them.

When Plassmann gave experimental volunteers what they thought was a discount wine, they liked it less than a supposedly high-priced wine, even though the wine in each glass was the same. "Price makes us feel a wine tastes better," Plassmann notes, "but that's a cognitive bias that arises from computations in the brain that tell me to expect it to be better, and then shape my experience so that it does, indeed, taste better."

Could the same sort of cognitive operation apply with regard to an ecological judgment? Plassmann thinks so: "It could be a moral concept, like 'This product is bad for the environment,' that drives the brain."

As every brand manager knows, a product's reputation can make it or break it. And reputation can be remarkably fragile; as neuroeconomic studies of preference show, a single note of negativity or positivity can skew our entire decision to buy. Our biases and expectations drive brain activity, which in turn shape what we do. That sequence from label to mental state to choice has profound implications for brand preferences. From this perspective, the ferocious marketing battles between rival brands are fought within the neural circuits of shoppers, where the telling moment comes in the second or two a customer contemplates a box of laundry soap.

"Most people don't buy the cheapest thing," O'Rourke points

out. "They pay more for what they perceive as good." He envisions environmental, health, and social welfare concerns entering the brand choice matrix, in addition to price and quality.

Still, a survey of twenty-five thousand customers across the economic scale by Marks and Spencer, the British retail giant, found that about a quarter of shoppers are simply not interested in whether an item carries a virtuous pedigree. Ten percent, on the other hand, will go out of their way to get a more ethical item. Those data points, if taken alone, suggest that those who are indifferent outnumber those who care by two or three to one.

But the most telling group in that survey was the large majority of shoppers who lie somewhere between the two extremes. Roughly two-thirds of shoppers, the survey found, care about ethical choices but want the decision to be easy, or are vaguely concerned about ethics but feel their shopping preferences won't matter. Radical transparency targets that two-thirds by making ethical choices easier, offering a shopper relevant data in a neat summary as she holds the item in her hand.

The two-thirds who care but want information with little effort are the swing voters, the crucial shoppers who might be encouraged to shop their values, but whose failure to do so breaks the demand–supply link between shoppers' choices and the products supplied. If there is no real market advantage to companies for adhering to ecological soundness, then there is less reason for them to shift how they make and transport their products. Taking the transparent marketplace to scale will depend on how large a proportion of shoppers in the middle ground use their ecological intelligence.

The Marks and Spencer survey results bolster the claims of

skeptics who argue that regardless of people's assurances that ethics matter in what they buy, most shoppers are indifferent to anything but cost, and transparency would make little or no difference. Witness the gap between how many people espouse green values and what they actually buy. Surveys of shoppers in the United States have found that around seven in ten think of themselves as "environmentalists," with about a third claiming they stopped buying a product because the company pollutes. Likewise, around three-quarters say they would not buy something made under bad working conditions; 86 percent in one survey said they would pay an extra dollar to be sure a twenty-dollar item of clothing did not come from a sweatshop.

That argument, however, assumes that virtue always costs more. Market realities make the picture murkier. Consider the ten most "toxic" shampoos and the ten least (as listed by Skin Deep, the website that evaluates the relative safety of personal care products). While the very worst, a kids' shampoo, is also the cheapest per ounce, the most *expensive* shampoo of the twenty is also on the "worst" list. In other words, cost and virtue cannot always be equated. For example, as oil costs have risen, businesses have been searching for ways to lessen its presence along their supply chain by switching to clean energy sources. Such sources may become cheaper than oil, once again breaking the link between high cost and improved ecological quality. Dow Chemical has committed to finding non-petroleum-based alternatives for its vast repertoire of industrial chemicals, a move likely to reduce the number of artificial toxins in nature. As cost equations shift, goodness may become cheaper—or at least increasingly competitive in terms of cost.

Nonetheless, cost remains key. Despite the willingness of some to pay a premium for eco-virtue, when it comes to what most people are willing to pay for, by and large only a fraction of shoppers seem to be guided by the ethical, environmental, or health impacts of products. One review of "green consumer" campaigns over twenty years found that only around 10 percent of consumers went out of their way to buy sound eco-products—presumably the same passionate group identified in the Marks and Spencer survey. Green campaigns do not seem to boost the numbers of green consumers much beyond this coterie of true believers. Environmental and public health activists have been discouraged by the repeated failure of their campaigns to motivate shoppers to buy more environmentally or socially sound products. Schemes ranging from educational programs in schools to eco-labeling have made little or no discernible impact in how people shop.

So what works? The experiment at Hannaford Brothers Company, the chain of supermarkets in Maine I mentioned earlier, has resulted in ready lessons for raising our ecological intelligence. One day shoppers found little stars perched next to the price tags of foods, rating the nutritional value of each item. Desirable nutritional choices received one, two, or three stars, for good, better, and best. Hannaford worked with a panel of expert nutritionists from institutions like Harvard and Tufts University to rate nutritional value. Foods earned points for vitamins, whole grains, fiber, and the like; they lost points for ingredients like bad fats, sugars, and salt.

Hannaford evaluated 25,500 products with the resulting formula, applying it to foods' ingredients lists and their nutrition panels. A host of products that food companies touted as "healthy choices" in fact received no stars, the worst rating—mainly because they were too high in sugar and salt. Only 28 percent of items on the store's shelves earned any stars; the rest got no rating at all.

Customers paid attention. A survey of Hannaford shoppers found that four in ten used the star ratings to guide their shopping fairly often—with sales figures revealing decided shifts in their purchase decisions. Hannaford estimates that those shifts were based on about a billion individual purchase decisions.

In the first year the three-star system was deployed, the stores saw marked sales gains for the most nutritious foods, those with three stars, and losses for those with two, one, or none. Three-star leaner cuts of meat increased 7 percent in sales, while ground beef, with no stars, dropped by 5 percent. Whole milk (no stars) dropped 4 percent, fat-free (three stars) gained 1 percent. Overall, packaged foods that earned stars had a jump in sales two and a half times greater than that for products that earned no stars.

The idea of nutritional labels came from focus groups with Hannaford shoppers about ways to make the time they spend in a supermarket more pleasant. Many shoppers complained of frustration and confusion in figuring out which foods were more nutritious choices. The star rating system, as Hannaford puts it, offers its "customers a useful tool that can help improve their shopping time with us."

As a Hannaford executive explained, the company's main motive for the rating system was to boost shoppers' positive feelings about being in its stores. The three-star system aligns with the chain's experience-based marketing strategy and transforms shopping into an education—with the dual benefits of helping customers find what's best for them and increasing the time they spend in a store.

The Delhaize Group, the Belgian company that owns Hannaford, plans to bring its ratings to other supermarket chains in its portfolio, one in Florida and another throughout the mid-Atlantic and Southeast. Delhaize may license the rating system to still others in regions of the United States where it does not operate.

Food marketers are noticing. Even though the shifts in market share were within only a single chain of stores, sales reps from several brands that lost market share approached Hannaford executives to see if making their product ingredients more nutritious might earn them a star or two. That once again suggests ways point-of-purchase data can create a virtuous change.

That potential should increase over coming decades. Stu Stein, then a student at Wharton, saw a talk I had given about ecological transparency posted on the Web, and posed this question on his website under the heading "Compassionate Capitalism": "If we had more knowledge about the things we buy, would it make a difference? If we knew that the washwater from the dye of one t-shirt might contribute to nearby children's risk of leukemia while another did not, would we care? I think so. My generation likes to do good by buying differently. When given the option to be virtuous, we take it."

But too often, he noted, they lack the information that would enable them to make a more positive choice. He proposed three things that would help: 1) knowing why they should care; 2) an easy cue for which choices are better; and 3) "a right decision that's as accessible as a wrong one." GoodGuide addresses the latter two, but not the first. The need to know why to care is really a call for ecological intelligence. Early signs suggest coming generations of shoppers will indeed care more than today's about the impacts of what they buy.

When I asked Thomas Ehrlich, a senior scholar at the Carnegie Foundation for the Advancement of Teaching, whether today's college students cared about these issues, he told me, "On campuses across the country there's been an explosion of student civic activities, particularly environmental projects and other forms of community service."

Baby boomers like me grew up during the early days of the Cold War. In my school days that meant regular "bomb drills" that reminded us we could be blown to bits in a nuclear war. Children today face what may prove, over the long term, to be an even more dire threat: the specter of drastic disruptions of life from global warming and the other ecological disasters we may have already set in motion.

Older shoppers may not have cell phones, be too set in their habits, or merely too lackadaisical as they shop, to use technologies like the smart bar code. But today's younger generations seem far more motivated to embrace them, growing up in an atmosphere of alarm about the future of their planet that stands to move them more strongly to action. If predictions of global warming are anywhere near accurate, Hurricane Katrina and her ilk herald a steady drumbeat of ecological disasters in the decades ahead. This sort of defining generational trauma seems likely to grow stronger as time goes on, as ecological momentum already unleashed bears more sad fruit.

While older generations of consumers may be largely set in

their habits, younger people are acutely aware of the need for an environmental bottom line. In a 2007 survey of American teenagers, half of the teens said that the degradation of the environment scared them. Most telling, almost two-thirds felt their generation will be more environmentally responsible than previous ones, with 78 percent believing they will have time to make changes that can repair the damage done to the environment.

This motivational difference makes younger generations more likely than older consumers to act on ecological transparency in their purchasing decisions, and to do so with greater urgency as the years go by. For starters, 80 percent say corporations should be held to a mandatory ethical code on their impact on the environment. Three-quarters say they would buy products or services that help the environment (whether they actually do remains an empirical question). More to the point, 83 percent said that, if it were easy to do, they would take action to help the environment—if someone showed them how. And that, in essence, describes the function of radical transparency: making it easy to help.

10

THE VIRTUOUS CYCLE

When I was a kid, one of my favorite treats was a French dough-nut, a fat pretzel of braided dough deep-fried in oil. The bakery was just two blocks away, a short bike ride; whenever I could scrape together enough money, I made the pilgrimage.

Little did I know the dangers lurking in that delicious fried delicacy, with all that sugar coating and its medley of fatty oils. As sensory psychologists tell us, the body's mechanisms for taste and smell have been fine-tuned to adore the sugars and fats that, well, make us fat. This neural strategy for surviving scarcity and famine presumably worked well in the hardscrabble days of prehistory; today it's an expressway to rotundity.

But the biggest danger lurking in those luscious French dough-nuts was one that did not exist until recent culinary history: trans fats, hydrogenated vegetable oil. Adding hydrogen atoms to cooking oils created saturated fats, gunk patented in 1903 that made baked goodies stay moist longer. The miracle of trans fats lent pastries and cakes a longer shelf life, let pie crusts (and French doughnuts) stay pleasingly crisp yet chewy. Trans fats were first marketed to the public as Crisco; I can remember the big can of Crisco in our kitchen—and in the kitchens in my buddies' houses—when I was growing up. Today Crisco has virtually disappeared from American kitchens.

Perhaps the first widespread public awareness of trouble with trans fat came from a 1993 report in the British medical journal *The Lancet*. Scientists analyzing data from the Nurses' Health Study, which since 1980 has tracked the medical destiny of more than eighty thousand nurses, noticed that women whose diets were high in trans fats had a higher likelihood of heart attacks. By 1997 the scientists had even more robust data to report: by then 939 nurses had already died from heart disease. The researchers calculated that switching from eating trans fats to nonhydrogenated ones would reduce a person's odds of heart disease by 53 percent.

But here was a case of unintended information hoarding: medical researchers were in the know, the rest of us clueless. Dr. Walter Willets of the Harvard School of Public Health and the lead scientist on the study of nurses, noted that of all the varieties of fat, from those in olive oil to those in butter, trans fat was the worst culprit, adding—back in 1997—that this little fact was "still unknown to most consumers." Indeed, at the time the Associated Press story reporting the study used the phrase "something called trans fat," to signal that readers were probably learning of the substance's existence as they read the article.

While in 1997 knowledge of trans fat itself—let alone its hazards—was barely beginning to dawn, that awareness grew quickly as a cascade of findings made clear the hazards in eating trans fat. In 2000 the FDA released a study estimating that removing trans fat from margarine and other foods could prevent about seven thousand deaths each year in the United States. The report suggested that labeling trans fats could have a meaningful impact by giving consumers a way to make more healthy choices.

Then came the death knell for trans fats. In 2001, the prestigious Institute of Medicine, a branch of the National Academy of Sciences, issued a report confirming that trans fat was strongly associated with heart disease, increasing the LDL cholesterol that clogs arteries and reducing levels of HDL, the "good" cholesterol that cleanses arteries. The conclusion: there is no "safe" level of trans fat in a food.

The U.S. Food and Drug Administration had already begun pondering whether to require that foods be labeled to reveal their amount of trans fat. Nutrition labels at the time included the total amount of fat in a food but made no distinction between, say, polyunsaturated fats, which are healthy, and trans fats.

Food manufacturers opposed labeling trans fats, complaining that there was simply no good substitute for hydrogenated oils, and that a host of foods would lose the taste, textures, and shelf life that customers wanted. Meanwhile, the food industry intensified research to find equally good-tasting alternates it could use to reformulate its products. By the time the FDA got around to requiring that foods show how much trans fat they harbored, major food companies had already found ways to drop hydrogenated oils and were proudly labeling once-guilty foods as "trans fat free."

In 2007 fast-food chain Dunkin' Donuts joined a multitude of other companies in announcing it would drop trans fats from its recipes, even its eponymous doughnuts (which for years had, literally, been dripping with the hydrogenated oil). Like every other major food company (including those that at first had complained that there was no substitute for trans fat), Dunkin' Donuts switched to a combination of more healthy oils to replace trans fats.

For more than a century hydrogenated oils had been seen as a magic ingredient that bestowed on hundreds of foods their lasting freshness, moistness, and crispness. But in just a decade the dawning of their downside in our collective awareness had turned hydrogenated oils into an object of disgust, even banned by law in some locales.

Early on, when the FDA began to hold hearings on listing trans fat on products, many companies opposed the proposed labels. At the time one newspaper article mentioned offhandedly that consumers concerned about health wouldn't touch products high in trans fat—"if they knew" which ones those were. Now we know, and as a result we are hard put to find anything high in trans fat to buy. Trans fat has virtually vanished from American food.

What's most telling about this saga is the mechanism that made trans fats vanish. The federal government never banned hydrogenated oils. No one told food companies they had to stop using trans fat. The crucial shift was in the *information available to consumers*. Trans fat stands as a textbook case of the potent market force that comes from full disclosure in labeling the things we buy.

As the public gets more finely detailed information on the various harms done by products, such cases of disappearing ingredients and abandoned industrial processes will no doubt proliferate. All it takes is a bit of radical transparency. Full disclosure has marketplace power, as a handful of earlier cases illustrates.

A Senate hearing on September 10, 2000, shocked drivers of SUVs—then the rage of the auto industry—with the news that these top-heavy vehicles were prone to deadly rollovers from something as mild as a blown tire. A total of 271 people had been killed in a spate of such accidents. One impetus for buying SUVs had been that people thought they were safer than smaller cars (as they indeed were in cases of a crash between an SUV and an auto with less bulk when there was no rollover involved). Congress, trying to find the best method to calm drivers' fears, turned to transparency: a law that required automakers to divulge to buyers the likelihood that an SUV would roll over.

The transparency system was a straightforward five-star rating based on government tests that instantly let a prospective buyer know if a given car was among the most or least prone to rollovers. Five stars meant the car had a 10 percent or less chance of rolling over in an accident; a car with one star had a 40 percent or more likelihood. And, to ensure the ratings were useful, the law demanded the stickers be placed right there on the auto's window in the dealer's showroom.

At first SUVs had a wide range of rollover ratings, with most very poor; thirty models were rated one or two stars, indicating a 30 percent or greater rollover probability. Just one SUV earned four stars, a less than 20 percent rollover chance.

But only four years later, the pattern had reversed: twenty-four models rated four stars, and just one was ranked with two stars. Consumer pressure had convinced automakers to stop lobbying against a standard for rollover safety (as they had for decades) and to speed up their R&D on technology for stability control, such as sensors for corrective braking.

The SUV rollover story is one of fifteen cases studied by researchers at Harvard University investigating when transparency produces beneficial marketplace changes. The focus of these studies ranged from the 2001 fiat that mutual funds disclose their after-tax returns to the 2004 ruling that auto companies collect and report consumer complaints about potential defects. In each one, a major, beneficial shift took place simply because consumers got new information about potential harms from standard practices or common products.

The Senate hearing on SUV rollovers was a benchmark in marketplace transparency. Congress's explicit rationale for subsequent tire-rating laws was that the information on rollover risk led buyers to choose safer cars, which in turn would lead automakers to improve the safety of the cars they made. And so it did.

Similarly, consumer demands for information led to industry action back in 1978, when a jungle of state-by-state energy efficiency standards for refrigerators was creating a compliance nightmare for appliance makers. The resulting desire of U.S. manufacturers for nationwide, uniform efficiency requirements led Congress to require that the Department of Energy set mandatory energy standards—not just for refrigerators but for nearly a dozen other electrical appliances.

Predictably, at first some industry advocates protested that the requirements were technically unfeasible. But, as so often happens, despite the protests manufacturers proceeded to develop refrigerators that were highly efficient—in fact, 10 to 15 percent better than the standards demanded. The ingenuity unleashed has resulted in today's kitchens having refrigerators that have larger capacities than those of previous decades and that consume a fraction of the energy. Energy use by refrigerators in the United States plummeted, and continues to drop as the years go on.

In neither of these cases did the government demand that industry meet a certain standard or decree any change. Rather, they simply required the informed to let the uninformed know critical information. If information moves markets, the advent of information symmetry shakes them.

THE MULTIPLIER EFFECT

Sequestered among New Jersey's anonymous landscape of industrial parks squats a vast factory complex dedicated to making bath and body products. The factory's main building, a massive 600,000 square feet, holds forty production lines. Every hour each line pumps out two thousand units, about two to three hundred boxes of shampoo ready for shipping.

A goodly portion of the shampoos in America's stores and beauty salons was born in the immense vats in this factory's mixing room, each vat the size of an upended cargo container—about 18 feet high and 10 feet across. A single vat holds 8,500 gallons, which turns out enough bottles of a shampoo to fill a slot on the shelves of every store in a national retail chain.

It takes an entire day to put the ingredients in a vat and another day to mix the batch. Then the shampoo gets piped into drums and tested for impurities. The drums are hooked up to one of the production lines, where that brand of shampoo gets pumped into bottles. The capacity of the plant: around eighty thousand units per hour.

Consider the scale of manufacturing versus what we buy: manufacturers think in batches of thousands of gallons, while a single bottle of shampoo represents a few ounces. But each single bottle represents all the others in its batch, about 108,800 standard ten-ounce bottles. However that bottle's worth of shampoo was made, whatever its ingredients, whatever its contribution to the devalue chain (the ways in which various points in its life cycle have negative ecological impacts), in the logic of the marketplace all these impacts are rewarded whenever someone buys a single bottle.

In this sense, a single customer switching a brand preference can have vast implications. For one, it gives every consumer a role in the business decision to continue the current way of doing things or to find alternatives. Just as single votes count in an election, the swinging of such purchasing choices in one direction or another decides the fortune of the brands competing for that person's dollar.

But the missing piece of the equation here is finding a way to let a company know precisely why we decided to buy, or switch from, its brand. Such an information feedback loop between shoppers' preferences and a business's response to how it does things creates a "virtuous cycle." When information about a product changes consumers' brand preferences, the resulting market shift in turn will lead companies to offer more of the improvements shoppers want. Simply providing information to buyers that changes their behavior leads sellers to change their business practices. A virtuous cycle connects what shoppers decide in the aisles of a store with what companies need to do to win their business.

One of the longer-playing virtuous cycles can be seen in the green building movement. We are nearing the end of that long era in the construction industry where, to maximize their profit, developers set their budget for a building's costs as low as possible, and architects, contractors, engineers, and everyone else who will build a piece of the complete building compete for their share of that fixed budget. That system provides incentive for bidders in turn to find ways to cut their costs to the bone to fatten their profits, in a race to the bottom: the subcontractor for the heating and cooling system, for instance, has every reason to install the cheapest he or she can find that will do the job and just meet building codes, rather than a higher-priced one that will save energy and money over the long haul for the tenants—the real customers of the building.

The fixed-budget system operated in the shadows of commercial development, out of sight of those tenants (and sometimes building owners) who would bear the higher operating costs. These crucial decisions were hidden in the construction bids and passed on to these customers for the life of the building. It was a classic case of marketplace information asymmetry.

Disclosure of the ecological downside of commercial buildings has arrived in the construction sector in the form of LEED (for Leadership in Energy and Environment Design), the certification system that has become the gold standard for green building. By alerting the world of building owners and tenants to the dangers of indoor pollution and better alternatives, to the high operating costs of cheap heating and air-conditioning, and to the many ways in which we can lower energy costs by using new design and material options, the LEED standards create ecological transparency where there was none before. LEED creates information symmetry by revealing the hidden costs to a building's owners and users of the old way of doing business in the construction world, and creates a virtuous cycle by offering ready market alternatives.

Commercial buildings in the United States account for about a third of our greenhouse gas emissions, and almost two-thirds of our energy consumption. The brick-and-mortar relics of earlier days that dominate the building stock in any city represent the greatest immediate opportunity for the real estate sector to go green. Converting a building to LEED standards represents low-lying fruit in upgrading our impact on the environment: the immediate payback comes in energy cost savings.

A study by the Green Building Council, which administers the LEED program, found that owners who retrofit older buildings on average get an annual savings of 90 cents a square foot; most earn back their investment within the first two or three years. Small wonder large building owners from Citigroup to property managers like Cushman & Wakefield are joining the movement. Other advantages include not just lower electric bills, but lower overhead expenses for things like cleaning, and healthier air inside as well—not to mention the increased comfort, health, and productivity of those who work in the building.

From the start, the small working group that kicked off the LEED movement realized that market forces would be the driver of this fundamental change. "The idea of market-based transformation" was a key founding idea, recalls Jim Hartzfeld, a founding member of the U.S. Green Building Council. "We realized that the voluntary response of the marketplace—generated by people's understanding that there were better ways to build buildings now, and it was in everyone's best interest to do it—was more powerful than imposing any kind of regulation."

The market results have been powerful. When LEED was introduced in 2000, there were 635 buildings worldwide that met the standards. Seven years later, over $12 billion in building starts had been designed to meet these green standards. LEED is fast becoming an industry norm for commercial properties, with many building codes worldwide adopting the standards for large buildings. As market demand has increased, so too has the supply.

The building industry is in the throes of waves of innovation, with a race to find new technologies that do everything from allowing a building's surfaces to be made with solar panels that generate electricity to geothermal heating and cooling systems that take advantage of the constant year-round temperatures of 50 to 55 degrees that lie several feet below the earth's surface. The construction industry's bar for green is in continuous upgrade. Industrial designers envision a coming generation of "living buildings" that will operate like an accessory to nature, producing more clean water and energy than they use. This virtuous cycle is moving into fast forward.

The larger accelerating force for such cycles may come from the cumulative force of institutional and business-to-business decisions rather than retail shoppers. If you are the purchasing agent for a large organization, your spending power has a much bigger impact. Mike Hardiman is one such big spender. As the director of purchasing for the University of Wisconsin, Hardiman spends upward of $225 million each year, about half of that for goods. The day we spoke, he was about to attend a meeting with other purchasing agents from the Big Ten schools, the huge state universities that, like his, buy massive amounts of supplies. "There's a large movement sweeping us up toward sustainability and social awareness, and we're nowhere near the crest. All of us purchasing agents are struggling with how to apply this.

"We already have a couple of mandates, like a requirement from the state that we buy recycled paper. Some major donors have given us funding for a very large new science center, and we're going for LEED certification. Other social issues have come up—we want to ensure the workers of contractors we deal with are paid living wages. We're part of a consortium of schools that has hired a third party to do an analysis of working conditions for our contractors."

Institutional purchasers like Hardiman are intentionally creating virtuous cycles via requests for bids on the goods they buy that specify incremental upgrades. The state of Texas has joined several others by moving toward updating its procurement practices to favor rewarding contracts to products that are more environmentally sound, including their life-cycle costs.

That strategy seems ripe for spreading to other institutional sectors. As Jonathan Rose told me, "My job as a builder is to select the material with the best backstory—the least environmental and health costs. Every design and material choice we make carries a market message. As the green building movement has grown in size and scale, there has been a tremendous response from manufacturers and suppliers to make more and more environmentally responsible materials. The green demand began with smaller, innovative firms but is rapidly growing as Fortune 500 companies and institutional investors demand healthier, greener products."

Rose and others see the power of collective action to create market pressure that encourages suppliers to upgrade materials. In time, he believes, the largest owners of buildings will do this for the things they continually replace or upgrade as well. Pointing to giant retirement funds that own trillions of dollars in real estate, he predicts that if these funds said they wanted "a certain improvement in the carpets, lights, or other fixtures they regularly replace in their buildings, then you'd start to see a continuous upgrade. When you drive key leverage points in an industrial system, the rest will follow."

This shifts the decision-making process for executives, in the view of industrial ecologist Gregory Norris. Management can now calculate, "If we get our environmental benefits to this threshold, then we could expand our market share this much. The more we move to the right on this graph of recycled content, for example, the more sales we'll get as we meet the threshold requirements for more buyers." This provides a concrete incentive for companies to justify the costs of finding ways to make the improvements needed to get to average or better for their industry.

In the past advocacy groups concerned with everything from saving the rain forests to ferreting out sweatshops would lobby governments to pass regulations to further their agendas. More recently many have switched tactics, trying to persuade shoppers to boycott products that displease them. The strategy boils down to creating collective consumer action—or the threat of such action—to shift markets to the kinds of products aligned with what they advocate. Such a market strategy can be far more effective and work far more quickly than regulation. It parallels the market pressure that many institutional buyers are applying.

Dara O'Rourke's hope for GoodGuide is "to provide a giant

lever that shifts markets to prod manufacturers incrementally to get better across the board." But that lever for change might be pushed for any of a variety of reasons beyond responding to a shift in the market, from ethical concerns and commitments to social responsibility to the effort to protect a brand's reputation. Here the old sixties slogan "Power to the people" takes on new force, empowering those in business who seek to promote the greener, cleaner, and more humane in the marketplace.

Radical transparency promises to create a marketplace mechanism that takes the consequence of shoppers' choices to scale: each individual purchase, aggregated with all the others, becomes tantamount to votes on the nature of the goods they buy. As businesses respond by making more of the improvements that shoppers want, shoppers can feel empowered by seeing that their ethical choices matter.

"You could make the argument that your bottle of pasta sauce makes a trivial contribution, but that brand's total impacts are the sum total of millions of decisions like yours," Gregory Norris argues. "If we can find a better choice, that's a vote, and every vote counts. Saying it doesn't matter what I buy is like saying it doesn't matter who I vote for. It's only our purchases that are driving this industrial machine. Companies tell me, 'I'm not paying attention until buyers care.' "

THE CHEMICAL STEW

Conventional wisdom posits a potential bonanza for companies that go green not merely in direct savings on energy costs, but also from the smarter products and processes they innovate that solve ecological problems. But looked at through another lens, the current tide of activity focused on global warming is just the first in a series of such waves likely to wash over businesses in coming years.

Most products marketed today are based on twentieth-century industrial chemistry. The twenty-first century will inevitably bring a more fine-grained understanding of how commonly used ingredients interact with human biology. Given the inexorable advance of science, eventually some of those substances will be implicated in processes that lead to disease of one kind or another.

The widespread fears about the heating of the planet are driven by a steady drumbeat of scientific findings, each hitting the media with a new wave of alarm. But just behind the current surge of fears about global warming, the next wave of dread to wash over us can be seen gathering a bit farther offshore. One inexorable force that stirs these waves is backwash from fast-moving scientific advances. Another is the ever-increasing zones of transparency created by the availability of information.

Put radical transparency together with, for example, medical findings about industrial chemicals, and we can see that one likely wave will be alarms about toxins: more compounds that are today routine ingredients in consumer products will become suspect. These anxieties may spread to seemingly innocuous industrial chemicals, simply because tomorrow's standards for toxicity will likely be more demanding than today's, as more information is spread more widely and the public's perception of danger becomes greater.

Another reason this may be the next major wave: While alarms about global warming and other planetary dangers have filled the news, they can seem to operate on too massive a scale and over too long a time frame to affect most people's everyday lives. But when it comes to protecting our own health and that of our loved ones, people pay far closer attention.

Consider a box of microwavable, butter-flavored popcorn. The label assures buyers that it has zero grams of trans fat and zero mg cholesterol. But the ingredients list fails to mention that the savory butter taste and mouthwatering aroma come courtesy of diacetyl, a flavoring long known by pulmonary specialists to cause bronchiolitis obliterans, a disease in which the small airways in the lungs become swollen, scarred, and, eventually, obliterated.

Victims can breathe in deeply but have severe difficulty exhaling. More commonly known as "popcorn worker's lung," the disease has sometimes led to the death of those who labor in popcorn factories or plants that produce candy and pastries, and even dog food, where diacetyl is used as a flavoring.

A canary in the coal mine for the rest of us was Wayne Watson of Centennial, Colorado. When Watson was diagnosed with popcorn worker's lung, his physicians alerted federal agencies that the threat had leapt beyond factory walls to consumers' homes. The resulting public alarm swiftly led the four largest U.S. makers of microwave popcorn to announce they were pulling diacetyl from the mix of ingredients.

In nature diacetyl occurs at low levels in butter, cheese, and some fruits, where it poses no danger. The popcorn companies were breaking no law by using diacetyl; the FDA had approved its use. And Wayne Watson had put himself at unusual risk; he dubbed himself "Mr. Popcorn" because he devoured two or three bags every day for ten years. He especially loved to fill his lungs with a deep inhalation of the buttery cloud of aroma released the moment he ripped open a freshly popped bag—in other words, the strongest dose possible.

His food fetish was a recipe for medical disaster. When heated, diacetyl becomes a vapor, the form that poses a danger to lungs. If breathed in over long periods, concentrated doses of this very vapor lead to popcorn worker's lung. When Mr. Watson's doctor went to his house and measured levels of diacetyl in the air right after he made popcorn, they were found to be as high as those in a popcorn factory.

So should we all shun diacetyl-laced popcorn? Maybe. Maybe

not. As one report on the case put it, "There are no warnings from federal regulators, nor is there medical advice on how consumers" should treat the news. And that's the quandary. The standards that the FDA, food industries, and even physicians use for determining consumer safety do not always match the recommendations of scientists who study the health impacts of the multitude of chemicals we imbibe.

Just what do we mean by "toxic," anyway? That question goes to the heart of a decades-long struggle over industrial chemicals waged between public health experts and the chemical industry. It revolves around a question that can be answered in many ways: what compounds are toxic to whom and under what circumstance?

The Flavor and Extract Manufacturers Association estimates more than one thousand flavoring ingredients may pose respiratory dangers to workers. No one knows how many other chemicals with potential dangers lurk in the everyday objects we use and foods we eat. Informed estimates put the number of man-made chemical compounds as high as 104,000. Of these, 10,000 are used yearly in volumes greater than ten tons. Only a fraction of these everyday chemicals have ever been tested for toxicity in adults, let alone on fetuses or infants.

When it comes to potential harm from the chemicals in what we buy, use, and own, while many dangers are suspected, almost all are "unproven," in the sense of achieving consensus on the verdict. Apart from a relatively small subclass of chemicals, like concentrated doses of vaporized diacetyl, the chain of causality from chemical X to disease Y in almost every case has yet to be investigated, let alone established.

When it comes to knowing which ingredient might be a medical concern, it's largely a guessing game. In some cases, science can identify certain ill effects from specific toxins and suggest a pathway consistent with those medical outcomes. But most of the apprehension centers on the simple fact that no synthetic chemicals are integral to the body, and at a high enough level or in various combinations, their presence might not necessarily be good.

But science cannot always predict what specific effects these exposures will have in a given person; the body's biological maze is simply too complex. These chemicals engage tissues in multiple ways. Some imitate the molecular structure of the body's own hormones, ending up lodged in the endocrine system; others mimic the chemical messengers that keep cells in the brain and body working smoothly together. Some are readily absorbed into body fat, while still others—particularly the large number made from petroleum—readily slip through the oil-based membranes that surround cells (petroleum-based chemicals harbor carcinogenic benzene rings). Once absorbed into the body's tissues, these chemicals can wreak havoc in any number of ways, none of which may be immediately obvious.

THE INFLAMMATORY SYNDROME

If you want to know what industrial chemical compounds Michael Lerner or his wife, Sharyle Patton, carry around in their bodies, just go to the Web page www.bodyburden.org. Lerner and Patton are both active in environmental health, the field that studies how the chemical by-products of industry and commerce impact the human body. They posted their analyses on the Web as part of an awareness-raising campaign.

Lerner, it seems, lugs around relatively high levels of methylmercury, inorganic arsenic, and polychlorinated biphenyls (better known as PCBs). These are but a few of the 102 industrial chemicals of 214 assayed by measuring metabolites in his blood and urine.

Patton's body, in addition to these, has relatively high levels of chlorinated dioxins and organochlorine pesticide residues, plus a generous helping of others that did not show up in her husband's tests.

Medical databases link, at various levels of certainty, each of these compounds with a distinct set of illnesses. Inorganic arsenic is a known carcinogen. BPA (bisphenol A), found in plastics, dental sealants, and the linings of tin cans, is suspected in certain birth defects and developmental delays in children, some cancers, and disturbances in endocrine and hormone function. Both chlorinated dioxins and PCBs come to us mainly in fatty meats, dairy products, and fish; like BPA, they may link to birth defects and developmental delays in children and to cancers, as well as to malfunctions of the nervous and immune systems. The pesticide residues enter our bodies via the foods they are used on, as well as in drinking water; they are associated with a similar roll call of disorders.

Stepping back and looking at the entire list of 214 industrial chemicals creates the creepy feeling that nothing is safe: toxins waft our way in house dust or air, from water and soil, or by off-gassing from a long litany of objects from paint and carpeting to computer consoles and furniture.

The body is an ecosystem of sorts, an exquisitely coordinated mass of disparate units functioning within a whole. And like any ecosystem, the body can be invaded by foreign substances that muck up the works. Quantifying how many such invaders our bodies harbor has been the quest of studies on bioaccumulation like the one Lerner and Patton participated in to assay this biological buildup over a lifetime. Bioaccumulation has become its own corner of medical science, with studies suggesting that virtually everyone alive on this planet harbors a stew of toxic substances.

By now thousands of people have been tested, and everyone has been found to harbor some version or another of this molecular stew. The biomonitoring program at the U.S. Centers for Disease Control has a massive project under way that measures people's exposure to toxic substances by assessing metabolites of toxins in their blood or urine. This gives a picture of what actually has been absorbed by our bodies, rather than what is in our proximity. This shift from measuring pollutants in our water, air, or soil to what has melded itself into our biology has led to related shifts in thinking about medical etiology and chemical risk.

One emerging medical model for these chemical invasions holds that ill effects can emerge slowly, over decades, from cumulative chemical exposures at doses so low they are measured in parts per million. For toxicology, this marks a shift away from the traditional approach of searching for a chemical's risk only at high doses from short-term exposures. The high-dose/short-exposure model applies more readily to, say, the safety of a painter who uses solvents on his job. But the alternative low-doses-over-decades model seems more apt for a child growing up with small daily exposures to risky chemicals from everyday objects—or to any one of us.

For instance, an emerging consensus in oncology holds that a person's lifetime exposure to many small amounts of cancer-causing agents can be just as toxic as a few big doses of carcinogens. This model of causation rejects the search for a single smoking gun—some substance that in itself fosters cancer—but rather looks to a person's lifetime, cumulative exposure to a wide range of chemicals that trigger cell mutation. This continual barrage of mutagens can finally overwhelm the immune system's ability to kill off mutant cells and so resist cancer. Our risk of cancer, in this view, reflects the sum total of day-to-day doses of carcinogenic molecules shed into our air, food, and water.

Dr. Martha Herbert, a pediatric neurologist at Harvard Medical School, points to the tens of thousands of manufactured compounds that are now found peppering nature in some three billion potential combinations, and the fact that no one knows all the ways these chemical concoctions might impact an infant's neural development. One of the greatest human dangers from this slew of molecules, Dr. Herbert reasons, comes when a child's fast-growing organs, budding central nervous system, and hummingbird-like rapid metabolism get exposed to—and voraciously incorporate—small amounts of foreign molecules, sustaining biological damage that may not surface for years.

The brain has a special vulnerability to interference from invading chemicals because, of all organs, it utilizes the widest variety of molecules to send the chemical messages that coordinate our mental life and biological functions. This very design means there are that many more ways molecules from outside the body can disrupt what goes on if they happen to interact with any of countless neural chemical reactions. Another reason for the brain's vulnerability is its rapid metabolism: the brain uses one-third of the body's energy supply, and thousands of chemicals affect its metabolic operation, which manages how well our cells handle energy.

A state-of-the-art analysis by Dr. Herbert and her colleagues of the genes commonly found in people with autism revealed that a large number have nothing to do with the neural specifics of autism, but rather reflect a person's vulnerability to environmental stress and inflammation. Dr. Herbert proposes that kids with autism have a genetic vulnerability to disturbances in their metabolism's management of how their cells handle oxygen and produce energy, and of their immune system's reactions to infections or allergens.

For these kids it takes less environmental stress to reach a tipping point into illness. Two things that can lead to this tipping point are systemic inflammation and what's called "oxidative stress," where too many free radicals—sticky molecules that cause havoc in our cells—lead to mutations of DNA and vulnerability to diseases like cancer. These two conditions go hand in hand with each other and, in combination with a unique susceptibility from other genetic patterns, express themselves in the spectrum of autistic disorders (as well as in seemingly unrelated symptoms common in children with autism, like diabetes, allergies, and asthma).

"What we are looking at is a breakdown of our body resiliency, our physical ability to bounce back from challenges," Dr. Herbert says. She sees this vulnerability as part of a much larger medical picture, one that may go a long way toward explaining the mystery of why the so-called diseases of civilization are increasing in affluent societies but are relatively rare in poorer ones. These include endocrine disorders like diabetes and autoimmune disorders like lupus, multiple sclerosis, and asthma.

As Dr. Herbert told me, she and her colleagues "began to wonder if all these different diseases aren't the same underlying biological process with different outward, visible end results. We're always producing free radicals, and in the right amounts they are part of how the cell balances itself. If they outpace the body's ability to clear them, you get three things: inflammation, oxidative stress, and trouble."

The immune system ordinarily produces short-lasting inflammation while fighting infections, but when a defect in turning inflammation off occurs, a condition that should only be temporary becomes ongoing. Dr. Herbert explains, "If the natural systems that clear free radicals get hit by a chemical that slows them down or otherwise interferes, you get stuck in a state where you run treacherously low on antioxidants, which shifts your biology to oxidative stress and chronic inflammation."

This model fits with a corner of biological science called "epigenetics," which studies, among other dynamics of the genome, how molecules from inside or outside the body turn our genes on or off. The chemical compounds known to cause oxidative stress and chronic inflammation, Dr. Herbert says, include "lead, mercury, alcohol, diesel fuel, pesticides—there's a litany that goes into the hundreds. We're all getting inflamed by this toxic cocktail. This seems to be a major common pathway for a host of diseases. The more toxins you dump in, the sooner it will occur and among more people."

There seems to be a tipping point where the body's burden of harmful chemicals overcomes its ability to handle them anymore.

The specific malady that results depends on what we're exposed to and how our unique genetic profile responds. Perhaps for some children the outcome may be autism. But other people with a different genetic profile or exposure at a different point in life might develop any of a range of medical problems from diabetes and ischemic heart disease to chronic obstructive pulmonary disease (COPD) and asthma.

This emerging causal model holds that all these diseases share a single root phase, chronic inflammation. Years of steady inflammation undermine the endocrine and cardiovascular systems, and the immune system's ability to fight the beginning of some cancers, while the constant irritation of lung pathways prepares the way for COPD. So medical science now proposes a new umbrella term: "chronic systemic inflammatory syndrome," which eventually can become life-threatening in any of several ways.

Take COPD, a precursor of emphysema, which has always been seen as a sad medical end stage for smokers. A worldwide study of COPD produced a surprising result: growing rates of emphysema in people who have *never* smoked. As more and more people live in cities where they breathe particulate-laden air, nonsmokers are developing COPD too. Over the lifetime of those living now in China alone, nonsmokers' exposure to polluted fumes will be responsible for almost two million "excess deaths," according to an editorial about the COPD findings in *The Lancet*.

COPD reflects the body's accumulated burden from exposure to lung irritants in the air—auto exhaust, cigarette smoke, dust, or chemicals like those that waft through an office from the computer printer. We all are susceptible. Worldwide, COPD rates are predicted to increase because airborne particles, like factory smoke, auto exhaust, and indoor pollutants, are all on the rise. By middle age, nonsmokers catch up with smokers in rates of COPD.

Whereas a lifetime accumulation from tiny exposures sets the stage for disease, the implication is that *any* exposures to chemicals that may enhance inflammation or otherwise hamper our body's function are a health concern. From that perspective, any synthetic chemical can be seen as a gamble with nature: who knows what unforeseen biological reactions it might trigger? No one does, at least for the vast majority of man-made chemicals our body takes in daily. All day long we play a game of chance, gambling that what's used to make the things we find so useful will not harm us in the long run.

How regulators think about toxicity makes all the difference in what we end up exposing ourselves to. In evaluating chemicals, European toxicologists start by measuring a substance's inherent toxicity. Then, if there is potential human toxicity, the panel weighs scientific evidence to assess the chemical's potential for harm. They are guided by a better-safe-than-sorry approach—called the "precautionary principle"—which means if a chemical is merely suspected of being harmful, it is banned.

Our approach in the United States assumes that even if a chemical has some inherent toxicity, it may still be safe to use under normal—or at least certain—conditions. The U.S. government requires conclusive evidence that people exposed to that chemical will be harmed before banning a suspect substance. Such definitive evidence of harm can be hard to muster; far more chemicals are deemed "safe" in this country than in Europe. As a result, there are countless chemicals commonly used in American products (and other countries with similar standards or with none at all) that are banned in European countries.

The stage for this dilemma was set long ago by a decision made in 1979, when the newly formed Environmental Protection Agency drew up a list of about sixty-two thousand industrial chemicals and ruled that their use could continue without any testing or review of any sort. Those grandfathered chemicals included some substances known to be highly toxic, like ethylbenzene, an industrial solvent that medical studies show to be a powerful neurotoxin. But the most disturbing problem, according to a report by the Government Accountability Office, is that thirty years later the EPA has required testing of only a few hundred or so of those chemicals. The rest are mysteries.

That contrasts to the approach being taken in Europe by a program called REACH (for Registration, Evaluation, and Authorization of Chemicals). REACH has an ambitious goal: testing and evaluating all those tens of thousands of chemicals that were grandfathered into use in everyday products by the EPA back in 1979—plus all the new ones that have come into use since then but have not yet been rigorously evaluated by an independent body. Starting in 2009, the European Chemicals Agency will publish lists of chemicals to be tested in successive waves, a heads-up for manufacturers who might want to start finding alternatives. For the chemicals that flow through the world economy, REACH will generate a new kind of periodic table, tabulating their hazardousness rather than their molecular structure.

"In concept I agree with what REACH is trying to do," commented a toxicologist at Procter & Gamble. "There are many chemicals in commerce today that were grandfathered into regulatory systems and for which there are little publicly available safety data. REACH is a way to make that information more available." P&G, he added, has long had its own standards for safety, whether or not the government required filing papers on a chemical's toxicity. As he put it, "We'd never put a chemical in the marketplace if it wasn't safe."

When I asked another toxicologist about the possibility that lifelong, cumulative exposures to otherwise "safe" chemicals might lead to an inflammatory syndrome, the idea was new to him. As a scientist, he raised pragmatic questions, like how to quantify an inflammatory response in people, and telling ones, such as whether studies have as yet shown a definitive relationship between a person's level of inflammation and lifetime accumulation of chemicals. His conclusion: "It's an interesting theory, and I can see it may have some merit. But there are lots of empirical questions. The science of toxicology has evolved over the last twenty years, and I suspect it will continue to evolve."

Some toxicologists argue their discipline may have a blind spot when it comes to the stew of chemicals we breathe, drink, or otherwise absorb over the course of life. One step in this awakening came in the journal *Neurotoxicology,* in a challenge to the methods used by toxicologists for decades to test the hazards of chemicals. Deborah Cory-Slechta, a toxicologist at the Robert Wood Johnson Medical School, found that exposing lab animals to the pesticides paraquat and maneb caused the degeneration in the dopamine circuits that underlies Parkinson's disease in humans. The damage occurred only if the exposure to one of the compounds was repeated (in this case, in utero and in adulthood) or through exposure to both pesticides in combination. Paraquat and maneb are quite distinct molecules, but the *mixture* or *number* of exposures produced the signature damage for Parkinson's.

Such findings—and there are dozens of others like these—create a paradigm challenge for toxicology: an exposure just one time to one of these chemicals resulted in no discernible damage. And up to this point that method—assessing the tissue damage from exposure to a single chemical or class of chemicals for a limited time—has been the gold standard in tests of a chemical's toxicity, our early warning system for protection. But it tells us nothing about how a given chemical might damage tissue if we are exposed to it in combination with others or over the course of a life span. The reality is that we all are exposed to a mix of countless chemicals continually, a predicament for which toxicologists as yet have no assessment method.

As Cory-Slechta points out, the standard methods of assessing safe levels of exposure to a chemical fail to address the environmental realities. Synergy among synthetic chemicals lodged in our bodies challenges the assumptions underlying risk analysis calculations. For one, these tests simply look to see if a compound kills cells. But very low doses may fail to kill cells while nevertheless damaging the cells' ability to signal other cells or otherwise interfere with their functioning. And, Cory-Slechta adds, a single-chemical, one-time exposure of healthy adults tells us nothing about how a substance might impact children, the chronically ill, or the aged—groups with greater susceptibility—nor about the realities, say, of breathing polluted air, a mixture of countless kinds of ultrafine particles whose chemical composition varies from place to place and day to day.

As Cory-Slechta diplomatically puts it to her colleagues in neurotoxicology, "Information on the scope and extent of chemical exposures in humans, while increasing, remains limited." Cory-Slechta proposes her discipline switch its thinking to a "multi-hit" model, in which insults to different target sites within a specific biological system, either over time from one molecule or all at once from many, harm a biological system. That, she adds, would be a major first step in toxicology's main mission, safeguarding human health. Current methods, she notes, may offer inadequate protection given this new understanding.

So what are we to do in the meantime?

THE AMYGDALA GOES SHOPPING

If you want to start a brand of shampoo, you might go to a gigantic personal care products factory deep in the maze of industrial parks scattered through central New Jersey, where they can offer ingredient design as well as manufacture it. You meet with a factory-based formulator, who will come up with a unique recipe for you. A businessman who is a partner in a hair care products company founded by a famous hair stylist told me, "Everybody in the business goes to these plants; they do the R&D for all the shampoos. There are no secrets in the industry—all the ingredients are listed."

Shampoo retails in a three-tier market—mass-market chains, hair salons, and upscale department stores—each with progressively higher price points. Products at the bottom, in the big-box stores, have little flexibility in ingredients. Those in salons and department stores have more freedom to pick specific substances without pricing themselves out of their market.

The giants in the industry do their own R&D and manufacture in their own plants. Nonetheless, they use virtually the same ingredients and methods. As in any business, cost considerations come first. The businessman told me, "When we looked for ingredients of our shampoo, it's not just what you want the shampoo to do for your hair, but the price point that determines what you can make. We told the formulator that we needed to hit a total cost of $2.85 in order to be able to sell to our customer—a big-box store that would retail the product.

"He said, 'You can't get what you want at that price.'

"But after several months and many rounds of sample formulations we ended up getting pretty much what we hoped for at that price point. But for organic ingredients we'd have had to pay much more."

Every shampoo contains four basic types of chemicals. The first is surfactants, cleaning agents that strip dirt off hair. But surfactants are harsh and can leave hair dry and brittle, so formulators add a conditioning agent to rectify the pH balance. Foaming agents make it bubbly; fragrances give a shampoo its unique identity. Shampoos can have dozens and dozens of ingredients fine-tuning their unique appeal in these four basic categories.

Not all those ingredients are necessarily benign. An industrial ecologist told me, indignantly, that he had recently learned that the shampoo he and his wife use contains 1,4-dioxane, a suspected human carcinogen. That chemical is not listed in the ingredients; it's there unintentionally in trace amounts as a residue from the chemical process used to make a foaming agent.

If you want to buy a completely safe shampoo, you might want to skip one that features a greenish-sounding name hinting at botanical wonders. Some of the fifty or so ingredients in this shampoo have been linked to cancer, reproductive toxicity in women, allergies, and disruptions of the immune and endocrine systems—to name just a short part of a long list. Not that a single rinse, or even years of hair washing, will trigger any of these maladies; using the shampoo may only heighten their risk a tiny, tiny bit, if at all.

By contrast, Skin Free Extra Moisturizing Soap & Shampoo Bar may be one of the safest shampoos around; its three simple ingredients—palm oil, cacao seed butter, and coconut oil—threaten no hazard to the health of those who use it as a shampoo. Or so I gather from Skin Deep, that cosmetics hazard–rating website (discussed in Chapter 8) operated by the Environmental Working Group, an outfit that crusades against toxic ingredients in personal care products. The average American woman applies one to two dozen personal care products daily, and Skin Deep tells which of these contain chemicals that might better be kept away from the body's biggest organ, the skin.

Despite the air of natural essences promoted by cosmetic packaging, beauty products depend greatly on synthetic chemicals for whatever elixir-like action they may have. In March 2005, the European Union implemented a rule requiring that any product placed on the body must be scientifically assessed for toxic effects. The chemicals in such products are successively being tested for "CMRs"—carcinogens, mutagens, or reproductive toxins—and any suspect chemicals found are to be banned from their ingredients or have their use severely restricted, at least in Europe.

But in the United States, the safety of the estimated 10,500 chemicals used in personal care products and cosmetics has been largely taken for granted—the Environmental Working Group claims that close to 90 percent have never been assessed by the FDA or the cosmetics industry. In the EU, these chemicals are being rigorously assessed quarterly by a committee of toxicologists drawn from scientific labs across the continent.

Drawing on such research, as well as on years of previous studies, Skin Deep evaluates the health risks of cosmetic ingredients by matching each one to what medical databases reveal about its level of hazard or safety. Using this methodology, for example, the website rates the Skin Free Extra Moisturizing Soap & Shampoo Bar as one of the top ten brands at the very safest level. In contrast, that shampoo with the eco-ish name languishes among the bottom ten of the 1,051 shampoos rated.

The website summarizes where a given shampoo lies along the safe-to-hazardous spectrum by giving it a green light for safe, yellow for moderate risk, and red for beware. This easy summary is probably all most consumers care about. But for those who want specifics, the website also offers a list that enumerates each ingredient in terms of the health concerns signaled by scientific findings. So, for example, the site says that BHA (a preservative that keeps the shampoo's oils from going rancid) has been linked to cancer, endocrine disruption, allergies and/or immunotoxicity, and organ system toxicity and has been found to accumulate in tissue, so that the more that is used, the higher these risks become. On a hazard scale of 1 to 10, BHA rates a 10.

This website evens the information symmetry between buyers and sellers when it comes to potential health risks in the 55,000 personal care products the site rates. When I mentioned the website and its evaluations to a high-level executive of one shampoo brand, he had never heard of Skin Deep and was surprised to learn that customers were using this data. Skeptical, he asked me whether shoppers would actually bother to go to a website to check on the safety of cosmetics they buy, let alone let it guide their choices.

Apparently they would. As of the most recent day I checked, since the website launched in 2004 there had been 64,328,621 visits. How many of those hits are from shoppers, and how many from cosmetics brand managers checking their products' ratings or from shampoo formulators, no one can say. In an ecologically intelligent world all three would be numbered among those millions. Think how many more consumers would use these ratings if they were available in stores, on the shelves next to the shampoo. If they were, I can't imagine any executive of a hair product not being aware of Skin Deep—and not reformulating their product to ensure a good rating.

From the perspective of neuroscience, Skin Deep caters to the apprehensions of the amygdala, the central node in our brain's radar for danger. These circuits continually scan for anything that might be a threat to us and triggers the fight-flight-freeze reaction that catapults us into a frenzy. When the amygdala goes shopping, it puts us on the alert for potential dangers in what we buy. The very possibility of hazard in a product triggers the brain's most primitive safety strategy: avoid what *might* be dangerous. Objective, rational evaluations of safety have nothing to do with it. The amygdala operates by an emotional logic, with a singular decision rule: better safe than sorry.

This overly cautious circuitry may have played a role, for instance, in the repulsion at made-in-China products that swept through America in 2007, starting with a series of alarms in the summer that reverberated through the holiday shopping season. For months the news featured a succession of widely publicized rapid-fire recalls of toxic pet food and toothpaste and lead-laced toys, all from Chinese factories. The panic over these marketing disasters witnessed the coining of a new term, "China-free," proposed as a label for products to reassure shoppers about their safety.

At the peak of the scare, product safety experts advised parents to find alternatives to toys made in China. That advice placates the amygdala, the brain's threat circuitry that drives jittery parents to be extracautious. This threat-avoiding strategy prevails even though the brain's centers for rational analysis may know full well that most playthings made in China are perfectly safe. The logical truism that all goods from China are not tainted (nor are all tainted products from China) matters little to the aroused amygdala. The amygdala's excess of caution has nothing to do with a rational weighing of risks and everything to do with how its design for survival pilots us through a world of potential dangers.

An initial scare primes the amygdala to be on guard against anything similar in the future. Specific circuits within the amygdala are specialized for the tasks of remembering a danger—and connecting a sense of fear or dread to the object. It evokes that same dollop of angst whenever that thing we dread comes our way again.

A neural snapshot of the shopper's radar for danger comes from the new field of neuroeconomics, which studies how a person's brain functions during, say, a purchasing decision. I spoke about wary shoppers with Tania Singer of the University of Zurich, who may be the first neuroscientist anywhere to hold a faculty position in an economics department. As Professor Singer told me, "When a mom sees a product that she thinks is poison, her amygdala gets her heart pumping. This alarm signal gets picked up by the insula," a part of the neocortex, the thinking brain, that has strong connections to the emotional centers. "The insula translates these feelings of alarm into words, interpreting them as the strong thought 'I don't like that product.' "

For instance, Jill Cashen, mother of a five-year-old, told *The Washington Post* she had confiscated every single doll in her daughter's collection of Polly Pockets when Mattel recalled some of them as a choking hazard. Even though consulting the Mattel website made it clear to her that most of the dolls had not been declared a hazard, Cashen was so alarmed that she seized even the innocent ones. As she explained, "I felt like we couldn't really be sure, so I took them all away," adding, "as a parent, it's really frustrating and scary."

That reaction—or, more accurately, overreaction—makes perfect sense to Baba Shiv, a professor of marketing at Stanford Business School, who studies the interplay between rational thought and feelings in purchasing decisions. "When cognition and emotion are involved in a decision, emotions outrule cognition most every time," he told me.

One of the strongest emotions is disgust, a vital reaction for the survival of any species. Nature has hard wired the brains of all mammals to recognize the smell, taste, and look of things that are toxic or otherwise nauseating. Better to have something that's suspicious and possibly dangerous elicit a spontaneous "Ick!" reaction than to blithely eat whatever we come across. This lifesaving design has morphed in humans to go beyond the realm of what we might eat to the range of what we perceive. Our brains find even weird beliefs or bad business propositions disgusting.

In an experiment, some restaurantgoers were served a sample glass of a "new California wine," while others who got the same wine were told it was a "new North Dakota" wine. In reality both wines were the same bargain bin Cabernet Sauvignon. But when patrons thought the wine was from North Dakota, they drank less of it, and, intriguingly, also ate less of their meal, compared to those who had that same wine labeled from California. There was, of course, nothing wrong with the North Dakota version except for people's expectations of what that wine might be like—and that dimming of prospective pleasure spilled over into how diners felt about their food.

When a wine label or a product brand fails to impress—or repels—us, our brain shows a lessening of activity in a strip of the orbitofrontal cortex, the neural zone that connects our thoughts to our feelings. In another version of the wine study, this one using brain imaging, volunteers were told that a glass of wine (again one and the same) was either from a cheap bottle or from a pricey one. The supposed high-end wine evoked higher activity in that orbitofrontal brain zone, signifying positive interest; the same wine masquerading as low end lowered activity, in a distinctive neural brain signature seen also when people feel disinterest, boredom, or disgust.

That same lowering of brain activity shows up when we face an unpleasant loss, whether when gambling or playing the stock market. If the loss really upsets us, that disappointment recruits the amygdala, which registers fear and feelings of aversion, and the insula, a site of disgust, among other states of mind. On the other hand, simply seeing the logo of a brand we like creates the opposite pattern, with the key orbitofrontal strip becoming more active in the brain reaction that promotes sales.

Hilke Plassmann, the neuroeconomist at Caltech who did the brain-imaging study of wine drinkers, says this boost indicates the "neural signal for brand preference. It creates the experience 'This is the brand I like.' Our cognitive model or expectation determines the neural activity. Deactivation in that orbitofrontal region is a sign something has a negative value. I would expect to see similar neural signs of disinterest or disgust if I gave you a chocolate bar or some orange juice and told you it was made with child labor."

Disgust reflects our hardwired programming, ensuring that we shun the rotten, the poisonous, and the revolting. Acquired distastes—things we learn to find disgusting—can become potent market forces. The negative market power of disgust may explain a common claim about marketing, that "bad news"—like revelations of sweatshops or toxic ingredients—has more impact on what people choose *not* to buy than does good news on what they buy. Campaigns to boycott products because of unsafe factories, or because fishing practices endanger dolphins, leverage this effect. A poll in Britain found that half of shoppers said they had punished a company by boycotting its products; an international poll found that between 40 and 50 percent of respondents had shunned a company's products for "poor practices."

"When you have an emotion like disgust, your reaction is not just psychological—it's neurological," I was told by Richard Davidson, director of the Laboratory for Affective Neuroscience at the University of Wisconsin. Davidson's research group made brain images while volunteers were given samples of five tastes that they had rated from highly pleasant to highly distasteful; as usual in these studies, the actual liquids were given with various positive or negative labels. When the cue was given that a taste was highly unpleasant—though in actuality it was only mildly so—the volunteers' brains reacted as though it were indeed extremely unpleasant.

"The cognitive cue overrides the actual experience," Davidson told me. "The information you have about a product is such a cue. Getting distasteful information about an item elicits the brain's response for disgust."

Shopper disgust has predictable consequences for marketing. "If you feel that kind of distaste for a product while you also consider another with a better profile," Davidson explains, "there's a contrast effect, which means you'll have an even stronger preference for the better one, because the other one seems so bad."

The contrast effect has been known for ages among salespeople. If you want a product to look good, first show the shopper an inferior product. If you want someone to buy an expensive item, start by showing them something even pricier. The mind's computations of value shift with the basis for comparison—all value is in contrast to something else.

When I described the notion of radical transparency to Craig Wynett, a creative director at Procter & Gamble, he zeroed in on the trade-off between short term and long term that is critical to the way people make choices. "We are hardwired to focus on short-term benefits at the expense of much larger, long-term rewards. From the evolutionary standpoint, this shortsightedness makes perfect sense—at least it did a hundred thousand years ago."

Wynett attributes this bias to the legacy of living on the African savannah, where life could end on any given day and the take-whatever-you-can-get strategy paid. "Many of the big problems people have, from weight loss to addiction, are the result of the shortsightedness we inherited from our primeval ancestors. When consumers are at the point of sale, what drives them is the present situation—getting a pleasurable experience or getting rid of a pebble in their shoe. If in the process we can solve some long-term problems, all the better. But the long-term benefit plays a remarkably small role in the choice.

"Happily for humans—and marketers of products with long-term benefits—our shortsighted bad habits are, at least theoretically, reversible. The newer areas of the brain, the frontal lobes, can shut down our instinctual behaviors. This is not easy, though. My suspicion is that even if you give shoppers at the point of purchase the kind of information that's focused on long-term benefits, it just won't *feel* like the right choice—especially if you have to pay 20 percent more for this benefit. Rationally, X may be better for the planet in the future, but Y seems better right now."

In Wynett's view, that decision-making matrix shifts when what's revealed about a product has direct benefit for the shopper. "At the point of purchase you think with your emotions. If you find a product might have toxins, there's an immediate payoff in switching away from it to a safer choice. The long-term benefit is as hot neurally as the short-term one. Your switch makes cognitive sense, not just emotional; it will be a rational impulse, not an irrational one.

"So the trick," Wynette added, "is to find elements of your product that appeal to consumers' sense of what is important to them right now, and to make sure that those elements compare favorably to the equivalent features of the competitors' products."

PLAYING IT SAFE

When Bakelite was invented in 1907, the substance was a wonder: a gunk that could magically take and hold any shape—its remarkable flexibility lent it the apt name "plastic." Bakelite was more durable and far cheaper than the Victorian-era materials it replaced, such as bois durci ("hardened wood") made from natural resins and an imitation ivory made from a creamy celluloid concoction extracted from wood fiber. With Bakelite a handy industrial application was found for an otherwise useless effluvium of the increasingly popular new fuel of the time, petroleum.

As the radio craze caught on, Bakelite found its way into American homes in the ubiquitous cabinets of tabletop radios, and found uses from the distributor cap of the Model A Ford to bangles and pool balls. During World War II, Bakelite and its close chemical cousins gave way to our modern versions of plastic, like vinyls. Like other plastics, vinyl hardens into a woodlike rigidity. But the addition of softening chemicals allowed vinyl to do what stiff Bakelite could not: bend a bit. To give vinyl the softness that makes plastic so useful in everything from IV bags in hospitals and "rubber" ducks in kids' bathtubs, phthalates are added, resulting in an oily-textured product with a long shelf life.

The Phthalate Information Center (an industry-sponsored website with links to the Vinyl Institute) describes the wide range of products that contain the chemical: "From their use in medical devices to toys to cars to homes, flexible vinyl products help make our lives better and safer. And in hospitals and emergency rooms, they help save lives. They make our homes more decorative, easier to clean, more energy efficient and durable. Flexible vinyl products are high-performing and cost effective; their performance is difficult or impossible to match with competitive substitutes. They save money for consumers."

On the question of phthalates' safety, the Center notes, "For more than fifty years, they have been a key ingredient in fragrances and in nail polish. One kind of phthalate fixes the fragrance in perfumes and other products to make it last longer. Another type is used in nail polish (as well as in tool handles and outdoor signs) to help prevent chipping and breaking. Safety reviews by European and American scientific panels have specifically cleared phthalates for use in toys and in nail polish. The different reviews use phrases such as 'safe as used,' or 'no concern,' or 'no demonstrated health risk.' No governmental review has found any phthalate unsafe as used in products for the general public."

That is all true, so far as it goes. But phthalates represent a large class of compounds in dispute. Public health activists and researchers in environmental medicine warn that "chemicals of concern," phthalates among them, contribute to or cause a wide range of disease, from autism and reproductive disorders to cancer.

That dance of accusation, defense, and counteraccusation occurs whenever an industrial chemical comes under question. Most of this argument goes on in the backstage of our collective awareness, surfacing in the media from time to time in reports of some alarming medical finding or other that will immediately be countered by soothing reassurances from industry.

The mile-wide gap in the scientific debate between environmental health activists and the chemical industry may never narrow sufficiently to reach consensus. But from a business perspective, there's a more significant conceptual gap: industry thinks about toxicity in one way; consumers in another.

A week or so after I decided not to give my grandson that little yellow-painted—and possibly lead-laced—toy car I mentioned in the opening pages of this book, I was in a store where I saw a rack of locally made wooden toys. One was a niftily designed car with an aerodynamic shape that swooped around in a way that let the passenger compartment double as a handle. The box it came in— itself made from recycled cardboard—assured me that the maple wood was sustainably harvested in Vermont and that the paints used were nontoxic.

That's the toy car I gave my grandson.

Did it matter to me that this car cost several times the price of the first car? A bit. After all, he could have enjoyed playing with either one just as much. But as I mulled it over, I recalled that his family lives in a small town where kids' toys are recycled via a community giveaway bin, finding endless new homes. The imaginative design was quite appealing, and this toy was bigger and better built than the first car.

But mainly I felt that my peace of mind about his well-being was well worth the premium. So I shelled out the extra few dollars.

That decision was in keeping with the paradigm of environmental health, the emerging medical specialty that analyzes how chemicals of concern impact our biology. We can't undo many of the toxins our tissues have accumulated—but we can stop adding more to the mix. The smart strategy here is to be wary and avoid exposure to potentially hazardous substances as much as possible. This school of thought tells us it's wise to be concerned and cautious, shunning products that contain chemicals of concern.

Even if these chemicals are not proven dangers (and it may never be possible to prove such danger to the satisfaction of all parties), the prudent shopper would likely avoid them when possible. Ecological health holds that any step that reduces biochemical stress on an organic system will have a cascade of benefits. Since our total body burden of toxins increases our risk for a range of diseases, the better choice is to avoid whatever adds to that malevolent accumulation.

When toxicologists in the United States assess a chemical's safety, they test for inherent toxicity—the hazard a substance poses to an organism, such as causing tissue damage in cell cultures or laboratory animals. They assume that this impact does not necessarily mean the same substance in a product will harm humans; more testing will be needed to arrive at a scientific consensus.

In contrast, the precautionary principle as applied in European countries means a chemical with potential risks can be banned despite the absence of a definitive scientific consensus. The EU already outlaws toxins that are common ingredients in much of the rest of the world, including the United States (an odd contrast to the slowness of many European countries to ban smoking in public places). So a prudent shopper would likely prefer products containing chemicals that are REACH-safe—if he or she only knew which ones those are.

To be sure, a plethora of U.S. government regulations strive to protect the public from toxic ingredients. But these standards for safe limits may include arbitrary boundaries, given some thinking in medical biology about how our bodies interact with environmental chemicals. Take the U.S. government's rule for lead—levels of 600 parts per million in a product are deemed safe and will not contribute to cognitive decline. But studies find that the loss of IQ points when a child has high lead levels in her blood are at the upper end of a continuous gradient—adverse behavioral and cognitive impacts don't abruptly begin with the arbitrary exposure level set by the government. So the American Academy of Pediatrics argues the limit should be far lower, just 40 parts per million. As Richard Canfield, a behavioral toxicologist at Cornell University, notes, "No one has ever found any evidence of a threshold below which lead has no effect" on a child's brain.

Those in environmental health and industrial toxicologists often apply different assumptions in judging toxicity. Such debates will never be settled—especially to the extent that those on either side of the issue argue from vested interest and each marshals evidence based on different underlying assumptions. In any case, there is no ultimate forum for determining the truth.

A toxicologist at a multinational consumer goods company offers a metaphor for thinking about toxicity in consumer products: Imagine a tiger in the wild and one in the zoo. The tiger itself is intrinsically dangerous, but the one behind bars is no danger at all. Chemicals in consumer products, he argues, are the same.

But that metaphor misses a point made by events at the San

Francisco Zoo the day before Christmas in 2007, when a tiger jumped over the wall and killed a zoogoer, mauling two others. Despite the zoo's implicit assurance that all was safe for visitors, the wall, it turns out, was three feet shorter than needed. Yet it had been in place for years. The zoo's administration was as stunned as anyone—they had assumed the wall was perfectly safe.

So it might be with industrial chemicals: as a steady stream of news items raises concerns about various suspected toxins in everyday items, the public grows more wary. In such an atmosphere of suspicion, a company's assurances that its products are utterly safe can ring hollow—once the amygdala goes on alert, suspicions rule over reason. Once a shopper loses trust in a product, brand loyalty evaporates.

And that is the point: at the moment of truth in a store's aisles, how *customers* perceive a product, matters more than how the manufacturer sees it. While companies can offer endless reassurances about product safety—and get federal regulators to agree with them—concerned customers are still likely to switch their purchase to a rival product they feel better about.

Such marketplace shifts make hair-splitting debates over what is or is not toxic a moot point. Even as that argument rages, it is being decided daily in the amygdalas of countless shoppers whose choices are swayed by the fact the toxicity issue has been raised at all. The amygdala shops for safety, driven by the neural "logic" of fear and disgust—just the chance that there may be danger to themselves or their family triggers the brain's alarm system, guiding a shopper away from a suspect product.

As information about the potential hazards of ingredients becomes available to customers in stores, many shoppers will go out of their way to avoid a product that is even potentially harmful. As Dr. Philippe Grandjean, head of the department of environmental medicine at the University of Southern Denmark, advises, "It is very unwise to wait until we have complete scientific truth. The prudent judgment is to protect human health."

An environmental health expert told me he became indignant when he noticed the sunscreen he was using on his small children contained oxybenzone, a chemical suspected of having carcinogenic properties when exposed to sunlight. "It's just what I don't want to put on my kids' foreheads. But if you tell this to companies, they'll say, 'Let's talk about risk assessment.' I say, 'No—I just want a sunscreen without any suspected carcinogens.' I like that sunscreen—I just want them to make it better."

Martha Herbert, the Harvard pediatric neurologist, observes that reassuring messages from companies that seek to discredit an unsettling research result about possible harmful impacts of industrial ingredients "are designed to calm the amygdala." By the same token, given the amygdala's worrywart role in decision making, it makes emotional sense that all of Skin Deep's evaluations are couched in terms of "concerns." Objectively speaking, there is no inarguable proof that even those shampoos rated most hazardous will actually cause or contribute to a serious health problem (minor troubles like rashes aside) in anyone who shampoos with them.

There may rarely be proof that a cosmetic ingredient poses a direct health threat, if only because most such hazards are cumulative and indirect, with a given chemical contributing to complex biological processes that might eventually lead to a disease. This complexity creates an inherent tension between the priorities of manufacturers and consumers.

Nonetheless, if I were a manager of a line of shampoo products, I'd much rather use ingredients that make my product last longer, smell better, clean more thoroughly, and build body in hair follicles better than my competitors'. In other words, I want to make the shampoo that consumers want to buy. Still, if I discover that some ingredient that adds one of these valued qualities has been found in a test on lab mice to have some untoward effect, it makes sense to drop it as an ingredient—even if there is no evidence showing a clear link to disease in humans.

Why? Consider how this piece of information affects a shopper browsing the shelf of shampoos in a local store. Given the new medical understanding of the danger to our body from the sum total of what we are exposed to—and following the precautionary principle—the safest bet would be to shop for items that minimize our cumulative exposures. If just as I'm deciding which shampoo to buy I discover a given brand contains ingredients that might be a health hazard, I will quickly choose the one that raises no concern.

The amygdala operates by a subcortical logic—the very possibility of a threat tips the scales toward a better-safe-than-sorry cost-benefit analysis. Business tends to operate via a cortical logic, deploying data in a rational manner. The discrepancy between the two modes of decision making can result in a disconnection, with consumers making purchase decisions from fears that hard-nosed business thinkers dismiss. In the future, though, as more product information makes its way to consumers, dismissing such concerns will almost always be risky, if not an outright mistake.

To the extent that chemicals are of genuine biological concern, they represent a novel case for economists, who deal with variables like cost and price but usually do not grapple with the environmental or health impacts for workers or consumers of chemicals in what we buy. But look at the debate over the safety of chemicals through the lens of marketplace information.

At present, consumer concerns have relatively little effect on the ingredients or chemicals used in the products we buy. But in a radically transparent marketplace, that equation shifts, allowing shoppers to make more informed decisions based on information that previously had been hidden. Companies may decide for any number of reasons to use chemicals of concern in their products. But once shoppers know what items contain those worrisome chemicals, they are less likely to buy them. And that will ultimately tip the scales for how things are made.

TOUGH QUESTIONS

With the advent of methods for radical transparency, what the marketplace offers today may become out of synch with what shoppers will want tomorrow. These new approaches to managing information herald a coming flood of data about the heretofore unnoticed consequences of a host of common ingredients in everyday products. What had previously been successful brands may be in danger of becoming tainted in our minds.

For companies, staying ahead of the waves of consumer preferences that point-of-purchase transparency seems on track to create requires early detection of which aspects of products are problematic, so that companies can develop better alternatives—sooner rather than later. To judge such risks, businesses need the executive's equivalent of mindful shopping, gathering new information and acting on it rather than reflexively denying the facts (as cigarette companies did for decades with evidence on cancer). Decision makers need to be among the first to know what's coming. And everyone in a core group of decision makers will need to see more clearly than ever before how to weigh the risks and realize the benefits.

Art Kleiner is editor in chief of the review *Strategy + Business*. When we met over lunch in the boisterous atmosphere of Metrazur, a restaurant perched in an alcove overlooking the giant concourse of Grand Central Station in New York City, I posed Kleiner a hypothetical business scenario: Let's say in the near future the field of epigenetics, the study of which molecules turn what genes on and off, begins to identify certain industrial chemicals as possible triggers of genes known to be active in specific diseases. Those chemicals happen to be crucial to a wide range of products. What should a company do? Kleiner rattled off a series of tough questions that skeptical executives would have to answer before considering changing their company's use of such chemicals:

Do we care about it? This raises the fundamental issue of values, priorities, and ethics. Executives who embrace social responsibility or environmentalism as a business imperative will answer this with an enthusiastic yes. Those whose business decisions are driven by financial concerns alone will drop the inquiry here, except to the extent that there may be easy cost savings. But there are a great many businesspeople who are somewhere in the middle—for whom bottom line concerns mix with other considerations—who might continue down this loose decision tree.

What would we lose if we ignore this? The answer may be company or brand reputation, or market share. Such an answer would likely revive the discussion even among those who initially answered no above.

How would we have to change our thinking? For a company to leverage this opportunity, its core group—the most influential decision makers—would have to come on board. The danger here is groupthink, the collective denial that the company's products have flaws or dangers. The cigarette industry's fight against the data on cancer stands as the classic case: the industry won a pitched legal battle for decades, but lost the war. Such groupthink can be seen in Detroit's resistance to hybrids before the oil price shock hit, even as Toyota's Prius grabbed market share from it. In contrast, the U.S. toy industry responded to revelations of high lead levels, and the ensuing enormous public alarm, by calling for an independent agency to inspect and certify the safety of its toys.

Another answer lies in shifting perspective beyond the short term. "We're caught up in the moment—it's tough to take the necessary corrective when there's no immediate crisis," a top executive at a global consumer goods company told me. "Part of making a decision like this is trying to find a net present value in these long-term choices."

One cognitive trap here involves the costs that have already been sunk into present ways of operating. The executive added, "If you've invested ten million dollars on Project X or a new factory, financial theory says that because that money's already spent, it should have zero effect on your decision for what to do next. But emotionally, almost no one can ignore it. The decision to pursue a short-term gain rather than to follow a long-term plan that might not pay back right away is, to some degree, a decision around risk. And for someone who wants to manage risk, the short term is the more appealing answer."

What's the harm? Is the evidence refutable? Raising the flag of doubt was the tactic deployed by the tobacco industry for decades to fight the accumulating medical evidence linking cigarette smoke to lung cancer. This tactic remains in use by many industries. Another version of this don't-rock-the-boat school of thought makes the counterargument that what we do is no worse than what our competitors are doing. These spins satisfy those who would rather not make any change at all.

What information exists that I need to be aware of? Answers here might come from Life Cycle Assessment, among other sources.

What are the costs of changing? Product ingredients have been chosen because they have some benefit—they add pliability, durability, shelf life, texture, and the like. Any switch in ingredients or processing risks a drop in quality, increases in costs, lower margins, and lower profits, not to mention a drop in sales—plus internal chaos in supply chain management. In the past, businesses contemplating such shifts did not have clear information on the risks and had to guess at the benefits of changing. But executives have had a much more detailed sense of the costs of changing, or good reason to fear what these costs might be. So the result has been inertia: why change?

Do we really want to know? "What if we find out we've been poisoning kids with additives in what we sell?" was the way Kleiner put it, posing an extreme case for facing discomforting facts. Finding out something like this would raise both emotional and legal issues. One corporate strategy has been to leave the actual risk unknown and justify any change a company makes on the grounds that customers want it, rather than admit some risk, which might open the way to liability problems.

If we decide to change, how do we titrate our response to fit the cost-

benefit calculus? Exactly when, fiscally speaking, does virtue pay? For instance, a book publisher tells me that he does not use recycled paper because at present it's too expensive. "But," he added, "we always talk about finding ways both to cut cost and do the right things—those imperatives fight each other. But one day those lines will cross. We're monitoring what others are doing about this, talking to paper mills about costs. Soon there will come a tipping point when one publisher makes the shift, and the rest of us will follow."

What are the logistics of change? Any major change will cost money and the aggravations of changing. Some suppliers might have to be dropped or persuaded to alter their practices or sources. Long-standing relationships and priorities might need to switch.

Are the changes worth it? Those executives who hold that the "business of business is business" will be more reluctant to change; their singular mission lies in maximizing shareholder value. Such executives will be reluctant adopters, at best—until they see how ecological transparency might help their company prosper. Kleiner's questions address the understandable skepticism of this group.

The subtext of these ten questions and their answers revolves around values, which dictate strategic priorities. These answers assume as the standard business mind-set a Friedman-esque guiding principle in which all that matters is the bottom line. Ecological changes are fine only if they bring no net effect in costs or increases in sales. This mind-set sees social responsibility as an irritation, a distraction from business fundamentals.

But that view becomes outmoded the more ecologically intelligent the public becomes, and to the degree that market shifts make such trade-offs pay. In theory, as marketplace transparency grows, stonewalling or ignoring data works less well; when we, the customers, know the facts, we will act on them anyway. Ecologically intelligent companies will be proactive: businesses will want to be the first to know about epigenetic data, collaborate with suppliers to make shifts, see marketplace feedback as actionable information, and perceive the change as a business opportunity that will bring added value, not just added costs.

THE ECOLOGICAL EVOLUTION

Throughout 2004 and 2005 Kerala, a state in India's south, underwent a severe drought, with a 60 percent decrease in annual rainfall. As crops failed, small farmers suffered an epidemic of suicide. But even as villagers ran out of water, the local Coca-Cola bottling plant near the village of Plachimada had no lack, even increasing its output. With the factory running at full tilt, its gates saw up to eighty-five truckloads of Coke drive off daily, each bearing more than ten thousand bottles.

That triggered a protest at the plant by local villagers that began on April 22, 2002, and continued for several years. Over that time the plant became a flash point, the bright red trucks a symbol of water profligacy and corporate indifference. The Coca-Cola company became vilified in the Indian press, where it exemplified how corporate operations helped cause the chronic dehydration suffered by millions of Indian villagers.

Decisions by the local village council and the Kerala courts led to the closing of the plant for seventeen months. Sales dropped throughout India. The company responded by pointing out that the Coke plant drew its water from a deep aquifer that, technically, had no immediate relation to the surface water local farmers used. The villagers were victimized by the drought, the company argued, not by the bottling plant's wells. And it pledged to put back more water into the local aquifer than it used.

The company had already begun to educate itself about water use. In 2002 Coke executives undertook an analysis of the world's supplies of fresh water, its growing scarcity, and the depletion of aquifers. But this top-down overview was of little relevance to local operations people who run bottling plants like the controversial one in Kerala. Internal studies revealed that operating managers simply regarded water from a municipality as an assured supply. They never asked the question "Where does that water come from?" Even when the occasional plant manager did have concerns about the local watershed, there was no support from the company for addressing them.

The company's attitude toward water management focused on operational performance—wastewater treatment and efficient water use within the plant. It typically had ignored not only where its water came from but also the overall availability of water for the local area. As Jeff Seabright, Coke's vice president for environment and water resources, admits, "It took a real wake-up call before we started to think beyond the four walls and pay attention to the larger system."

In a world where 40 percent of people have no reliable source of safe drinking water and shortages daily destroy habitats, that attitude could not last. Coca-Cola convened meetings on water at each of its twenty-three divisions throughout the world and had local managers complete an exhaustive three-hundred-question survey to identify the water issues at each site. By raising the entire organization's awareness of water use, the iniative began a companywide conversation, with people who usually did not talk to one another now engaging the issue together. At that point, as Seabright tells it, the company realized it lacked crucial expertise in aquatic ecosystems and the dynamics of watersheds. It turned to the World Wildlife Fund for help.

That created a small crisis for WWF, which had long taken contributions from corporations (as well as the general public) but maintained its distance and independence. WWF had to rethink its strategy and mission, realizing that it could gain leverage by partnering with business. Suzanne Apple, the WWF coordinator of the Coca-Cola project, points out that Coke is the world's single biggest customer for sugar, as well as purchasing large numbers of aluminum cans and immense amounts of glass, tea, and a long list of other items. "If we can work with a company like Coca-Cola and shift their purchasing to sustainable sources," she observes, "it can have a huge impact."

But the issue at hand was water, more particularly the mindset that viewed water only in terms of its use in products, cleaning, and processing, or of challenges like how to reduce the water used to make a liter of Coke from 3-plus liters to somewhere under 2.5 liters. WWF expanded that myopic view by analyzing a bottling plant's total water footprint, from suppliers through distributors and retailers. Sugarcane, it turns out, requires some of the most intense water use of any crop. That expanded analysis concluded it takes more than 200 liters of water simply to grow the sugarcane that goes into that one liter of Coke.

Coca-Cola had discovered its devalue chain. Insights like these shifted the scope of thinking about water from the single watershed a bottling plant draws on to all those watersheds tapped at any point in the company's supply chain. Coke needed to consider all the major uses of water, as well as the ways and rates at which those sources were renewed. In Seabright's words, "If we are wasting water or polluting we have no legitimacy to stand on."

This second wake-up call enlarged the mission of Coke's water initiative to look at its total water demand, as well as that of its suppliers, to get them to see themselves as part of a larger system whose water use could be measured and improved. That also got Coke to look beyond its own business to see the need to engage other corporate partners to build political will for the overall management of water. The CEO Water Mandate, one expression of this initiative, evolved under a United Nations umbrella. It urges companies to show progress in areas that range from water use in their direct operations, supply chain, and watershed management to becoming more transparent about all this.

The target of ecological transparency is being met at Coca-Cola in part by asking auditing firms to measure and report on their water use in countries like India so that they have verifiable benchmarks against which to show improvement. Companies meeting the Water Mandate pledge to set incrementally better targets for their water use, to help their suppliers become more water efficient, and to do what they can to help with local water shortages and improve water cleanliness. At its Plachimada plant, Coca-Cola installed a sophisticated rainfall-harvesting system designed to recharge local groundwater reserves. It also dug a bore well for the nearby village, sending over two tankers of fresh water daily to keep the well filled.

As for its worldwide operations, Coke has taken a fresh look at water management. In 2006 Coca-Cola and its franchisees processed 80 billion gallons of water, some ending up in drinks, but most used in making the drinks. Coca-Cola has set measurable targets for itself toward the goal of ensuring that by 2010 all wastewater from Coke plants worldwide is returned to the local water supply clean enough to support aquatic life.

The company has been making efforts to understand the watersheds where it operates and the local social and economic issues surrounding water, and undertaken the responsibility to lead in this area globally. In July 2007, Coca-Cola's CEO, E. Neville Isdell, announced to the triennial UN Global Compact Leaders Summit that his company's guiding principle in the years ahead would be "We should not cause more water to be removed from a watershed than we replenish."

That shift to sustainability as a means to create value can be seen in terms of five discrete stages in the evolution of a business, each with its own drivers, in the view of MIT's Peter Senge and his colleagues at the Society for Organizational Learning. The earliest stages describe the conventional business response, as reflected in the assumptions behind Kleiner's questions. The assumptions include that accommodating to ecological needs will be costly, unnecessary, and bad policy.

This results in companies digging in their heels, denying the need, sowing doubt. Any move toward ecological improvement comes from reaction to outside pressures, whether regulations that require lower air emissions or some activists picketing an annual meeting. And those moves are limited to doing the least amount necessary to meet minimum requirements. Lee Scott, Wal-Mart CEO, admits the retailer's initial conservation initiatives were driven by the need to protect its sullied image.

A more proactive approach begins in the next stage of Senge's model, with voluntary compliance; the drivers here often come from the realization that taking environmental measures can save money and improve reputation and brand value. The surge in companies finding ways to save on energy exemplifies this, from Wal-Mart dropping $25 million per year in diesel costs by putting small generators in the cabins of its trucks to Adobe Systems retrofitting its headquarters to LEED standards and saving the $1.4 million in costs within ten months. Such benefits to the bottom line can create a virtuous cycle, as the initial savings lead to a search for more ways to find such gains.

Beyond this search for savings comes the next level in Senge's progression, integrating sustainability into a company's strategy, typically by discovering a range of ecologically sound business opportunities. For a public company to reach this stage requires meeting the constant challenge of showing it can be profitable as it becomes more ecologically intelligent. The internal signs that a company has reached this benchmark include shifting responsibility for sustainability from an executive whose main job focuses on stakeholder management to leaders of business units and corporate executives like COOs. In a company sustainability holds a meaningful place in strategy and its implementation, shaping capital and budget allocations, core operations, and R&D. It drives the pursuit of significant new markets and the rethinking of supply chains alike.

Procter & Gamble aims to integrate sustainability into strategy. "We use Life Cycle Assessment a lot in our sustainability program," says Len Sauers, vice president for global sustainability at P&G. P&G did extensive life-cycle analyses for energy impacts of its product lines for everything from disposable diapers to shampoos. The very worst impacts turned out to occur not during transport or extraction of raw materials but during the phase when customers used certain products. The singular villain was consumers' need to heat water for laundry detergents.

"That was by far the biggest contributor to our company's entire energy footprint," says Sauers. As a result, the company's R&D unit developed Tide Cold Water, a laundry detergent that cleans clothes without consumers having to heat the water in the washing machine. According to Sauers, if everyone in the United States converted to such a detergent, it would reduce by 3 percent the total household energy use (a savings of nearly 90 billion kilowatt hours) and eliminate up to 34 million tons of carbon dioxide release (roughly equivalent to 8 percent of the Kyoto Agreement target for the United States).

There are, Sauers says, no adverse trade-offs to using Tide Cold Water and one great advantage: it is no more expensive than regular detergents and cleans just as well. P&G calculates that the money saved in energy costs from not having to heat laundry water is equivalent to the price of the box of detergent—in this sense, "it pays for itself." In an ecologically transparent marketplace, Tide Cold Water represents an optimal product, at least in terms of its energy profile.

P&G market research finds that up to 10 percent of shoppers will "inconvenience themselves"—for example, pay more—to get an environmentally superior product. But up to an additional 75 percent will buy sustainable products if they have no adverse trade-offs like higher price or poorer performance. "We think we make the largest impact by targeting the huge middle," Sauers says. "With Tide Cold Water the price is the same and the quality is the same—there are no trade-offs. As a company we think this is the way we can make the biggest difference. LCA let us discover this."

Another incremental improvement by P&G can be seen in its "compaction" initiative, which involves finding ways to get the same effect from smaller amounts of their products. For instance, a liquid laundry detergent that used to require half a cup per load has been concentrated so that one-quarter cup suffices. That, says Sauer, means "the bottle is smaller, you need less shipping material, and get more energy savings by increasing transport efficiency. If this were done with all laundry detergent in the U.S., we'd take 140 million pounds of materials out of the system from what's not used and eliminate 42 million distribution miles."

One motivator for companies like P&G has been Wal-Mart's eco-friendly packaging mandate, which demands its suppliers minimize packaging. Charmin toilet paper and Bounty paper towels now both come in a version with far bigger rolls, resulting in less space needed per unit for packaging and during transport. Other benefits include using fewer cardboard cores for the rolls and having fewer wrappers end up in landfills.

"Our company is dedicated to finding more and more incremental improvements like this," Sauers reports. LCA analyses show that after heating water for cleaning clothes, the next major contributors to the company's energy footprint are the materials used in making laundry products and disposable diapers, and home use of dishwashing soap and shampoos (these no doubt also result from the use of heated water).

"The company's latest five-year business goals for sustainability target finding at least twenty billion dollars in innovative sustainable products," says Sauers. "Several such product initiatives are already in the development pipelines. Every business unit is working on sustainability now, and we expect them all to be contributing. We're looking at our supply chain and asking suppliers to bring new ideas to us for product improvement."

What P&G's business strategy now seeks, as Sauers puts it, is "innovation, which leads to a better product, at lesser cost, that's more environmentally sustainable, with no trade-offs to the consumer. We've integrated sustainability into the rhythm of our business."

At the apex of corporate ecological intelligence are companies founded with this mission foremost in mind. Typically the founders foresaw these business opportunities while competitors were still at the stage of mere compliance; these visionary entrepreneurs made ecological goals part of their mission from day one.

Take Eosta, Europe's largest distributor to retailers of organic produce, a $100 million business. Volkert Engelsman left his job as an executive in the commodities division of Cargill to found a company that would intentionally contribute to a better environment, health, and social responsibility. He told me, "We saw we could only do this if we financed the company in a way that we'd be held responsible for all three of these goals. So our start-up capital was from green investment funds. The financial bottom line is our barometer for success, but not the only one."

Eosta stands as the exemplar of an ecologically intelligent company, practicing the three swarm rules: *know your impacts, favor improvements, and share what you learn.* Buy one of Eosta's mangoes or oranges, and you'll find a sticker with a three-digit number on it. Go to the website www.natureandmore.com, punch in that number, and you will find a message from the farmer who grew it along with a profile of his operation and its merits. For example, Fazenda Tamanduá, a mango farm in the equatorial state of Paraiba in Brazil, introduced a new variety that needs less water to grow and a drip irrigation system to optimize a scarce water supply in this parched climate, sharing the methods with smaller local farmers.

An interview with the farm's owner, Pierre Landolt, reveals that he left Europe to start the farm back in 1977, hoping to bring better agricultural technologies to a poverty-stricken region with a tough climate. A slide show takes you to the mango grove and shows an aerial view of the spread, and workers sorting and boxing the mangoes for shipping. A chart displays results from an independent evaluation, from wages and salaries and an atmosphere of respect to irrigation and pest management through innovation— the operation's most outstanding rating.

"We're trying to build awareness bridges," says Engelsman, "so customers can know about our growers. These are local communities and we know these people, whether in Egypt or Brazil. We want to highlight their contributions."

That awareness serves to decommodify Eosta's products. While for most food distributors a banana is a banana, Engelsman sees a premium in personalizing the shopper–grower relationship. "We serve an awareness elite, people who are concerned about health, the environment, social issues," he told me. "We don't try to compete with the lowest prices but to capitalize on the benefits of our growers—they're not just organic but also socially and environmentally responsible."

If a grower's produce has a higher ranking on the Eosta scales, his fruit will sell at a higher price. "We might charge twelve euros for a high ranking, ten for a lower one," says Engelsman. "We pass that increase on to the grower; we take a fixed commission. That rewards the good things they are doing."

Engelsman believes in the power of a transparent marketplace—transparent in the cost chain as well as the quality of Eosta's produce. One way Eosta embodies this transparency can be seen in what it calls a "trace and tell" system. Every fruit or vegetable it sells can be tracked back to the specific grower it came from and its ranking displayed. "Today's customer has health, environmental, or social concerns that he supports by giving to causes like Greenpeace," Engelsman told me. "We want to let our customers use their buying power to support what they believe in, and we can only do that by giving them full information, the whole story behind our products: who grew it and a threefold quality rating that reflects its ranking on healthiness, environmental, and social qualities."

Eosta puts great effort into rating its products, hiring outside experts in nutrition and ecological impact to assess every crop of fruit and vegetables it sells. Independent auditors evaluate the three aspects of, say, an apple to come up with its rankings. A grower wins higher social ratings by, for example, contributing to local schools or clinics, profit sharing with employees, or cultural efforts like putting on a music festival for the community. "Social indicators vary by local reality," says Engelsman. "If a farmer in

Zimbabwe tells us all their workers' children go to school, that's an achievement—but not in New Zealand."

The environmental ratings revolve around water conservation, composting, and other indicators of organic farming best practice; auditors travel to each farm twice a year in scheduled visits and twice a year unannounced. And the health ratings are based on the nutritional qualities, taste, and other attributes of the food itself as it arrives at Eosta's warehouses. Fazenda Tamanduá, that farm in a semiarid region of Brazil, for example, rates four of five stars on both ecology and social responsibility. To know how its mangoes rate on health, you'd need to get one from a recent shipment.

Many retailers that carry Eosta's produce value its ratings as bulletproof ecological transparency, according to Engelsman. Some retailers that carry Eosta brands, he says, want to avoid the kind of scandal that hit a major British supermarket chain when the BBC ran a documentary revealing that its organic peanuts from Asia were harvested using some child labor. In such an environment, brands will win by monitoring and anticipating consumer preferences and hot spots proactively, changing ahead of the curve, and reassuring the marketplace via transparency.

Most Eosta suppliers are in the Southern Hemisphere; transportation is one of the company's major ecological costs. "We launched a climate-neutral program to offset all our emissions. We do a full LCA on all greenhouse gas emissions throughout our supply chain, from farm to plate, under the supervision of Germany's national certification agency."

More proactively, Eosta has driven an innovation that lessens release of methane, a greenhouse gas. "If you collect all the green waste from a city and throw it on a landfill, it starts rotting," Engelsman says. "You cause anaerobic fermentation that makes methane. But if instead you put green waste in compost and keep turning it in the right way, you avoid methane emissions and end up with stable compost that will increase your soil fertility—which replaces mineral fertilizer—and increase the soil's water-holding quality so there's less runoff. You also enhance the pest resistance of crops.

"On the other hand," Engelsman adds, "if you use the nitrogen fertilizers standard in conventional farming, you'll get greater yields but the crops will be more susceptible to pests, so you need pesticides. Producing and applying fertilizer contributes sixteen percent of all global greenhouse gases, especially nitrous oxide, which is three hundred times more aggressive than CO_2."

The company managed to get Kyoto-approved carbon credits for the composting done by the organic farms in its supply chain. Eosta has set up joint ventures with these local farmers and co-operatives to produce compost that will replace nitrogen fertilizer in several developing countries. Selling their carbon credits provides the farms a supplementary income stream.

"We're taking this to scale in a joint venture with the World Bank," Engelsman says. "You can do this with any field crop—citrus, avocado, anything. Most agriculture takes place near rivers and in deltas, where chemical fertilizer runoff causes eutrophication. The World Bank has financed a program to hire people to cut back the algae this causes before it chokes off the oxygen aquatic life need. But we said, instead of burning the algae or other alien vegetation, we'll use it for compost and gradually replace the need for mineral fertilizers that cause the problem in the first place."

Eosta represents the new breed of start-ups and entrepreneurial outfits that incorporate ecological intelligence into their DNA from the start. But the more common path for companies is to retool an existing mission to embrace sustainability and other hallmarks of ecological intelligence. That was the case at ABC Carpet & Home, a trend-setting retailer in Manhattan. Paulette Cole told me that when she took over as owner and CEO in 2004, "We decided we should become mission based and use our platform to lead a paradigm shift in retail, using beauty as a tool for change. We do green with style."

One of the first initiatives was a letter the company, a founding member of the Sustainable Furniture Council, sent to its furniture suppliers, most in North Carolina. "We told them we were going to educate our consumers by putting labels on furniture explaining responsible forestry. We see ourselves as a model for other stores; we believe we will increase the demand for responsibly managed woods. So we invite you to get on board.

"Many of our vendors took us pretty seriously, though some were skeptical," Cole said. "You're asking a business to add costs and work." So ABC Carpet & Home partnered with nonprofits like Rainforest Alliance, asking them to provide their services to and share their expertise with furniture makers, like criteria for responsibly managed wood and where to source it. They warned them about countries where paperwork "certifying" sustainability was often a cover for black market woods and educated the companies about healthy forestry practices.

"We're sharing this information with our suppliers so we can get the products we want," Cole said. At the time we spoke, about 40 percent of ABC Carpet & Home's reproduction furniture offerings bore a "goodwood" label, certifying that the wood is either reclaimed or ethically logged. That label is one of more than a dozen the retailer uses to educate its customers and reassure them of the ecological pedigree of its products. Other eco-items include organic bedding; formaldehyde-free upholstery; linens made from organic cotton, silk, and natural dyes; and "Organic Baby & Little Ones," toxin-free products for children.

A 3,500-square-foot space on the third floor shelters ABC Home & Planet, which consolidates sustainable offerings from the rest of the store's six floors. Museum-like displays educate shoppers about, for example, the differences between organic, natural, and cruelty-free wool, organic cottons, and natural dyes. Altogether the retailer's offerings are tagged with any of thirteen different labels, each telling the product's ecological backstory. "We're educating our customers and modeling for other retailers," says Cole.

Ray Anderson, CEO of Interface, a carpet tile company, remembers his conversion experience well. It began at a sales meeting in 1994, when he was asked to give his reps some talking points on Interface's environmental philosophy. His reply was "That's simple. We comply with the law."

That less-than-inspiring response led Anderson to ponder the environment more deeply, until he had an awakening: "I realized I was running a company that was plundering the earth."

So Anderson set his company the task of becoming what he calls a "restorative enterprise," one that takes nothing from the earth that cannot be replaced, regenerated, or recycled. This ecologically intelligent enterprise, he was determined, would do no harm to the biosphere; Anderson has resolved that his business will be completely sustainable. His concern about environmental crises comes coupled with a vision for business, the realization that the only institution powerful and pervasive enough to turn these problems around is "the institution that was causing them in the first place: Business. Industry. People like us."

14

THE PERPETUAL UPGRADE

Wherever you live, whatever you do, you are very likely to have something in your home or workplace made by FiberMark, a manufacturer of papers, packaging, and a host of related things that permeate the manufacturing universe. Its products range from Bible covers to wallpaper, from the fancy boxes for Hermès scarves to the lowly file folders ubiquitous in offices. One of the world's leading providers of packaging and paperboard, Fiber-Mark has managed to reverse the dominant flow in the global supply chain: its factories in the United States ship packaging to China, Thailand, and just about everywhere else in the world where things are made. Those packages, in turn, stream through the world's retail outlets.

The company's Brattleboro, Vermont, paper mill offers its customers two hundred different colors and grades of paperboard.

FiberMark's Brattleboro plant became the first manufacturer in that green state to switch from burning fuel oil to used vegetable oil for powering the factory's turbines, drying papers, and heating the plant. At first, Vermont's Department of Environmental Conservation required a test run of the oils to see if the fumes would make the picturesque town reek like a fast-food kitchen. Satisfied, the state let the company proceed, and today a FiberMark tanker truck makes a daily journey to Manhattan to collect used cooking oils from restaurants there.

The switch lowered the plant's fuel oil use by almost 75 percent, and emissions of sulfur dioxide and nitrous oxide, both causes of acid rain, continue to fall with each gallon of vegetable oil burned. The air quality inside the factory has improved enormously, and what had been a steady odor from the fuel oil has largely vanished; vegetable oil burns far more cleanly.

That environmentally conscious decision was as much about saving fuel costs as saving the planet. But FiberMark has pushed ahead on other environmental fronts, particularly in making more and more of its packaging from recycled paper fiber. Some of FiberMark's clients had already been asking for recycled papers—particularly those in the university market. But when I asked FiberMark CEO Anthony MacLaurin if he had switched to recycled paper because of demands from customers, his reply was "Not really. We believe this is where the world is going—so we're bringing it to our customers."

Packaging from FiberMark holds a slot in a vast number of product supply chains, so whenever FiberMark upgrades its methods, all those products share in the ecological benefit. As Gregory Norris observes, "When anyone in your supply chain makes a smart move, it makes your product greener too—as well as the purchases of everyone who buys your product. That ripple effect turns thousands of upstream suppliers into your allies, to the extent any of them make improvements."

When Gregory Norris walked me through the details of an LCA for a recycled glass jar, with its overwhelming list of negative impacts, he pointed out that each one represented an opportunity to explore whether some industrial upgrade—a different chemical here, a novel process there—might improve the jar's overall footprint. "Any of these negative impacts are a waste, in the colloquial sense—an unintended consequence that smart design can reduce."

Norris has a vision for a way to churn out an endless stream of such ecological upgrades throughout the world of industry and commerce. Earthster is a free, open-source, Web-based program that will offer businesses LCA-driven windows into supply chains and create an online bazaar for upgrades. When we spoke, Norris and his colleagues were hard at work developing the prototype for this gigantic piece of ecological transparency software. The consortium backing Earthster's development included Dell, Owens Corning, Stonyfield Farm, and the state of Texas, among others; all these organizations are prospective users.

Earthster seeks to give B2B (business-to-business) shoppers a way to signal producers about the ecological improvements they want to see in products over their life cycles. By design the program will give producers all along supply chains a way to benchmark themselves against averages for their industry, and let companies looking for upgrades know they are better by posting their product and process scorecards on environmental, health, and social indicators. In theory, the LCA methodology offers a clear avenue to identifying the progression of gains to be had from supply chain upgrades for any product.

Earthster's strategy depends on social computing to build a collaborative database. "I publish my LCA data for the screws I sell," says Norris, "and you use my screws in your product. You can plug my data into the LCA database for your product. That way we build a database together. We want a system where people anywhere along the supply chain can help us gather information on a product's impact."

To speed the spread of useful innovations, Earthster will highlight products or processes whose record for reducing impacts is better than the industry average. "If your vegetable oil has a better carbon footprint than most, we want to call that to the attention of any potential customers."

Benefits for buyers are built in, too. "Earthster lets you search the database for which product is better than average on, say, environmental impact. You can change your purchase accordingly and calculate the environmental benefits of switching. For instance, if a glass factory switched to renewable energy, it would reduce the global warming potential from making their product by fifty percent. We hope to promote just that kind of upgrade."

That feature should appeal to buyers for organizations that have mandates to make their purchases more environmentally friendly and who need to document those benefits. Earthster can also help buyers who have a particular concern like climate change or off-gassing find the better products and report the specific benefit.

Norris envisions that "Earthster will allow, say, the state of

Texas to tell its suppliers, 'Next year we will purchase thirty million dollars in your product category, and the following list of environmental impacts are important in our choice. We'll give preference to companies that are good in these ways, or getting better.' "

The specific preferences could be detailed in any number of ways: an improvement in an item's overall impacts as evaluated by an LCA, better life-cycle water efficiency, a carbon footprint 20 percent below sector average, or fewer particulates emitted, to name a very few.

Institutional customers can choose the upgrade that targets the most problematic aspects of a given item. For vegetables that need lots of fertilizer, the targeted problem might be eutrophication of water ecosystems due to irrigation runoff carrying nitrogen or phosphorous from chemical fertilizers, depleting oxygen, and choking aquatic life. Adding this requirement to a purchasing policy that favors food from local farms would also help protect the area's rivers and lakes.

Norris predicts, "If a huge institutional buyer like Texas says to its global suppliers. 'We're spending this much on your product group, and we care about the following variables over and above cost,' it will create a new category of performance characteristics." Instead of cost and quality being the sole basis for purchases, doing the least harm becomes another selling point.

This is not hypothetical; the trend started a while back. A global manufacturer of heavy equipment, Norris told me, won a huge order from a foreign government because it was able to respond overnight to questions from the purchasers about the precise recycled content of the metal in its bulldozers. "In the global competitive environment," Norris added, "this already matters. If you sell to governments, you need this information."

Governments have begun to pool their criteria, multiplying the beneficial market impact of their "RFQs," or requests for quote, which they routinely use to solicit competitive bids. In the United States, state purchasing agents are already consulting with one another to find common ground and standardize their requests, giving them greater market force. The conversation has begun, Norris says, that will allow companies that put in these bids to compare, for instance, how California's specifications match those from Texas for recycled content or lower carbon footprints in the carpet they want to buy.

The public sector, from universities and hospitals to towns and cities, states, and provinces, has started adding these mandates to its purchasing specifications, with the trend certain to grow stronger. One of the tougher problems for purchasing agents with ethical mandates of one sort or another is how to get the hard data that would guide them.

As Mike Hardiman, who directs buying for the University of Wisconsin, complained, "All of us in procurement are struggling with looking into the supply chain in depth—we're seeking how to do that in a smart way. It's one thing to say you're concerned about workers' wages, but when you're buying something like a copier, you're dealing with a complex supply chain where different factories in different places make different parts. How far can you go in tracking down the data you need?"

Norris's hope is that Earthster will one day give such industrial buyers the kind of information they need to "show a metric for how much good we've done in the world—that our choices, for example, have reduced this kind of pollutant by that much.

"Say a manufacturer responds to Texas's request to upgrade their environmental performance," he adds. "They're not where they need to be yet; they've got too many toxins in their supply chain. They could use Earthster to find that a big problem is in their aluminum, from releases of dioxin during its manufacture, based on generic data for the aluminum industry.

"Then they have to track down a supplier with great environmental management or with high recycled aluminum content. So in the next step an engineer designing a product or a purchasing manager at the product site calls the environmental manager of an aluminum producer and says, 'Please go into Earthster and calculate your level of toxic release.' If they find it is better than average, then the engineer can recompute their own performance and show Texas they now meet the purchasing requirement.

"If that environmental manager finds out they are worse than the average toxic release for their industry, and wants to keep the Texas business, then we would record their present levels as a benchmark for progress. Once they find ways to lower their release, they can show a reduction from that benchmark in pollution per product sold.

"Progress is a game that every company can play," says Norris. "Everyone can get better incrementally—and we need them to. The idea is not just to make a few green companies rich but to spread progress everywhere in the economy."

As huge institutional buyers and retailers pressure their suppliers to improve, those suppliers will pass that pressure down their supply chain. Anyone who has a way to improve some aspect of products' LCAs can let that be known on Earthster. So the industrial designers, engineers, or chemists searching for ways to upgrade can more readily find the innovations that will help them get there, in a kind of Craigslist for ecologically minded industrialists. Norris sees Earthster as "facilitating the link between green buyers and sellers" in the enormous B2B bazaar, where companies buy from other companies.

GoodGuide aims to offer a complementary service to companies, a market-sensing feature that might prove immensely helpful in strategic decision making. "We can analyze billions of purchasing decisions to see what really matters to shoppers," O'Rourke told me. "Do shoppers care about carbon footprints? Chemicals of concern? Maybe having phthalates loses sales. We'll aggregate data on what customers prefer, and we'd like to make these analytics available to companies so they can change their products accordingly. We want to feed the data back at the level of manufacturing, to accelerate virtuous cycles."

Earthster and GoodGuide, operating in tandem one day, could well aggregate the cumulative choices of individual shoppers, institutional buyers, and B2B purchasers, creating a powerful market force favoring incremental improvements. "GoodGuide allows people to pick small, proximal goals for change, rather than a gross all good or bad," says O'Rourke. "That lets companies respond by gradually upgrading. We're adding the information that will create the incentive for companies to keep upgrading. As one company upgrades, that will pressure others to match it. Now that Timberland puts carbon ratings of its shoes right on the box, other companies should feel pressure to disclose the same information. That competitive pressure creates real incentives for products and companies to get better."

Of course, O'Rourke adds, "We're not there yet. There's no way for us to know who is just greenwashing and who is making a genuine change for the better—managing their supply chains better to reduce toxins and environmental impacts, to improve working conditions. There's no market feedback as yet to reward doing good. At present we have very poor information, and so we make poor decisions all the time. We need to add the solid data for shoppers that will create the virtuous circle, where companies sell more product and see their stocks rise—do better by doing good."

That continual upgrading would occur, for example, if the goal for a brand was simply to be better than the sector average. As poor performers reach average and average ones respond by getting even better, standards inexorably rise for all. As an executive at a global company told me, "If we put everything out on the table and someone else runs with it, that just lifts the bar for everyone, including us. If one player changes, the rest will have to."

As O'Rourke sees it, "If companies start paying attention, it will motivate them to disclose more and better information to consumers, kicking off a process of continual improvement, as consumers demand more and more of the companies they buy from."

Are major companies paying attention? Take Andy Ruben, who was appointed by Wal-Mart CEO Lee Scott as the first vice president of the company's sustainability initiative. When we spoke, Ruben had just left that post to head Wal-Mart's private-brand sourcing strategy, a position where he felt he could more directly influence operations. "Our CEO sees sustainability as fundamental to our business strategy," Ruben told me. "The company started on this defensively at first, but by now it's fundamental."

When I asked Ruben what he thought of the approach to ecological transparency being taken by GoodGuide and Earthster, he replied, "What's in the black box of the ratings? If they had a great box, we might want to use it" for purchasing, just as institutional buyers could use it as a screen.

Ruben sees the need to go beyond what he calls "eco-think." He told me, "Getting to fifty percent recycled content in packaging is good so far as it goes. But we don't just want someone slapping eco-labels on a package. We want to reinvent the system to minimize or completely get rid of the packaging. Why redo everything and label it green? We want to open up a candy store of innovation—more than just green: smart.

"To me all negative impacts of products are a discovery about unintended consequences," Ruben says. "There can be thousands of consequences from a single decision, and we may be seeing just ten of these unintended impacts. The most competitive companies will engage to uncover these unnoticed impacts and make better decisions. Simply put, they will become more competitive by seeing their business in a broader light.

"We think of ourselves as buyers of products on behalf of our customers," Ruben reflects. "We have two hundred million customers and sixty thousand suppliers. That's our lever: to buy better products for our customers. So we see one of our roles as creating the demand so suppliers will try to find the innovative alternatives everybody needs. That can move things faster, so it will ripple through the supply chain."

One place Wal-Mart started was packaging. Everyone has had the experience of opening a cereal box and realizing the top portion is all air. It turns out, Ruben tells me, that the amount of air can depend on the line speed at which cereal goes into its packaging. "The box is larger than needed and gets shipped all over the world that way. There could be big savings in finding how to keep up line speed while adjusting how the boxes are filled, so we can end up with a smaller box. Now that you identify the problem and the market for the solution, you create an incentive for innovation.

"We recently put in place a packaging scorecard to measure the efficiency of a product's packaging. I was at a packaging conference where I heard about a manufacturer claiming that they could improve their Wal-Mart packaging score from a four to an eight—a big jump. This is the more competitive market of innovation that I am talking about. When the companies that make use of such broader innovations gain market share, everyone wins."

Wal-Mart has also begun measuring energy use for its goods in seven product categories and will eventually apply this data to choose suppliers for products ranging from DVDs and vacuum cleaners to toothpaste and soda. Wal-Mart's eventual goal, according to John Fleming, chief merchandising officer: "removing nonrenewable energy from the products Wal-Mart sells."

Well and good if you have the market heft of Wal-Mart. Smaller retailers in some sectors are finding that they can gain greater leverage in their supply chain by working together with similar companies than any could achieve on its own.

"We see sustainability as a team sport, both vertically down into the supply chain and collaboratively," Kevin Hagen, director of corporate responsibility at outdoor goods co-op REI, told me. REI has been working with Organic Exchange, a not-for-profit that sources cotton, to find the textiles for its organic clothing line.

At the early stages of the supply chain, few brands actually have direct contact with suppliers (who may be suppliers to suppliers of their suppliers), and so have little influence on how they operate. That's one reason the Organic Exchange was created. Says Hagen, "The Exchange broke a logjam in everyone's supply chain. It used to be that dye houses had no lot control; all the fabrics that came into a house were treated as interchangeable. Organic cotton went in, but there was no way to know what came out. No longer—the Organic Exchange has helped the industry develop 'chain of custody' tracking, so now when organic fabric goes in, we know what comes back."

Hagen adds, "It's largely a problem in industrial design; in our business there are a number of problematic industrial processes involved in our products, like dyes and waterproofing, a soup of chemicals that does all kinds of things. As one lone brand we have little opportunity to affect these outcomes, but as a collaborator with other companies, we can all have an effect. We can articulate our desires for specs and allow the supply chain to respond. We want lots of innovation and development in the supply chain."

The Outdoor Industry Association, which numbers companies like Nike, Patagonia, and Timberland among its members along with REI, has been the main vehicle for this sector to work with its supply chain for ecological upgrades. Hagen says, "The Outdoor Industry Association's Eco-Index group has over one hundred brands of outdoor products working together to create specifications for environmental attributes that can help motivate the innovation we want in the supply—and we can make the reward worth the change.

"Suppliers will innovate if the market is there. But first they have to know what outcomes are important and how it affects their competitive position. Often the right change reduces costs and improves competitive positioning. We disagree with the idea that it's all about paying more to be green."

While before such supply chain change had been spotty and ad hoc, Hagen adds, "Now we're getting systematic metrics. The Outdoor Industry Association Eco-Index is intended to help measure suppliers' eco-performance with LCA-type analysis that gives scores on issues such as energy use, chemistry, and waste. And we offer advice to suppliers on how they can improve their scores— eliminate toxic chemicals, reduce waste. We are driving toward minimum required thresholds for everything we design—the outdoor industry can take a unified stance for all our products. It's not that our customers are forcing us to do this, but we see a connection between getting people outdoors and how we run our business."

LCAs would do well to include positive impacts along the supply chain as well as negative. Remember that Gregory Norris's analysis of the Dutch power grid found that the relatively small amount of economic activity in the 10 percent of its supply chain that was in impoverished countries accounted for enormous health benefits to people there, dwarfing the harms to health done by the grid's pollution. Norris uses World Bank databases to argue that the boost to health from people getting jobs will be greater the lower the mean life expectancy of an area—especially when enhanced economic activity expands social services like education and medical care. If that increased cash flow ends up largely in the pockets of just a few or of people in other countries, of course, then locals benefit little.

One way to increase positive social impacts is through Fair Trade certification, which ensures that producers in developing countries are paid reasonable wages and have safe and just working conditions. "Some customers, a small percentage, are willing to pay more for fair trade coffee because of its virtue," says Ruben. "Many of our customers either can't or won't choose to pay more, so the overall societal change is limited.

"Working with Café Bom Dia and Paul Rice of TransFair, we were able to relook at the coffee supply chain through a broader fair trade lens. By creating longer-term relationships with growers in Brazil, we found efficiencies in colocating roasting, bagging operations, consolidation points, and more. In the end we are able to offer a better-quality coffee, fair trade certified, for under six dollars a pound. That's less than half of what others are doing by simply finding fair trade coffee and selling it.

"One of the best parts of this win was that this coffee displaced a few major brands of traditional coffee—not because customers were demanding fair trade but because it was a better-quality coffee that was more affordable. This creates a much larger win both for customers and the coffee growers."

Ruben hopes for a continuing cascade of such wins: "We need a systems perspective on how we're operating today to see the thousands of places we can do better." When Wal-Mart asked its truck drivers not to idle their diesel engines anymore—and installed smaller generators just to power the truckers' cabins—the company saved $25 million a year. Comments Ruben: "That went straight to the bottom line. And because trucking and retail are a penny business, we just created thousands of environmentalists. Others have a choice either to compete or to live with being less competitive."

But Ruben sees Wal-Mart's leverage point not so much in finding such solutions, but rather spurring them by creating a vigorous market for upgrades. He told me, "Our role is to create the marketplace in an opaque supply chain—to surface information that makes the supply chain improve. It's not an LCA on every product but a systems view that perceives unintended harm and aims to profit from improvements, all in a consumer-driven economy. Businesses must create customer value to survive over the long term. That's what makes this broader systems viewpoint and resulting innovation so exciting. It's a competitive business strategy."

Another crucial feature: collaborative learning and knowledge sharing. Says Ruben, "We have suppliers we intend to stay with, so we can make this a real, shared strategic relationship. We will make this shift, but we need to figure out how to do it together."

Ruben sees that the LCA methodology, which pinpoints what needs to improve, offers only part of the solution. "That's necessary, but not sufficient. The crucial next step: innovation."

Ruben, for one, is bullish about finding points for upgrade innovations throughout the supply chain. "This is the largest strategic opportunity companies will see for the next fifty years," Ruben predicts. "This is the most exciting time to be in business, with more opportunity to create change in the world than ever."

THE NEXT FIFTY YEARS

There are, literally, millions of ways to upgrade our collective ecological footprint. Take that glass jar. To melt sand into glass, manufacturers of everything from glass containers and auto windows to hybrid products like fiber optics depend on massive furnaces that can run for as long as ten years at a stretch at more than 2,000 degrees Fahrenheit. But industrial glassmakers use a basic design for furnaces that has seen little change since it was first developed in the 1850s.

To be sure, there have been small improvements here and there, like using pure oxygen to improve energy efficiency a bit. That drive to experiment with new methods has accelerated with higher energy costs. One innovative furnace design would improve heat transfer by, in effect, turning the oven upside down, bringing the usual twenty-four hours needed to melt sand down to just three. That shift could save vast amounts of energy—but as yet the improvement yields smaller batches with bubbly glass that breaks more easily. Another radical switch uses microwave ovens instead of the traditional natural gas but again yields batches too small for industrial production. As Ian Kemsley, the inventor of the microwave glass oven, notes, "We're making glass essentially the same way as the ancient Romans. There's tremendous waste and a huge amount of money to be made by innovating."

Here ecological intelligence takes the form of rethinking our entire legacy from earlier days, when processes and inventions came online without regard for their impacts. Upgrading this legacy may present the biggest business challenge of the twenty-first century: we need to reinvent everything, from the most basic platforms in industrial chemistry and manufacturing processes through the entire supply chain and life cycle of products.

We face a toll from fundamental decisions reached many years ago: choices about how to engineer and manufacture, about energy sources, about what chemical compounds to use—decisions made without regard for the impact to the commons, the planet we share, and our bodies. To be fair, the industrial chemists and engineers of earlier centuries had far, far less information about the adverse impacts of the substances they used and how they used them than is the case today.

For the most part, cost and marketing considerations have held sway—sound business practice. But in the near future those calculations will need to consider, too, the risks of ignoring the dawning ecological transparency in the marketplace. And, perhaps more to the point for many executives, strategic thinkers will see new business opportunities opened up by that very transparency.

The possibilities for radical innovation and clever upgrades seem endless. Researchers in New Zealand mapped the genome of ruminant animals like sheep and cows to discover the genes that regulate flatulence, in order to develop a vaccine that will greatly reduce "flatulent emissions" from livestock—which now account for 28 percent of human-related methane buildup. Meanwhile plant-breeding geneticists in the United Kingdom are attacking methane emissions via genetic improvements in digestibility, sugar content, and protein-breakdown enzymes in grazing grass.

Environmental scientists at Spain's National Center for Biotechnology have developed software that identifies whether a molecule will biodegrade well. The software analyzes, for example, whether a variety of plastic will break down completely as sun and water melt it, or if it will hold together for a thousand years. This test for biodegradability opens an entirely new criterion for materials selection.

The Paris Metro's new line uses old technology in a holistic way. The standard technology generates electricity from the friction produced when a train brakes and then uses this energy to boost the same train when it starts or accelerates. The Metro went beyond thinking about trains one at a time to envisioning them as parts of a system. On the new Line 14 the electricity all the trains make by braking is fed back into the power system so that any train can draw on it, reducing the energy needs of the line by 30 percent.

Such systems analysis suggests another range of ways to rethink how industrial systems impact those in nature. Take plans for a paper plant to be located in the South Bronx. The plant was designed to use recycled paper harvested from recycling as its pulp stock, not that from trees. "There's more paper fiber per acre in New York City than you can get from an acre in the Amazon," says Jonathan Rose, who helped draw up the plans. "It's in the recycling bin or the garbage."

Paper plants use huge amounts of water, so the site was chosen to be close to a sewage plant; the paper would be made using cleansed sewage water rather than devouring fresh water. For years New York City newspapers got their newsprint delivered daily in enormous rolls shipped by truck from Maine or Canada. Locating the plant smack in the environs of the city avoids that long journey. No trees cut, no fresh water used, no diesel-puffing tractor trailers rolling along for hundreds of miles—three natural systems where impacts are minimized. "Why do we have pollution?" Rose asks. "Pollution is a sign of incomplete consumption— something being wasted. When we see buildings, factories, cars or power plants as isolated entities, we lose the benefits of systems efficiency."

Other gains could be found by using LCA methods to ratchet up current standards for green certifications of all kinds. LEED ratings for green buildings exemplify this opportunity; so far that certification is based on a relatively narrow slice of what goes into a building and how it gets used. The LEED governing group has been working with industrial ecologists to help them introduce LCA into their green building standards.

"LEED is a first step," commented Pedro Vieira, a member of the Consortium on Green Design at the University of California at Berkeley. "But it only touches the surface—you can do an LCA of a building, assessing all the individual materials, water and energy used, as well as the logistics of producing them."

The sand used to make cement, for instance, typically is excavated from a riverbank and then sent to a facility that sorts rocks and sand by granularity, grading them by size. Next the finest sand goes to a coal-fired kiln to be mixed with other minerals, and the whole batch is cooked at 2,642 degrees Fahrenheit. Most of the batches end up in cement in trucks that mix in water and chemicals while hauling it all to a construction site. Excavating, transporting, and heating cement are extremely energy intensive, accounting for about 3 percent of the world's greenhouse gases.

When a building's life ends, an average 25 percent of the structure's concrete is recycled: walls and slabs are crushed and sorted for their next use, typically in roads or new buildings. "If we increase the concrete recycling rate to fifty percent," Vieira and his UC Berkeley thesis adviser, Arpad Horvath, calculated, "it would mean the equivalent of taking approximately six hundred thousand vehicles off the road for a year" in terms of reducing its contribution to global warming.

This list goes on indefinitely. These advances and their ilk will be the stuff of headlines for the next century in basic and applied sciences as well as in environmental studies and ecology—and the basis of bottom lines in business. We need a continuous cascade of such improvements throughout the industrial enterprise if we are to bring the human endeavor beyond harm's reach, so that commerce supports the earth's carrying capacity rather than threatening it. The big question: can we do it?

SECOND THOUGHTS

Let's not be naive about business realities.

Mondi, based in South Africa and London, sells paper and packaging materials in thirty-five countries and has been a leader in its sector in environmental upgrades. In the 1990s Mondi was among the first large paper companies to produce totally chlorine-free office paper by improving bleaching practices, and it continues to search for ecological upgrades.

Wolfgang Schacherl, a Mondi executive, told me, "Environmental advantages have always been one of the pillars of our market positioning, so we need to do continuous R&D and invest in innovations to maintain that position. We find our customers will usually stay with an environmentally upgraded product even if the cost is a bit higher. But at the end of the day cost and performance are by far the most overwhelming decision criterion"— not environmental excellence.

Mondi product design engineers developed a single-ply paper for bagging industrial goods like fertilizer that replaces two- or three-ply papers. The bags use less paper but are stronger and stiff enough to withstand even tremendous pressure while being filled with cement and the stresses of being shipped around the world. Another innovation, an "airstream" bag design for high-speed filling, replaces a petroleum-based wrapping with a paper-based one, supplanting a nonrenewable resource with a renewable one.

Mondi uses LCA methods, among others, to figure long-term targets for environmental sustainability, though it does not evaluate all the impacts across all its product groups. For its paper products it does a yearly update on its plants that analyzes energy, water use, emissions, and wastewater per ton of paper. For many industries, impact assessments of chemicals over product life cycles are a legal requirement in European countries; Sweden and Finland have the highest environmental standards for entering their markets.

Yet, as Schacherl told me, "Procurement departments have a larger range of considerations than environmental impacts alone—cost, for sure. It's not always possible to make environmental-friendly products at the same low cost."

When will the tipping point come? "If we look at how corporations are rated in the financial markets, fiscal performance is, of course, most important," Schacherl said. "But there's also a slight trend to evaluate environmental performance, too. The London Stock Exchange now rates companies on a sustainability index. But these are new considerations; it's unclear what the market impacts from this will be. If financial analysts started recommending investment in more sustainable companies, that would help."

Still, Schacherl has witnessed a gradual shift. "Ten years ago no one asked what forests we cut our trees from, and now we need to prove we use sustainable methods and follow Forest Stewardship Council rules. If we learned that something we used in making paper was troubling, we'd drop it immediately. We've positioned ourselves as the high-quality eco-brand."

But, he added, he didn't think that would matter at all to companies at the low end of the paper market, whose marketing strategy was simply to make their paper the cheapest. That premise applies to world commerce, as well; take First World versus Second World economies. The countries of the Second World—like Brazil, India, Russia, and China—harbor the growing new consumer markets whose spending power drives much of the world economy's growth. For billions of shoppers in these economies cost alone will likely prevail as the hallmark of bestselling products.

It may take decades for the first-tier market's desire for impact transparency to reach or permeate these second-tier economies. The market segmentation that separates high-quality/low-impact goods from low-cost/poor-impact ones will likely prevail for decades in these bustling economies. On the other hand, if global retail giants like Wal-Mart apply their huge advantages in seeking ecological gains from their suppliers, the cost equation might change radically. Even in Second World economies, this business strategy conceivably could drive down the market share of low-cost/poor-impact products. If so, accumulating forces could tip toward a worldwide virtuous cycle.

GETTING IT RIGHT

Three years after a disastrous infestation of drinking water by a toxic microbe killed more than one hundred people in Milwaukee, the U.S. Congress passed a law in 1996 requiring disclosure of toxins in community water supplies. The law required that local water authorities throughout the land regularly test their water supply and inform their customers of any contaminants.

The devil was in the details. Somehow the regulations mandated a treacherous combination of inaccurate analyses, idiosyncratic ratings, and a failure to link any of this to the actual level of health threat. To compound the problem, all this inadequate data was displayed in a complex table rife with arcane technical terms that a chemist could love but hardly anyone else could comprehend. Plus, the already hard-to-decipher data was as much as a year out of date.

The upshot was a series of public health disasters. Some cities were reassuring their citizens that their drinking water was perfectly safe based on assays at the filtration plant, while ignoring microbes or toxins the water might pick up as it wended its way through hundreds of miles of creaky piping. In most cities much of that piping contains lead, which leaches into the water and puts children at risk. A decade after Congress passed that benighted law, the Environmental Protection Agency estimated that 10 percent or more of Americans still were drinking tainted water daily.

Simple ineptness or poor execution may be the greatest threat to the best-intentioned transparency efforts in the marketplace. There are other risks: radical transparency is itself an untried intervention in a complex system and as such may have any number of unintended, even unfortunate, side effects. There are many caveats and cautions. For one, as some argue, only top-tier brands, which are the most reputation-sensitive, may be affected. Bottom-tier firms, whose business model centers on having the lowest-cost products, often with unknown brand names, would likely not be affected by the market pressures transparency creates.

Another concern: misguided good intentions could mean sourcing or other nightmares for companies trying to respond to market shifts. Say, for instance, a critical mass of consumers stampedes away from products with a certain ingredient that happens to hit the headlines and get carried far and wide via some digital tidal wave. Yet we will still want the products to maintain whatever beneficial texture or other quality that ingredient lent, even if no suitable replacement has yet been found.

That catch-22 could be compounded by others, like the predicament of needing to manage suppliers who may not agree to change their practices. For instance, Dara O'Rourke, whose early research was on supply chains, tells me that many global running shoe brands depend for manufacturing on a single Taiwanese firm that, through a holding company in Hong Kong, operates a vast network of factories throughout China and beyond. This shoe maker can keep its costs rock bottom by, among other practices, making all the shoes for the various companies in the same way. The company has so much power in its industry that a lone shoe brand might not be able to dictate changes it wants to make. Says O'Rourke, "In this kind of global supply chain situation, an individual brand is meaningless" and might well be powerless to insist on manufacturing changes that the market favors but the manufacturer opposes.

A publisher told me, "I print my books in China, because I can find cheaper four-color presses that can print on green paper. There's now one company in China that has built a Forest Stewardship Council–certified paper mill; that means, for instance, it gets its wood pulp from sustainably grown forests and the mill minimizes its use of water. Environmentally, this is the best in China. But this company is owned by a bigger Chinese corporation that has another division notorious for clear-cutting rain forest in Indonesia. When this was discovered, the FSC pulled the green mill's certification because the parent company was doing the wrong thing. So there's no Chinese FSC-certified paper mill at the moment. That raises the question, do I import green paper from Europe to China? It's not energy efficient to ship paper, and it's not cost effective for me.

"I tell myself, I probably should use that green Chinese paper mill, because they are trying to do the right thing. Even if I can't say it's FSC-certified, it still has another kind of green certification. Am I upset they lost their FSC certification? That's the way you put pressure on them to improve. But should my business go to them? It's the best paper I have available in China, and they've invested millions in this plant—shouldn't I support that?"

Then there are the difficulties of verification down through the maze of a global supply chain. As one businessman bemoaned, "Things change week to week, and people make different judgment calls up and down the line. One source we depend on for 'green' stock couldn't get enough raw material from his supplier one week, so he just switched to another supplier whose products were readily available but not sustainably made. It's just like at home: most days we rinse and recycle our plastic and glass containers—but sometimes they're just too yucky to wash, so we toss them in with the rest of the garbage."

As the triple bottom line (which reports environmental and social responsibility initiatives in addition to the standard financial metrics) becomes a fixture in corporate reports, companies are looking to auditing firms to certify how well they are doing. When I asked the head of one of America's Big Four auditing companies about auditing such impacts, he told me this was "one of our better-growing lines of business. How else do you know how much water you're using in India?"

As it happened, a week or so later I was talking with Dara O'Rourke, who over the course of seven years inspected working conditions in more than one hundred factories throughout the developing world for organizations like the Swedish government and the World Bank. At one point a consortium of universities asked him to report on the factories that supplied them with clothes emblazoned with their school emblem.

Three of those factory inspections were done in tandem with auditors from one of those Big Four consultancies. O'Rourke's report on their audit was sobering. O'Rourke shadowed the auditors as they inspected three garment factories, one each in China, Korea, and Indonesia. In the factory outside Shanghai, for example, the official auditor took a rather random forty-five-minute walk through the factory, during which he missed several hazards to workers' health: workers wearing flip-flops and with no gloves or eye protection operating hot-dye machines; safety guards missing on machine chains and sprockets; workers cutting by hand without protective gloves.

Workers were interviewed about the company's labor practices in the presence of managers, who knew what they were being asked—ensuring that the answers would be sanitized—rather than off-site and in confidence so workers could open up. In short, what struck O'Rourke was not what the auditors found but what they missed. The auditors noted a series of minor violations but found the factory to be in "acceptable" compliance, based on reassurances by factory managers that problems would be remedied. In O'Rourke's view, the auditors, with their extensive training in fiscal details, were not up to the challenge of a social audit.

O'Rourke also questioned the standard practice of letting consulting firms that provide their services to a company also monitor the impacts of factories that supply those companies, because of potential conflicts of interest. In a transparent system, the most credible evaluations are by completely impartial third parties. O'Rourke suggests that corporations monitor factories in their supply chain in a more transparent way, making their methods and findings public and so subject to verification.

O'Rourke also proposes that different factories and firms harmonize their audits, so consumers can compare them. Procter & Gamble's director for sustainability insists that there need to be transparent definitions that can be reviewed by third parties for several key questions: What is a "sustainable" product? What is a "renewable" material? What qualifies as "packaging reduction"? Standardized industrywide metrics and ongoing measures would be the greatest help here.

In seeking ecological upgrades in supply chains, says Wal-Mart's Andy Ruben, "The verification elements are extremely important." He cites the availability of wild-caught seafood, which came about because of a system of certification that showed where fish had been caught, to ensure it was not from a zone where the species was in a state of collapse. Similarly, an advantage for Wal-Mart of buying fair trade coffee turns out to be verifiability, because the coffee comes directly from the farmers rather than through middlemen who can make tracking the origins of the coffee impossible, let alone, for example, whether it was grown organically.

A while ago I was visited by two friends from Shanghai, one a high-level executive at China's largest real estate developer, the other a leadership coach for several CEOs of Chinese corporations. The big buzz in the Chinese business world, they told me, was what Wal-Mart had done with its Chinese suppliers. Wal-Mart, though the world's largest retailer, owns no factories but buys everything from toys to TVs from thousands of factories globally. Wal-Mart has taken steps toward ensuring ethical sourcing by sending its own inspectors to these factories—in 2006, the company inspected nearly 8,900 plants worldwide, with 26 percent of those visits unannounced.

Wal-Mart's two hundred or so inspectors rate each factory on working conditions, safety, and environmental practices. Most factories with problems like failure to pay overtime get warnings and guidance in how to improve; Wal-Mart sees this as an opportunity to educate factory managers and upgrade conditions. But those factories with repeated or egregious violations such as physical abuse, child workers, or prison labor are barred forever from supplying Wal-Mart. Nearly twenty factories suffered that fate in the 2006 inspections; many more received warnings and advice on improving.

It would seem an overwhelming task to audit factories in the turbulent realm of Third World entrepreneurs, where suspect plants can be operated out of sight or be closed down only to reopen as something else doing the same things, or where hidden "shadow factories" actually produce the goods supposedly made in the show factories inspectors know about.

But many companies are taking steps to ensure that their goods are clean. In January 2007, the world's four largest retailers—Wal-Mart, Britain's Tesco, France's Carrefour, and Germany's Metro—formed the Global Social Compliance Program to develop a uniform code for workplace standards in the factories that supply them worldwide. This would mean the world's major retail companies have a single standard for how workers are treated, covering their health and safety. It forbids child and slave labor and racial and sexual discrimination, and mandates fair treatment and wages. This group of giant companies intends to enforce the code by having its own independent monitors audit factories.

Adding bottom-up reports from the factory floor might make such social audits more credible. As one executive for a multinational retailer told me, "If an issue like the health implications of a product is our goal, we run up against a lack of transparency in the supply chain. We need to make it okay for people on the scene with cameras and cell phones to say what's going on. We need more eyes and ears who have the brains of an industrial ecologist. That would give us data points we never had before. We need to let people in the supply chain report up. If I could do it, I'd set up a reward system that makes the supply chain transparent. The trouble is, there may be more money for some supplier in adulterating a product than in fixing it."

Gregory Norris notes that the state of Maine has a law that says when city or state agencies buy clothing like police uniforms they need to be sure the textiles used are sweatshop free. "But nobody can certify that now," he notes, "because the global textile marketplace is such that you go out of business if you don't have sweatshops somewhere in your supply chain. This economic pressure for sweatshops means any data you do get is slippery.

"Many folks are trying to get this right," Norris adds. "The Gap, like Nike, is looking at their supply chain." When the Gap received negative press over sweatshops, it instituted a model factory audit system, publishing its findings in the social responsibility section of its website.

The retailer, Norris recounts, "began by saying they were going to audit all their suppliers. But top-down audits fail to uncover all the bad issues and do not necessarily lead to real improvement. If Gap drops a supplier who then gets new customers, then nothing changes—it doesn't improve working conditions for anyone. So the Gap is moving toward long-term engagement with their suppliers rather than audits alone. That way they can help the suppliers learn how to get better, and Gap can get to the levels of worker safety they want."

Gregory Norris was consulted by a multinational that was measuring the ecological performance of its suppliers in Asia; the company has been discovering that they can make engineering changes to reduce emissions, and that there is local financing available for the new equipment they need. The limiting factor turned out to be that the plant managers knew little about alternative energy—the company needed to show the suppliers how to measure their CO_2 emissions and get the engineering expertise to lower it. Increasingly companies trying to green their supply chain are realizing the value of a sustained engagement with valued suppliers, which allows them to build the capacity they need to meet environmental goals.

Then there are the limits of what LCA itself can do. For one, existing Life-Cycle Assessment information has many gaps and often offers industry averages for the upstream components of items but not for finished consumer products: there's an LCA for a glass jar but not for a jar of pasta sauce. Most of the LCA data provides information that matters to industrial engineers, such as for materials like plastic resins, metals, or the various grades of a manufacturing ingredient. Another limitation of the LCA methodology reflects its strength: being empirically based, the measure is being constantly refined, a perpetual work in progress. Every time an industrial ecologist adds the results of an LCA for a specific product, that strengthens the overall database.

Another limit to the usefulness of LCAs lies in the conventional underlying business model. Typically consultants to industry develop proprietary LCA software, charging companies for access to their data and software. Whenever a consultant does a study for a company, that data goes into his or her database. The company needs to pay a fee for using it, say, to find the carbon footprint of a peach.

Norris is working with colleagues to enable a new business model that turns the conventional logic on its head—with each industry contributing data on its own operations into a common data resource, so that each company essentially brings one morsel to the table and everyone can feast from the potluck banquet, gaining access to data from all the others that have contributed. This, in effect, creates an LCA information commons for industry.

That commons could help industries meet market pressures for upgrades, such as those from large organizations. As Mike Hardiman of the University of Wisconsin told me, "We at the university are trying to be leaders in improving our world; we feel that's part of our mission." But large buyers like Hardiman are frustrated in that mission by the present lack of standards and benchmarks that will let them track how well they are doing. Hardiman believes a solid certification system would make all the difference.

"ISO certification credentials companies for having high-quality controls in manufacturing that let manufacturers find suppliers with high standards. But there aren't any such standards yet that address social consciousness issues. If there were, they would be a benchmark that would guide our purchases. In a global business environment, that lets you know who you're buying from."

Finally, are radical transparency and all its incremental improvements enough? The adequacy of perpetual upgrades alone was questioned from a surprising source: John Ehrenfeld, the executive director of the International Society for Industrial Ecology. One of the founders of the field, Ehrenfeld fears that in terms of the massive challenges facing our planet, these gradual improvements may be too little, too late.

Ehrenfeld points out that simply reducing our unsustainability results in a host of technological fixes that leave untouched the underlying causes of these problems. Increasing the fuel economy of cars as the main strategy for reducing the environmental impacts of driving is such a partial solution: Although gasoline needed per mile has dropped over the years, the number of miles driven (at least before the oil price shock) has risen so greatly that it has canceled out any benefits to the environment. Says Ehrenfeld, "This strategy is shortsighted to the extent it shifts the burden away from developing better transportation alternatives."

Ehrenfeld, who retired as director of MIT's Program on

Technology, Business, and Environment, notes that, from the global perspective, the rate of change toward greater sustainability must outpace increases in overall industrial output to ensure that eco-upgrades matter. Examining corporate and government data on gains in eco-efficiency, Ehrenfeld concludes that they are too small as yet to offset the growing threats. He calls for industry to make more radical leaps, finding innovations that greatly expand the current range of ecological choice. In addition to discovering better choices among present technologies, he also calls for product innovations that "radically reduce the amount of stuff that humans all over the globe use to produce well-being."

If industrial ecology had a statesman, it would be Ehrenfeld. He brings a larger perspective to the minutiae of Life Cycle Assessment by questioning what it all means with a radical premise: "The global industrial system is broken; the environment would rather not have us here at all. Reducing unsustainability, though critical, does not create sustainability. The planet needs to be restored to a healthy state. We should go beyond the goal of merely lessening our harmful impacts and seek true sustainability"—the flourishing levels of health, vitality, and resilience that allow both humans and Earth's ecosystems to thrive.

"Of course we need every possible eco-efficiency, any solution that reduces unsustainability," Ehrenfeld is quick to note. "Everything that makes the next thing we buy less negative is necessary; every such action helps." But, he adds, "the vision of what we need to be truly sustainable goes way beyond this. We need to look at the whole consumer mentality."

DOING WELL BY DOING GOOD

Centuries ago when villagers would share a common grazing area, some farmers abused the privilege by overgrazing their herds, destroying the pasture's value to all. The contemporary equivalent of this tragedy of the commons can be seen in the business model that has been dubbed "take-make-waste." Environmental activists who coined that phrase charge that the free market has a glaring blind spot: it ignores the cost of commerce's destruction or consumption of nature itself, the planet's common.

Throughout history companies have been able to consume or pollute air, water, or land with little to no consequence. The costs—such as damage from floods and the expense of treating respiratory disease or cleaning toxins from soil—are borne by the general public. Whatever form such abuse of nature's commons takes, the laissez-faire mishandling of any public resource can be seen as unsustainable and ethically unacceptable. Ethical judgments aside, there has been a practical problem in dealing with this abuse: calculating the actual cost of such damage to nature.

But new methodologies now allow the quantification of "natural capital," the economic value accruing from nature. One model for this can be seen in the efforts of the Canadian Boreal Initiative, a consortium of environmental groups and companies like Suncor Energy (natural gas) and Tembec (a paper and pulp giant) that have huge investments in the vast forest that spans most of the Canadian north. Working in tandem with the native peoples whose land lies within the region, the Initiative has conducted a systematic estimate of the yearly fiscal worth of the pristine, sprawling Mackenzie Valley, a virgin forest zone in the Northwest Territories. The Valley contains a large part of the vast boreal forest that spans most of the Canadian north—the world's largest remaining intact woodland.

The Valley's natural capital—the sum of ecological services like absorption of carbon dioxide and other greenhouse gases, pests eaten by birds, clean water—has been put at roughly $378 billion. That figure dwarfs the annual economic value in the same region from extractive industries like mining, whose operations inevitably destroy a part of the common itself—and which in the past have never been charged for that destruction. That estimate offers a model for calculating the cost to a common of any commercial activity that diminishes these ecological services and so allows a rational basis for "taxing" the activity.

A parallel calculus for the public health risks of industrial processes yields a similar measure for analyzing air emissions from industrial supply chains. Combining LCA with epidemiologic databases, researchers at the National Center for Environmental Research estimated added cancer cases per $1 million output for certain industries in the United States due to the release of toxic chemicals during manufacturing.

From the perspective of a product's life cycle, we usually do not know the extent to which harmful impacts are passed on to the public. If a factory releases toxins that increase the rate of cancer or kill fish in a local river, or if a product's disposal releases toxins like mercury into the landfill, the company has passed off hidden costs of that product to the people and communities that will suffer or pay for repairing the damages.

One policy solution for this dilemma, proposed with increasing frequency in recent years, is to tax companies for the harms their products cause over the course of their life cycle. That tax could take the form of a proportionate payment to an organization that remedies the damage, such as a wind farm that reduces the equivalent amount of greenhouse gases emitted by an industrial process. Such a tax converts the damage to the common into an operating cost borne by the business, so forcing the price of the resulting commodity to reflect its adverse impact. Transferring the cost of harm to the company that does the damage would create strong fiscal incentives to find ways of doing business that will reduce such costs.

One fundamental dilemma of the tragedy of the commons boils down to how to handle challenges of vast magnitude and regulate business on a global scale. Nations send out fishing fleets that have incentives to catch as many fish as they can—which depletes the fishing stock available to everyone. The Maldives are threatened by rising sea levels from global warming, with the United States the largest contributor to greenhouse gases. Pollution from China affects Japan. And none of these players need bear the cost—fish are free to anyone who catches them; the people of the Maldives are powerless to reduce American greenhouse gas; people suffering from respiratory disease in Japan can do nothing about China's coal-burning plants.

With such dilemmas in mind, the economist Joseph Stiglitz argues that holding corporate interests above all means that harm to the global environment and public well-being are inevitable. He would turn to rules from governments or bodies like the WTO to remedy the abuses. As one chemist who does basic research on toxicity put it, "The function of government is to offer incentives through regulations. That way, the new research becomes part of the cost structure."

We can't always wait for government solutions. Political realities may make promises of beneficial shifts attractive, but not the pain of those shifts—politicians too often defer the pain until they will be out of office. Depending on governments and their policies to patrol the world of commerce has notorious pitfalls; governments are notoriously slow and awkward when they try to regulate commerce. And corporate self-interest typically dictates that companies oppose such government restrictions. Mandatory carbon caps, the banning of chemicals, enviro-activists picketing corporate headquarters all nudge commerce toward more ecological transparency. There is no doubt a place for such interventions. But these are sticks.

Radical transparency holds out the carrot, the promise of business opportunity waiting to be seized. The free market itself could foster an alternative or complementary mechanism for making damage to the commons consequential to a company, through systematically revealing that harm to consumers. And if a company takes steps to compensate the commons for damage done (e.g., as a member of the Forest Stewardship Council, which requires a company to plant trees to replace those it lumbers) or raises local health and education standards by bringing jobs to poverty-stricken areas, that, too, would be transparent.

Radical transparency would let the marketplace reward the good regardless of whether the damage was "taxed." As a former U.S. government economist, who asked to remain anonymous, told me, using the dynamics of the free market in this way "bypasses the ineptitude of government. It lets the market show what matters—you don't need to wait for governments to act."

Stiglitz proposes that global economic success depends on getting the right regulatory balance between markets and government. As an executive at a Fortune 50 company put it, "Customer shifts and government regulations are the two things that can change the business reality in the right direction."

Stiglitz, who pointed out the ways poor information cripples markets, sees economic indicators alone as markers of efficiency that are insufficient for our times. Free markets, he says, result in too much pollution and too little of the basic research needed to make radical leaps toward sustainability. Lately he has joined a chorus advocating a "green net national product" that, along with fiscal measures, takes into account depletion of natural resources and environmental degradation to replace the standard gross domestic product, the measure of a nation's income and economic output, as the index of an economy's robustness.

Something akin to that dual measure makes sense, too, as a

metric for a company's dual bottom line: eco-efficiency measured as the ratio of economic value added versus ecological impacts. That gives a more ecologically intelligent accounting, one that weighs financial success in light of its net harm: both the value chain and the devalue chain. Some companies already have begun to operate along these lines. BASF, the German chemical product company, uses such a measure of eco-efficiency to choose among alternative processes and options, seeking strategic choices that yield both financial and ecological gains.

When I asked the head of product innovation at a global company how an ecological transparency system might change the business landscape in years ahead, he mentioned two probable ways thinking might morph. The first would be a shift in the value basis, adding a product's ecological impacts into the equation. The second will come in the scramble to rethink how products are made, to maintain a brand's market position.

Then there are the initiatives of companies that embrace a triple bottom line, where environmental and social impacts matter as well as financial outcomes. Historically corporate responsibility has gone through distinct phases. The first, exemplified by Andrew Carnegie, saw industrial robber barons amass great wealth and later become philanthropists; Carnegie's public libraries dot the United States. The Robin Hood phase sees companies charge premiums for green products and then give a portion of profits to worthy causes.

In the third stage, growing rapidly these days, companies integrate sustainability into their business strategy. This "requires rethinking the business, the product, and the solutions, so you have mutually reinforcing benefits," in the words of Kevin Hagen, director of corporate social responsibility at the sporting goods co-op

REI. He cites how REI has been reexamining its corporate footprint, trying to go from "do less bad, to do more good."

"There's a difference between just trying to be green and finding sustainable business solutions," Hagen observes. "The first can have unintended consequences and may or may not work in its business implications. The second is thoughtful, has metrics, and contributes profitably to the business. We're getting beyond either/or, sustainable or profitable—they're not mutually exclusive. It's not about trade-offs or finding the balance between the two. Success is when these are mutually reinforcing—the more green we can be, the more money we make."

Hagen points to a decision made, after REI assessed its carbon footprint, to shift from relying on conventional power from the electric grid and natural gas for its operations to renewable energy. "We identified price volatility as a business risk we had not identified before," says Hagen. "So both to eliminate CO_2 emissions and hedge energy costs, we looked for renewable sources wherever we could—we're now at twenty percent renewable sources. That decision has insulated us a bit from the rising costs of energy."

When the bottom line is the sole arbiter of decision making, some or many of the changes ecological transparency demands may seem unreasonable or at the very least risky strategic targets. They can be made more readily to the degree that there are clear or likely competitive advantages. But that decision becomes much easier for organizations that have adopted an ethical bottom line so that impacts on the planet matter, impacts on health and on people matter. When these enter the equation along with cost, business calculations render different decisions.

Mike Hardiman told me that several years ago the Wisconsin

state legislature mandated all government agencies buy recycled paper, regardless of cost. "When the requirement started, the cost differential between virgin and recycled used to be large, but now the gap has closed. If someone doesn't start the trend by making a principled stand, we won't see the changes we need in industrial methods and materials."

Corporate social responsibility represents a mixed picture across companies, with some setting high standards for themselves and their sector, others making idiosyncratic or halfhearted efforts, and still others using toothless measures that may merely sound good to whatever stakeholders care. "The triple bottom line is a desire, not a hard metric," says Pavan Sukhdev, an accountant who directs the Green Indian States Trust in New Delhi and consultant to InfoSys and WinPro. "With the present loose definitions of the triple bottom line you can tell your own story most any way you want. But we'd never allow that range of flexibility for fiscal accounting."

The worst cases are the companies where corporate social responsibility has become the front line in a bitter war between business ethics and shareholder value, with companies espousing aspirations that fiscal realities stymie. As the head of corporate compliance at a national apparel firm confides, for many in top management ethical mandates like those for corporate social responsibility are just an "irritant"—something they have to put up with or pay lip service to. In the words of this executive, "If I could walk into my CEO's office and say, 'Look, here is proof that the customers are stopping buying from certain brands based on their ethical sourcing practices,' then they would pay attention."

COMPASSIONATE CONSUMPTION

"For years," laments Robert B. Reich, professor of public policy at the University of California at Berkeley and former U.S. secretary of labor, "I've preached that corporate social responsibility helps the bottom line. Respect the environment, your employees, and the community, I argued, and they'll not only respect you back; they'll buy your products."

Reich goes on to explain why he's changed his mind, making a provocative case that the socially responsible gestures companies make are mere public relations gambits, ways to burnish their public image, cut costs, or dodge more government rules. And, he adds, "That's the way it should be. Companies aren't moral beings. They exist to make money for their shareholders by hanging on to customers."

That pretty much sums up a core debate in business ethics, the classic predicament that pits doing good against doing well. Two bibles in this argument are economist Milton Friedman's *Capitalism and Freedom,* which argues that corporate profit is the sole moral basis for business operations, and philosopher John Rawls's *A Theory of Justice,* which has shaped the views of those who argue that a moral basis for business must be social responsibility.

In the gritty arena of day-to-day business decisions, to the extent executives put profit as the primary driver of strategy, other goals become secondary. As Reich observes, objectives like social responsibility or minimizing environmental impacts can be pursued only to the degree that they help the bottom line—like the easy cost savings from lowering energy costs. But when the price of doing the right thing threatens profitability, those good things are skipped.

As Milton Friedman famously put it, "The social responsibility of business is to increase its profits." Within the terms of Friedman's argument, a strong ethical case can be made for *not* making changes—no matter how virtuous—if they will harm profit. That sets up the win–lose: either doing well or doing good.

At this point Reich throws up his hands, saying it's hopeless to try to reason or moralize companies into virtue. He favors coercion through government regulation—after first closing down the lobbying by business interests that he sees as paralyzing government action in the United States. That tactic could take years, decades, or forever to achieve.

Radical transparency offers a third way out of this dilemma: make goodness pay. Eco-transparency transforms the core assumptions of this discussion itself, morphing the business model to create a market reality where doing good becomes synonymous with doing well.

Making visible the hidden impacts of our choices holds a bold solution, one that goes beyond the tired tactic of instilling environmental fears and even beyond hopes about innovative greener and cleaner alternatives for industry. Those virtuous technologies will matter little if the marketplace fails to make them financial winners.

Beyond these fears and hopes lies full transparency about the impacts of what we buy. To the extent that transparency allows shoppers to vote with their dollars for more ecologically intelligent technologies, ingredients, and design—and so shifts market share toward them—commerce will reform itself, not just in the name of responsibility but in pursuit of profit.

Activists decry the threats of global warming, the pollution of our bodies, sweatshops, and the like, while many businesspeople have argued for greening and social responsibility as good for the corporation. Yet the fundamental tenets of capitalism have put those two camps at odds: executives are paid to maximize company shareholder value and quarterly earnings, not to support the common good. This antagonism between corporate goals and those of the public interest creates a quandary for those many executives who seek both to please their shareholders and to pursue the best interests of the public. But radical transparency unites what had seemed polarities: the self-interest of a company aligns with the best interests and values of the consumer.

This conceptual sea change reorients capitalism to embrace the public interest as an arena for competition emerges where ethics, innovation, and initiative are dependably rewarded in sales. This shift replaces a win–lose assumption of profit versus virtue with a win–win proposition. Whether our purchases add up to a few dollars at the local store or millions through business-to-business transactions, we incentivize business to make positive changes by voting with our dollars. Each of us becomes an active player in determining the course of the planet, our health, and our common destiny.

The movement toward such transparency augurs a day when the free market will forcefully operate in the public interest. Radical transparency offers a mechanism for commerce-based improvements, where market forces rather than governmental fiat bring about desired changes. It creates a genuinely positive impact on a firm's bottom line from the missions of responsibility that so many corporations already call their "second bottom line"—but that today may lose money. It catalyzes an immense competitive arena for innovation, entrepreneurial genius, and smart strategic planning to create wealth. And in doing so, it moves us all toward a more viable and healthy planet.

One critique of globalization holds that it creates a social and environmental race to the bottom in developing countries where factories compete to supply the cheapest goods most quickly. The marble tiles, handmade carpets, and labor-intensive lingerie sold in the First World are too often made by laborers in the Third World who work deadly long hours, for pitiful wages, under dangerous or unhealthy conditions—millions of children among them.

Governments in such countries have objected to having labor standards part of trade agreements; some economists fear that such standards might punish developing economies should multinationals pull investments from subpar suppliers. Michael Hiscox (the Harvard professor who conducted the experiment that showed shoppers would pay more for ethically made towels) argued at a conference on globalization at Princeton University that a market-based tactic might well work more effectively than trade agreements. A certification for products that met higher standards for working conditions, environmental sustainability, and so on would alert concerned shoppers, many of whom, his study found, are willing to pay higher prices to reward such virtuous goods. That might make virtue pay a good way down the supply chain.

Consider what this might mean for the impact of the world's richest consumers on the working and living conditions of the world's poor. Another great injustice of global warming can be seen in the sad fact that the world's poor will suffer most greatly from global warming, while they contribute least to the cause. The habits of the rich most intensely fuel the planet's global warming—and so the rich bear the greatest ethical burden to change.

The one billion denizens of the developed world consume at a rate thirty-two times greater than the world's poorest citizens. This vast share of humanity's footprint on the planet means a thirty-two times greater rate not just in using limited resources like oil or lumber or fish but also in producing waste like greenhouse gases, plastics choking marine life, and a sea of other stuff moldering in landfills.

Social geographer Jared Diamond, who makes this observation, notes that this rate of consumption will become utterly unsustainable as millions from countries like China and India reach for the lifestyle of the world's affluent. He suggests that if consumption were to grow more efficient—using alternatives to fuels that produce greenhouse gases, sustainable lumbering and fisheries, and the like—we would stand a better chance of dodging a planetary collapse from this unparalleled human binge. That greater efficiency would be far more easily reached if the marketplace were transparent: if it were crystal clear to us which things we buy contribute to health, sustainability, and social equity—and which worsen things.

With the right information at their fingertips, the wealthiest consumers could do more than achieve more sustainable consumption for themselves. Shopping would become an opportunity for compassion, with purchase decisions whose effects could ripple through global supply chains, so leveraging better environmental, health, and working conditions for the world's poorest.

Shoppers in Berlin or Brooklyn or Beijing could make informed choices that would speed the conversion of China's power grid from coal-belching plants to alternate sources, reduce the clouds of toxins that a Mexican farmworker inhales, upgrade working conditions in sweatshops in Vietnam, or enhance the health of miners in Africa. That means, in turn, not just better life circumstances for Chinese, Mexicans, Vietnamese, and Africans but also more virtuous shopping choices available to these target nations as they in turn become more affluent. In a transparent marketplace, shopping becomes a geopolitical act.

In short, radical transparency holds the potential to better align what sells with the public good. It changes consumers from helpless cogs in a vast machine into a force that matters—whether those consumers be concerned moms or purchasing agents for a huge organization. A transparent marketplace alters the fundamental balance between businesses and their customers, allowing shoppers to vote with their dollars with unprecedented precision.

This informational fix has been a missing piece in the free market system all along, one that holds the promise of ending the eternal tension between profit and public welfare. Radical transparency changes the rules of the game for business. In an ecologically intelligent economy, executives will be paid to maximize shareholder value by being responsive to the public good. As market forces align corporate and public interests, commerce takes on a new role as a tool for our collective well-being.

A boost in ecological intelligence seems essential for our species to adapt to the singular challenges of these times. Ian McCallum, a South African physician and naturalist who writes about ecological intelligence, points out that while our planet seems destined in the years ahead for shifts in weather that threaten our fragile niche, the planet itself can continue long after our species has gone. To avert this fate, he says, we don't have to fix the planet but rather our relationship to it.

He would have us consider the distinction between healing and mending. Mending suggests the quick fix, the Band-Aid that, while helpful, does nothing to resolve the underlying problem. Mending can be compellingly seductive, an endless stream of fixes that never truly heal. Healing goes deeper, to the root causes, and brings a profound change of attitude. Healing perceives the hidden patterns that connect and sees everyone as having some part in the solution. The root meaning of "heal" is to make whole again.

"We have to stop speaking about the Earth being in need of healing," McCallum observes. "The Earth doesn't need healing. We do."

ACKNOWLEDGMENTS

Ecological intelligence is by its very nature widely distributed among far-flung networks of people; each of us holds at least a small part, some of us quite a lot. In my explorations I've been helped along the way by countless individuals, only some of whom I can acknowledge here.

First there are the many insightful people who appear in this book, who educated me as I interviewed them. I learned a huge amount from these conversations and am enormously grateful. In addition to those I've quoted directly or cited in the text, I have major debts to the following: Larry Brilliant sparked my thinking about all this in the first place. Shoshana Zuboff and James Maxmin, in their groundbreaking book *The Support Economy,* helped me understand the marketplace power of people "voting with their dollars." Ben Shedd first demonstrated for me how to make bar codes transparent. Michael Lerner inspired me with hard data on ecological health. Early on, Myla Kabat-Zinn and Gary Cohen flagged for me the hidden ecological risks in everyday items. Art Kleiner helped me see the problem from the executive's perspective; Steve Tuttleman offered key insights into business realities and sensibilities. William McDonough opened my eyes to a realistic path to reengineering the built world.

Other helpful ideas and suggestions came from Jessica Brackman, Jacalyn Bennett, Richard Boyatzis, Matt Breitfelder, Elizabeth Cuthrell, Steve Dane, Richard Davidson, Jake Davis, Darcy Rezac, Robin Elson, Deborah Gannon, David Goehring, Joseph Goldstein, Charles Halpern, Kate Harper, Mellody Hobson, Russell Jaffe, Jon Kabat-Zinn, Lord Richard Layard, Tom Lesser, George Lucas, Harper Marshall, Charles Melcher, Daniel Melcher, David Meyer, Robert Ornstein, Stephan Rechstaffen, Diane Rose, Jeff Sable, Sharon Salzberg, Ed Skloot, Vikram Soni, Maggie Spiegel, Richard Weinberg, and Weijun Zhang. This list acknowledges but a few of my many benefactors along the way.

Jonathan Black provided dogged, crucial research help. Rowan Foster did as-needed searches and kept the whole shop running. And, as always, my wife, Tara Bennett-Goleman, has been a priceless fount of insights, wisdom, and nurture.

NOTES

CHAPTER ONE: *The Hidden Price of What We Buy*

cheaper toys are more likely: Christopher Beam, "Why Do They Put Lead Paint in Toys?," www.slate.com. August 15, 2007.

various levels of lead: Jeff Karoub, "Groups Release Guide to Toxins in Toys," Associated Press, December 5, 2007.

clueless as most of us: And, for the record, I did not coin the term "ecological intelligence"—it's been knocking around for years.

toll these decisions have: The passage is from the foreword to the paperback edition of my book *Vital Lies, Simple Truths: The Psychology of Self-Deception* (New York: Simon & Schuster, 1986), p. 13.

boiled down into evaluations: Industrial ecology for the moment remains largely an academic discipline that caters to the needs of industry, with its proprietary databases closed to the public eye. But an article in the *Journal of Industrial Ecology* called for the discipline to apply its analyses to weigh the relative impacts of competing products, tag harmful impacts, and make those evaluations public in simplified forms that would help shoppers making decisions at the point of purchase as well as progressive firms that could use these metrics to upgrade their products. Dara O'Rourke, "Market Movements: Nongovernmental Organization Strategies to Influence Global Production and Consumption," *Journal of Industrial Ecology* 9, nos. 1–2 (2005): 115–128.

CHAPTER TWO: *"Green" Is a Mirage*

poses a riddle: Bhadantacariya Buddhaghosa, *The Visuddhimagga, or Path of Purification,* trans. Bhikkhu Nanamoli (Boston: Shambhala Publishers, 2003), chapter 18, paragraph 25.

to name but a few: Juan Carlos Alonso et al., "Design for Environment of Electrical and Electronic Automotive Components Based on Life Cycle Assessment," *Gate to EHS,* March 17, 2003, pp. 1–7.

belonging to the God Indra: See, for example, Francis Harold Cook, *Hua-Yen Buddhism: The Jewel Net of Indra* (University Park, PA: Penn State Press, 1977). Indra, a Vedic deity, is the archetypic lord of lords; as the god of war and storms he bears some resemblance to the Teutonic god Thor.

repeating and reinventing itself: The Ouroboros has also been seen as symbolizing creation out of destruction, primordial unity, and the dual nature of all things, among many other interpretations.

refusing plastic bags in stores: "Anya Hindmarch Talks about Bag Craze on Eve of New York Launch," www.ecorazzi.com, July 17, 2007.

Eager buyers lined up: Lisa McLaughlin, "Paper, Plastic, or Prada?," *Time,* August 13, 2007, p. 49.

merits of paper versus plastic: Martin B. Hocking, "Paper versus Polystyrene: A Complex Choice," *Science* 251 (1999): 504–505.

forgoing pesticides in cotton: John C. Ryan and Alan Thein Durning, *Stuff: The Secret Lives of Everyday Things* (Seattle, WA: Northwest Environment Watch, 1997).

foods marketed as healthy choices: Andrew Martin, "Store Chain's Test Concludes That Nutrition Sells," the *New York Times,* September 6, 2007, C3.

plucked from the aisles: TerraChoice Environmental Marketing, "The Six Sins of Greenwashing" (2007), www.terrachoice.com/Home.

NOTES

CHAPTER THREE: *What We Don't Know*

20 percent less snow: Christoph Marty, "Regime Shift of Snow Days in Switzerland," *Geophysical Research Letters* 35 (2008): L12501.

10 percent of coral reefs: Roberto Danovaro et al., "Sunscreens Cause Coral Bleaching by Promoting Viral Infections," *Environmental Health Perspectives* 116 (2008): 441–447.

Harvard psychologist Dan Gilbert: Lecture at PopTech Conference, Camden, Maine, October 2007.

molecules nature can absorb: William McDonough and Michael Braungart, *Cradle to Cradle* (New York: North Point Press, 2002).

"development" can hide the extinguishing: Vikram Soni and Sanjay Parikh, "Justice for Nature," unpublished manuscript, 2008.

CHAPTER FOUR: *Ecological Intelligence*

"ecological intelligence": My exploration of ecological intelligence goes down very different paths from those taken by Ian McCallum, whose book *Ecological Intelligence: Rediscovering Ourselves in the Environment* (Golden, CO: Fulcrum Publishing, 2009) offers the eloquent insights of a physician, Jungian analyst, and poet. I had begun writing about ecological intelligence before I came upon his gem of a book.

uniquely human ability: Gardner has flirted with this talent, speculatively adding to his initial list of seven what he calls "naturalist" intelligence, for those who have extensive knowledge of the living world. People gifted in this realm can make critical distinctions and detect the hidden patterns and order in nature, as Linneaus did. Howard Gardner, *Intelligence Reframed* (New York: Basic Books, 1996).

all-encompassing sensibility: Ecological intelligence as I describe it here does not meet the formal requirements of an "intelligence" as studied by psychometricians; I use the term as a heuristic for the capacity to perceive connections between human activities and their range of consequences in natural and social systems.

Evolutionary anthropologists recognize: Esther Herrmann et al., "Humans Have Evolved Specialized Skills of Social Cognition: The Cultural Intelligence Hypothesis," *Science* 317 (2007): 1360–1366.

CHAPTER FIVE: *The New Math*

one-fifth that for trucking: Emissions for container shipping are rated at 52 grams of CO_2 per ton of cargo per kilometer transported (for trucking, 252 grams; for shipment by train, 200 grams; and for air cargo, 570 grams). Tyler Colman and Pablo Päster, American Association of Wine Economists Working Paper no. 9, "Red, White, and 'Green': The Cost of Carbon in the Global Wine Trade," October 2007.

from New Zealand: Caroline Saunders and Andrew Barber, "Comparative Energy and Greenhouse Gas Emissions of New Zealand's and the United Kingdom's Dairy Industry," AERU Research Report no. 297, July 2007. It would be intriguing to see if environmental scientists at a British university would come to the same conclusions about lamb from New Zealand.

Long-stemmed roses: "The Good Consumer," *The Economist,* January 17, 2008, economist.com.

just over the Channel: Michael Specter, "Big Foot," *The New Yorker,* February 25, 2008.

the liquid is boiling hot: Scott Belcher, "Bisphenol-A Is Released from Polycarbonate Drinking Bottles and Mimics the Neurotoxic Actions of Estrogen in Developing Cerebellar Neurons," *Toxicology Letters,* January 30, 2008, pp. 149–156.

our planet's natural reserves: Soni and Parikh, "Justice for Nature."

pills in our medicine cabinets: Bethany Halford, "Side Effects," *Chemical and Engineering News,* February 25, 2008, pp. 13–17.

male minnows stopped making sperm: Karen A. Kidd et al., "Collapse of a Fish Population after Exposure to a Synthetic Estrogen," *Proceedings of the National Academy of Science* 104 (2007): 8897–8901. Even though the human body excretes these estrogen compounds in the form of a metabolite, in wastewater treatment plants bacteria cleave to the metabolite and re-create the original compound.

260 excess cancer cases: Dinah Koehler et al., "Rethinking Environmental Performance from a Public Health Perspective," *Journal of Industrial Ecology* 9 (2005): 143–167.

terribly unsanitary conditions: Associated Press, "Probe Targets Brazilian Ethanol Company," March 11, 2008.

comparing the harms from pollution: Gregory Norris, "Social Impacts in Product Life Cycles: Towards Life Cycle Attribute Assessment," *The International Journal of Life Cycle Assessment* 1 (2006): 97–104.

toll of Dutch shopping: Durk S. Nijdam et al., "Environmental Load from Dutch Private Consumption," *Journal of Industrial Ecology* 9 (2005): 147–168.

number of lethal accidents: Leif Barthel et al., Department of Life Cycle Engineering, University of Stuttgart, "Social LCA: Analogies and Differences to Environmental LCA," presentation at the Third International Conference on Life Cycle Management, Zurich, August 27–29, 2007.

"working seconds per process": See, for example, Cecilia Makishi et al., "Social LCA—Requirements and Needs," presentation at Life Cycle Assessment/Life Cycle Management annual meeting, October 6, 2006.

case of ecotourism: Norris, "Social Impacts."

CHAPTER SIX: *The Information Gap*

lack of available information: Years after his first article proclaiming that greater information enhances efficiency, Stiglitz coauthored another claiming that there are upper limits to how readily information can be shared, so optimal efficiency remains an elusive dream. See Sanford J. Grossman and Joseph E. Stiglitz, "On the Impossibility of Informationally Efficient Markets," *American Economic Review* (June 1980): 393–408.

"information asymmetry": Joseph Stiglitz, *Globalization and Its Discontents* (New York: Norton, 2002).

ignorance cripples market efficiency: The range of prices for an identical item, like a used car, represents the level of ignorance in a market, while sound information on prices and value lessens the amount of ignorance and by zeroing in on the fair market value of that car narrows the range of prices.

hampers market fairness: The insight that information matters economically allows computations of the costs of ignorance. One formula measures how our personal welfare changes simply by virtue of having sound information about a product, using contaminated foods as the case in point. The equation boils down to: If we're clueless, we might buy the tainted hot dog or cat food; if we're in the know, we'll avoid it (economists, of course, state that self-evident proposition in more nuanced and technical terms). W. Foster and R. E. Just, "Measuring Welfare Effects of Product Contamination with Consumer Uncertainty," *Journal of Environmental Economics and Management* 17 (1989): 266–283.

even then the explicit labeling: David Mattingly, quoted in Tom Mueller, "Slippery Business," *The New Yorker,* August 13, 2007, p. 42.

bout of hyperactive frenzy: D. McCann et al., "Food additives increase hyperactivity in three-year-olds and in 8/9-year-old children in the community," *The Lancet* 370 (2007): 1560–1567.

fight over label design: M.F. Teisl et al., "Can Eco-Labels Tune a Market?," *Journal of Environmental Economics and Management* 43 (2002): 339–359.

"green" certification programs: See, for example, the Green Seal program, www.greenseal.org.

they crave information: Teisl, "Can Eco-Labels?"

In economic theory: Archon Fung, Mary Graham, and David Weil, *Full Disclosure: The Perils and Promise of Transparency* (New York: Cambridge University Press, 2007).

CHAPTER SEVEN: *Full Disclosure*

shift from one brand: To be sure, subtle cues can also shift choices. But the consciously decided preference should be less vulnerable to change later on from subtle cues alone.

in line with your conscience: Raina Kelley, "Day 31: The End my Friend," September 21, 2007, blog.newsweek.com/blogs/freegangirl/.

"prime" the mind: See, e.g., John A. Bargh, "The Automaticity of Everyday Life," in R. S. Wyer (ed.), *Advances in Social Cognition,* Vol. 10 (Hillside, NJ: Erlbaum, 1997).

CHAPTER EIGHT: *Twitter and Buzz*

revolution catalyzes new forms: Clay Shirky, *Here Comes Everybody: The Power of Organizing without Organizations* (New York: Penguin Press, 2008).

advocate of ethical leadership: See, e.g., Bill George, *Authentic Leadership* (San Francisco: Jossey-Bass, 2003).

the three-star ratings: Andrew Martin, "Is It Healthy? Food Rating Systems Battle It Out," the *New York Times*, December 1, 2007, p. C3.

there are lots of holes: Rich Barton, interviewed in "Chat," *Wired*, December 2007, p. 267.

viral marketing class: Q&A with two Stanford Facebook class teams that reached 1M users in thirty days, November 25, 2007, www.insideface book.com.

more than a million: Paul Hawken, *Blessed Unrest: How the Largest Movement in the World Came into Being and Why No One Saw It Coming* (New York: Viking, 2007).

court-ordered shutdown: For one activist account of the Plachimada Coca-Cola plant incident: D. Rajeev, "India: Everything Gets Worse with Coca-Cola," Inter Press Service, August 22, 2005.

Their goal: a single standard: Ian Pearson, quoted in James Kanter, "A Low-Carbon Diet," *International Herald Tribune*, June 7, 2007, p. 13.

CHAPTER NINE: *Fair and Square*

the Fair and Square batch: Michael J. Hiscox and Nicholas F. B. Smyth, "Is There Consumer Demand for Improved Labor Standards? Evidence from Field Experiments in Social Product Labeling," Department of Government, Harvard University, unpublished manuscript, February 2008. A similar sales bump happened when the labels were put on candles, albeit not quite so strongly.

eco-products cost 2 percent more: GreenBiz, "FSC-Certified Wood Outsells Non-certified 2 to 1," www.greenbiz.com/news, January 13, 2004.

socks were priced the same: Monica Prasad et al., "Consumers of the World Unite: A Market-based Response to Sweatshops," *Labor Studies Journal* 29 (3): 57–80.

wine in each glass: Hilke Plassmann et al., "Marketing Actions Modulate the Neural Representation of Experienced Pleasantness," *Proceedings of the National Academy of Sciences* 105 (2008): 1050–1054.

a quarter of shoppers: "The Good Consumer," *The Economist*, January 17, 2008, www.economist.com.

would pay an extra dollar: O'Rourke, "Market Movements."

also on the "worst" list: The ratings are at www.cosmeticsdatabase
.com/browse.php?maincat=haircare, while prices were taken from Web
marketing sites and retailers.

"green consumer" campaigns: J. Makower, "Whatever Happened to
Green Consumers?," Organic Consumers Association, July/August 2000,
www.organicconsumers.org/Organic/greenism.cfm.

little or no discernable impact: O'Rourke, "Market Movements."

Hannaford Brothers Company: Andrew Martin, "Store Chain's Test Concludes That Nutrition Sells," the *New York Times,* September 6, 2007, C3.

billion individual purchase decisions: That estimate was in a news release from Hannaford stores on September 6, 2007.

"Compassionate Capitalism": Stu Stein, whose student blog has disappeared (he has since graduated from Wharton), was commenting on
my talk "Why Can't We All Be Good Samaritans?" at the 2007 TED conference, www.ted.com/speakers/view/id/178, in Monterey, California.

survey of American teenagers: A random, representative sample of 767
teens from 13 to 19 years old, mean age 14.6 years. JWT survey, "Ten Stats
about Teens and the Environment," *New York,* March 2007.

CHAPTER TEN: *The Virtuous Cycle*

came from a 1993 report: W. C. Willett et al., "Intake of Trans Fatty Acids
and Risk of Coronary Heart Disease Among Women," *The Lancet* 341
(1993): 581–585.

already died from heart disease: F. B. Hu et al., "Dietary Fat Intake and
the Risk of Coronary Heart Disease in Women," *The New England Journal
of Medicine* 337 (1997): 1491–1499.

labeling trans fats: FDA, "Food Labeling: Trans Fatty Acids in Nutrition
Labeling," *The Federal Register* 68, no. 133 (July 11, 2003).

dripping with the hydrogenated oil: There's more to the trans fat story,
though. Dunkin' Donuts, like many other food companies that now claim
their foods are "trans fat free" still includes up to half a gram of the stuff per
serving. Federal regulations allow foods below the half-gram threshold to be
labeled as having "zero grams" of trans fat. Associated Press, "Time to Make
the Donuts . . . Healthier," *Daily Hampshire Gazette,* August 27, 2007, p. D1.

which ones those were: Kim Severson, "Hidden Killer," *San Francisco Chronicle,* January 30, 2002, p. 1B.

transparency: Fung, Graham, and Weil, *Full Disclosure.*

Energy use by refrigerators: A 1973 federal mandate was not implemented because by 1978, when energy standards were ready, President Reagan opposed them. Even so, the industry began increasing energy efficiency on its own, and individual states went ahead to impose their own requirements. By 1993, a national standard was implemented by the federal government under President Clinton. David B. Goldstein, *Saving Energy, Growing Jobs* (Berkeley: Bay Tree Publishing, 2007).

enough bottles of a shampoo: The math: 8,500 gallons equals 1,088,000 ounces. If the bottles are 10 ounces each, that would make 108,800 bottles. The two major drugstore chains in the United States each has about six thousand stores. Each store stocks three or four units of each product (with additional stock held in the chain's distribution centers). So it takes twenty-four thousand units to fill the shelves for one product at all the stores.

imposing any kind of regulation: Jim Hartzfeld, quoted in Peter Senge et al., *The Necessary Revolution: How Individuals and Organizations Are Working Together to Create a Sustainable World* (New York: Doubleday Currency, 2008), p. 21.

CHAPTER ELEVEN: *The Chemical Stew*

"popcorn worker's lung": Gardiner Harris, "Doctor Links a Man's Illness to a Microwave Popcorn Habit," the *New York Times,* September 5, 2007, p. A23.

pulling diacetyl from the mix: Associated Press, "Microwave Popcorn to Omit a Risky Chemical," the *New York Times,* September 6, 2007, p. C12.

should treat the news: Associated Press, "Heavy Popcorn User Ailing," *Daily Hampshire Gazette,* p. 4.

may pose respiratory dangers: David Michaels, *Doubt Is Their Product* (New York: Oxford University Press, 2008).

man-made chemical compounds: One commonly cited source for estimates of numbers of chemicals: *Guide to the Business of Chemistry, 2006 Edition* (Arlington, VA: American Chemistry Council, 2006).

concoctions might impact: Actually, the combinatorial possibilities are much greater. The approximately three thousand most-used chemicals, if studied in groups of three, could be combined in about 85 billion ways. Since tests of body burden have measured around two to three thousand chemicals each (far less than the 85,000+ chemicals in the federal registry) and yet have found easily one to three hundred chemicals in each person, the combinatorial possibilities are vast. And that is just the combinations of the chemicals themselves—this does not account for dose, timing, genetic individuality, concurrent infections, or other concurrent health issues, such as stress, immune impairment, and so on.

the brain's vulnerability: Martha Herbert et al., "Autism: A Brain Disorder, or a Disorder That Affects the Brain?," *Clinical Neuropsychiatry* 2, no. 6 (2005): 354–379.

environmental stress and inflammation: Martha R. Herbert et al., "Autism and Environmental Genomics," *Neurotoxicology* 27 (2006): 671–684.

endocrine disorders like diabetes : Kevin Becker, "The Common Variants/Multiple Disease Hypothesis of Common Complex Genetic Disorders," *Medical Hypotheses* 62 (2004): 309–317.

a tipping point: Oxidative stress and inflammation are themselves markers of allostatic load, a broader index of stress the body undergoes versus its ability to stay resilient in the face of these biological challenges.

worldwide study of COPD: A. Sonia Buist et al., "International Variation in the Prevalence of COPD," *The Lancet* 370 (September 1, 2007): 741–750.

according to an editorial: "Beyond the Lungs—a New View of COPD," *The Lancet* 370 (September 1, 2007): 740.

may still be safe: The complexities of environmental–physiological interactions clearly allow for safe exposure to some toxins in controlled amounts. As encountered in nature, botulin bacterium, an anaerobic toxin, sometimes called the world's most deadly poison, can paralyze and kill a person within days. But with the tiny, harmless amounts delivered in Botox injections, the targeted muscles relax for about three months, making facial wrinkles disappear. Even botulin, then, can be used safely under the right conditions.

methods used by toxicologists: Deborah A. Cory-Slechta, "Studying Toxicants as Single Chemicals: Does This Strategy Adequately Identify Neurotoxic Risk?," *Neurotoxicology* 26 (2005): 491–510.

CHAPTER TWELVE: *The Amygdala Goes Shopping*

Skin Deep: Skin Deep Cosmetic Safety Database, www.cosmeticdata base.com.

close to 90 percent: the estimate was made by the Environmental Working Group, www.cosmeticdatabase.com/research/whythismatters.php.

recent day I checked: July 28, 2008.

China-free: Food for Health, a U.S. company, announced plans to mark its products "China-free" soon after a tide of health and safety scares about goods from China. "China-free," *Time,* September 3, 2007, p. 17.

collection of Polly Pockets: Hannah Schardt, "Polly Pocket: Safe and Sound Toys," the *Washington Post,* September 2, 2007, p. NO6.

"new California wine": Brian Wansink et al., "Fine as North Dakota Wine: Sensory Expectations and the Intake of Companion Foods," *Physiology and Behavior* 90 (2007): 712–716.

than does good news: O'Rourke, "Market Movements."

chemical comes under question: For a more detailed account of the economic and political dynamics behind scientific debates of toxicity and safety see David Michaels, *Doubt Is Their Product* (New York: Oxford University Press, 2008).

as applied in European countries: David Vogel, "The Hare and the Tortoise Revisited: The New Politics of Consumer and Environmental Regulation in Europe," *British Journal of Political Science* 33 (2003): 567–568.

arbitrary exposure level: Toxicogists still quote Paracelsus, the ancient Greek physician: "The dose makes the poison," meaning that some substances may be safe at low doses but harmful at higher ones, and the higher the dose the more dangerous. But that misses subtleties; with lead, for instance, even minimal levels of exposure have a negative impact on IQ, and at higher levels the added rate of IQ decline slows. Low doses can make a great difference. R. L. Canfield et al., "Intellectual Impairment in Children with Blood Lead Concentrations Below 10 Micrograms per

Deciliter," *The New England Journal of Medicine* 348, no. 16 (2003): 1517–1526.

lead has no effect: Richard Canfield was quoted in David Leonhardt, "Lessons Even Thomas Could Learn," the *New York Times,* October 24, 2007, C3.

to protect human health: Dr. Philippe Grandjean was quoted in Marian Burros, "Studies Link Other Ills to Mercury, Too," the *New York Times,* January 23, 2008.

CHAPTER THIRTEEN: *Tough Questions*

Raising the flag of doubt: See, for example, Michaels, *Doubt Is Their Product.*

ten thousand bottles: Alexander Cockburn, "How Coca-Cola Gave Back to Plachimada," *Counterpunch,* April 16/17, 2005.

to put back more water: "The Coca-Cola Company Addresses Allegations Made about Our Business in India," www.thecoca-colacompany.com/press center/viewpoints_India_situation.html, posted June 1, 2004.

a real wake-up call: Quoted in Senge et al., *Necessary Revolution,* p. 78.

can have a huge impact: Senge et al., *Necessary Revolution,* p. 84.

wastewater from Coke plants: Dane Lawrence, "Water Investment Sends Coke Back to Basics," *International Herald Tribune,* June 6, 2007, p. 7.

five discrete stages: Senge et al., *Necessary Revolution.*

Kyoto agreement target: I interviewed Len Sauers on May 27, 2008. He was interviewed in *Brandweek,* May 20, 2008.

CEO of Interface: Anderson, cited in Senge et al., *Necessary Revolution.*

CHAPTER FOURTEEN: *The Perpetual Upgrade*

ecological transparency software: Earthster, www.earthster.org.

products ranging from DVDs: John Fleming, quoted in "More Firms Focus on Climate Change," Associated Press, September 25, 2007.

dwarfing the harms to health: Norris, "Social Impacts."

huge amount of money: Ian Kemsley is quoted in G. Paschal Zachary, "Starting to Think outside the Jar," the *New York Times,* June 15, 2008, www.nytimes.com.

enzymes in grazing grass: Michael T. Abberton et al., "The Genetic Improvement of Forage Grasses and Legumes to Reduce Greenhouse Gas Emissions," paper prepared for the Food and Agricultural Organization of the United Nations, December 2007.

test for biodegradability: "Software Predicts if Chemicals Will Biodegrade," *New Scientist,* June 9, 2007, p. 29.

plans for a paper plant: Allen Hershkowitz and Maya Lin, *Bronx Ecology: Blueprint for a New Environmentalism* (Washington, DC: Island Press, 2002).

CHAPTER FIFTEEN: *Second Thoughts*

search for ecological upgrades: Mondi is listed on both the Dow Jones and the FTSE4Good sustainability indexes as a top company in its sector.

infestation of drinking water: Fung, Graham, and Weil, *Full Disclosure.*

in tandem with auditors: Dara O'Rourke, "Monitoring the Monitors," unpublished manuscript, MIT, September 28, 2000.

Wal-Mart has taken steps: Thomson Financial, "Wal-Mart Reports Labor Violations," August 15, 2007.

made in the show factories: Alexandra Harney, *The China Price* (New York: Penguin, 2008).

fair treatment and wages: Bill Baue, "From Competition to Cooperation: Companies Collaborate on Social and Environmental Issues," Social Funds, January 19, 2007, www.socialfunds.com. That approach has been spreading to other business sectors; automakers including Ford, GM, and Honda have launched a similar project on socially responsible management of their supply chain.

too little, too late: John R. Ehrenfeld, "Eco-Efficiency: Philosophy, Theory, and Practice," *Journal of Industrial Ecology* 9 (2005): 6–8.

host of technological fixes: John Ehrenfeld, *Sustainability by Design* (New Haven: Yale University Press, 2008).

CHAPTER SIXTEEN: *Doing Well by Doing Good*

take-make-waste: Paul Hawken, Amory Lovins, and L. Hunter Lovins, *Natural Capitalism: Creating the Next Industrial Revolution* (Boston: Little, Brown, 1999).

NOTES

the planet's common: Peter Barnes, *Capitalism 3.0: A Guide to Reclaiming the Commons* (San Francisco: Berrett-Koehler, 2006).

public health risks: Dinah A. Koehler et al., "Rethinking Environmental Performance from a Public Health Perspective: A Comparative Industry Analysis," *Journal of Industrial Ecology* 9 (2005): 143–167.

corporate interests above all: Joseph E. Stiglitz, *Making Globalization Work* (New York: Norton, 2006).

part of the cost structure: John Warner, as quoted in Mark Schapiro, *Exposed* (White River Junction, VT: Chelsea Green, 2007), p. 187.

financial and ecological gains: Cited in Ehrenfeld, "Eco-Efficiency."

"they would pay attention": The head of corporate compliance at an apparel company was quoted in Alexandra Harney, *The China Price: The True Cost of Chinese Competitive Advantage* (New York: Penguin, 2008), p. 233.

"they'll buy your products": Robert Reich, "No Obligations," *Condé Nast Portfolio*, January 2008.

millions of children: Megha Bahree, "Child Labor," *Forbes*, February 25, 2008, pp. 73–79.

market-based tactic: Michael Hiscox, "Fair Trade as an Approach to Managing Globalization," paper presented at the conference "Europe and the Management of Globalization," Princeton University, February 23, 2007.

thirty-two times greater: Jared Diamond, "What's Your Consumption Factor?," the *New York Times*, op-ed, January 2, 2008.

our species has gone: McCallum, *Ecological Intelligence.*

Earth doesn't need healing: McCallum, *Ecological Intelligence*, p. 14.

RESOURCES

- www.DanielGoleman.info for Daniel Goleman's blogs and appearance schedule.
- www.morethansound.net for the audio series "Dialogues on Ecological Awareness," Daniel Goleman in conversation with leading thinkers.
- www.goodguide.com for evaluations of health, environmental, and social impacts of products.
- www.earthster.org for ecological supply chain innovations and life-cycle evaluations.
- www.environmentalhealthnews.org for daily updates of scientific findings on health and the environment.
- www.cosmeticsdatabase.com for Skin Deep, the database of ingredients in cosmetic and personal care products.

INDEX

INDEX

ABOUT THE AUTHOR

DANIEL GOLEMAN is the author of the international bestsellers *Emotional Intelligence, Working with Emotional Intelligence,* and *Social Intelligence,* and the coauthor of the acclaimed business bestseller *Primal Leadership.* He was a science reporter for the *New York Times,* was twice nominated for the Pulitzer Prize, and received the American Psychological Association's Lifetime Achievement Award for his media writing. He lives in the Berkshires.

www.danielgoleman.info
Author photograph: Steven Edson